BUILDING BRIDGES

**"An average teacher instructs.
A better teacher explains.
A fine teacher demonstrates.
An exceptional teacher inspires."**

Not just anyone can teach bridge effectively, but my friend Jeanne Wamack is blessed with an exceptional teacher's most vital attributes: a profound love of the game and the earnest desire to share it with others, and the amiability and charisma to maintain the interest of her students - and this is no easy task - for a period of weeks.

For many years, at the Birmingham Duplicate Bridge Club, Jeanne has introduced aspiring players to the joys of bridge. The book you are holding is a product of her diligence and determination to impart her knowledge and respect for the game to others. Read on and benefit from Jeanne's expertise.

Frank Stewart

Internationally syndicated bridge columnist and author

What do students and teachers say about <u>Building Bridges</u>?

Jeanne Wamack has written the perfect workbook for bridge players of novice level and beyond. Each chapter comprises a comprehensive topical explanation followed by exercises with a thorough answer key. The chapters systematically build on one another. By the conclusion, the reader will have an encompassing knowledge of bidding, defense, and play of the hand. This solid manual bears multiple readings. I continue to learn something new each time I review *Building Bridges*.

                                                                             M. K. Professor, Samford University

I went from knowing nothing about bridge to loving it so much that I play multiple times per week. I owe this newfound love of mine to Jeanne Wamack's *Building Bridges*. Her book gave me a great foundation in the basics, with which I do quite well. Being a believer that the basics bid correctly will get you just as far as playing dozens of conventions, this well written and fun to read book taught me what I needed to know to begin playing. Now, I'm slowly expanding my game in order to play with more experienced players. I cannot recommend Jeanne's book enough for new players. You will enjoy her writing and teaching style. Building Bridges made me fall in love with bridge.

                                                                                    C. S. Sales Manager, AT&T

Building Bridges forms a highway. In the beginning, some students have never shuffled a deck of cards. As a certified EasyBridge! instructor, ACBL club director, and cruise line instructor, I feel the key to bridge club growth is promoting beginner lessons. Lessons need to be fun and stimulating with extensive reinforcement in a logical learning progression. After assisting Jeanne for over seven years, from her early lessons to her book of today, I have seen her material develop in substance for the student wanting to "grow" forward. Highly recommend Jeanne Wamack's book to all who desire to begin the wonderful journey into the bridge world.

                                                                  E. R. Bridge teacher, Silver Life Master

I was in Jeanne Wamack's first bridge class. She was a wonderful teacher who turned this former Goren bridge player into a lover of duplicate bridge. When she realized the book in use did not give adequate information, she distributed many handouts and sent emails to provide the extra information for her students to understand duplicate bridge. This led her to begin the process of writing a book for beginning bridge players. Following several years of developing and revising, she has created a fantastic book, *Building Bridges*, for those who want to play or teach duplicate bridge. It is a totally inclusive book filled with explanations and examples that will be your go-to reference for a lifetime of good bridge.

                                                                       L. G. Educator and Principal (ret.)

Building Bridges is a wonderful book for those who want to learn to play duplicate bridge. The chapters cover everything from explaining what duplicate bridge is, through bidding conventions, defense, card play, scoring, and bridge etiquette. Each chapter is clearly written for easy comprehension and at the end of each chapter is a practice and application section. This book is ideal for either learning on your own, or even better, as a text book for an instructor to use with students. Each chapter flows logically to the next and effortlessly leads the student along the path to being a competent beginning bridge player.

                                                    A. F. Retired Federal Criminal Investigator
                                                                     Classroom assistant for over eight years.

We thoroughly enjoyed the classes. We learned how to play the game, something we've wanted to do for a long time. *Building Bridges* is *NOT* a boring bridge book! It is a pleasure to read and it is easy to understand. Jeanne is a talented writer and teacher who makes learning fun, and by association *Building Bridges* makes learning fun too.

                                                                            C. D. Educator, and
                                                      B. D. Certified Dale Carnegie Course Instructor

BUILDING BRIDGES
*An **introduction** to the card game of bridge*
by
Jeanne R. Wamack
"Queen Jeanne" to her students

Welcome to the wonderful world of bridge! No other card game is as challenging, entertaining, rewarding and aggravating as bridge! If you are a new student, stay the course because it will be worth the effort. If you are returning to this great game or are updating your skills to learn the latest "technology," good for you because bridge has changed since Charles Goren developed his theories of the game long ago. New theorists have appeared, their ideas have improved our game, and the evolution continues.

Through this sixteen week program, you'll learn the basics of Modern Standard American style bridge. You'll be able to play with anyone else familiar with Standard American, perhaps with minor adjustments as slight regional variations do occur. Chapter one addresses the etiquette of duplicate bridge, but the GAME of bridge is the SAME regardless of which approach you decide to take - social, duplicate, or both.

How to Use This Manual

In the first section of this book are the series of lessons, each accompanied by practice and application. Attend class, absorb information from the discussion and subsequent card play, read the chapter at home, then test yourself. As a whole, most beginning bridge programs are longer, but players often want to end classes earlier rather than later and participate in games. *Building Bridges* acknowledges this, but in order to capitalize on the quick turnaround there is a **PRICE:** you **MUST** follow up your class with the practice and application exercises. Review each topic since **REPETITION** is truly the best way to learn. *If you fail to complete these tasks, you will never really master the game.* Don't worry; each lesson is only a few pages. If some of the information in a chapter seems to be too much for the moment, scan it, then take in the summary or highlights of that lesson. You may study in depth at a later time. We cannot cover every nuance during class, so most chapters have a further explanation of the main concept. In some of the chapters may be found additional information titled, "For Future Study." This is to help you become a more insightful player. *Do not try to learn this material until you have spent even more time at the bridge table.* Rome wasn't built in a day!

Should you be unable to attend classes in your area, read this manual to familiarize yourself with the game, then search for a local bridge club or social group with whom to develop your playing skills.

The next section contains Appendix A where you will find several useful study guides - the popular Bidding Flow Chart, the Point Scale, and more. I recommend using the material in Appendix A for quick personal review sessions since each chart represents a synopsis of valuable information. Appendix B is for the advanced beginner.

After you begin playing regularly, reread the chapters as the lessons will take shape the more time you invest in the game. Hopefully many of your questions will be answered within these pages as you play and gain confidence. You will find there are many helpful tips throughout the book: it is intended to be used for reference as you develop your technique, discovering the ingenuity of the game. However, one book cannot teach you everything about bridge, so start on your journey from here.

This material is copyrighted. You may neither reproduce nor share this manual in any form. Books may be ordered from the address below. **Please respect copyright laws.** Should you be viewing the slide show and would like copies of the charts, they are duplicated in this manual.

I suggest you join a local bridge club. Clubs often hold low-level games for beginners and friendly, helpful players are already at the club waiting for you! Many bridge clubs offer continuing education opportunities as well. You'll also want to join the **ACBL** (the American Contract Bridge League). Membership fees are inexpensive. They support and promote the game, are a tremendous source of information, publish an excellent monthly magazine, and record points earned by members.

Enjoy your future bridge ventures!

Sincerely,

Jeanne Wamack

2315 Fox Glen Circle • Birmingham, AL 35216
(205) 616-3724 • jwamack@aol.com

Building Bridges © 2022 Jeanne R. Wamack May not be reproduced in any form.

Table of Contents

1. **Mechanics and Etiquette: Be Technical and Ethical** — 3
   Suits and ladders/Boards and boxes/Abbreviation key

2. **Basic Blocks: Bidding the M and m's, Part One** — 9
   Opening a major suit and responses

3. **Basic Blocks: Bidding the M and m's, Part Two** — 13
   Opening a minor suit and responses

4. **The Rule of 20 + 2 and Preemptive Bidding** — 17
   Two more ways to enter the auction/For Future Study

5. **One No Trump Opening Bids and Conventional Responses, Part One** — 20
   The PIG and Jacoby Transfers

6. **One No Trump Opening Bids and Conventional Responses, Part Two** — 23
   The PIG and Stayman/Standard American responses with interference/For Future Study

7. **Overcalls** — 27
   Long suit level one/Long suit level two/TOX/NT overcalls/Bidding over a preempt/Overcall summary
   For Future Study

8. **Bidding After Interference from the Opponents** — 31
   The negative double and the positive cuebid/For Future Study

9. **Leads** — 34
   Good leads...and not such good leads

10. **The Finesse** — 38

11. **Play of the Hand** — 41
    Suit contract or No Trump contract/ATAC/For Future Study/The odds

12. **Defense** — 46
    Tips: Leads/Signaling/Defensive play/ALAS/For Future Study/Dummy's duties

13. **BIG HANDS** — 50
    Inviting game/Forcing game/Fine tune your hand with distribution points/For Future Study

14. **HUGE HANDS** — 56
    2NT and responses/2C and responses

15. **Blackwood and Gerber** — 59
    For Future Study

16. **Complete Scoring and *more* on Offense/Defense** — 61
    How duplicate scoring works/Strategy/Penalty Xs/Extra tips

17. **BONUS CHAPTER: Rebids and Review** — 71
    Requested by students: a review session

18. **For Home Study: More Bridge Etiquette, Tournaments, and Final Thoughts** — 78
    Table etiquette/Tournaments/Partnership agreements

Appendix A: Bridge definitions/Charts/Lead table/The Point Scale/The Breakdown of Points — 82
    Convention card and instructions/Questions for a new partner/Study Guides/Flow chart

Appendix B: Forcing, Non-forcing and Game forcing bids/Penalty doubles/Misc/Tournament Tips — 105

INDEX — 108

Building Bridges © 2022 Jeanne R. Wamack May not be reproduced in any form.

Lesson I - Mechanics and Etiquette   NOTES:

"Let's start at the very beginning, a very good place to start." says Maria in <u>The Sound of Music</u>.

Bridge is a card game played with a deck of fifty-two cards. Each deck comes with fifty-four cards, including two joker cards, but we do not use the jokers in bridge. Bridge is a PARTNERSHIP game: you and your partner work together, I repeat, WORK TOGETHER to win. Your partner is the person sitting across the table from you, and the other players are your opponents or "frenemies." They may be your friends, but they are friendly enemies at the bridge table.

Each time you play duplicate bridge, the set up will be the same. In the middle of the table you'll see trays made of plastic or metal with playing cards divided into four compartments. These are ***duplicate boards,*** and there are usually two-four at each table. All the boards are numbered. Players sitting in the **same** position at each table throughout the room play the **same** boards using the **same** cards. After play, the cards are put back into the **same** slots, then the boards are passed en masse from table to table. In most card games (and in social bridge) the cards are shuffled after play is over, but in duplicate bridge you do not reshuffle the cards. THE BOARDS REMAIN IN THE CENTER OF THE TABLE, EVEN DURING PLAY. This ensures that the correct set of cards go back into the proper slot for the next player. You'll have room.

Under the boards, there will be a large card which is either laminated or in a plastic envelope. This is a **guide card** which informs you of your table number, pair number, and whether you are sitting north/south or east/west. Don't forget your **pair number** or your **direction**. In order for everyone to play different boards and pairs, some players will move from table to table as the boards do.

Your table will have four ***bid boxes***. The bid box holds all the calls a player may make in the game of bridge. To make a ***bid*** or ***call*** (take a turn at the appropriate time), the bidder will remove the card he wishes to display from the box and put it on the table. The box is divided into two sections. In the front section are red, blue and green cards that may be pulled out one at a time. In the larger back section, the bidder grasps the card corresponding to the numbered bid he wishes to make, then he'll pull out that card PLUS ALL THE CARDS BEHIND HIS BID CARD. He'll glance at the top card to be certain it is his intended bid, then he'll place the bid on the table with the number and symbol facing away from him for the other players to view. Each subsequent bid is placed on top of the previous bid, without covering the previous bid, so that **every bid is easily seen,** creating a horizontal row of overlapping bids. After the bidding is over, all the cards taken from the front section will go back there. All the numbered cards on the table will be pushed together, already in perfect order, and slipped into the back of the bid box behind the unused bid cards.

At your table, in addition to everything else, you may see a small plastic box with a keypad. It is for recording scores. There are three scoring methods. One is a wireless system allowing North to enter the scores into a central computer. Using the box at your table, North types in the scores answering onscreen prompts. A second method is a piece of paper, called a ***traveller,*** on which is written all the scores for the single board. The traveller is folded and tucked into its corresponding board, then accompanies the board around the room. The third method is a small card known as a **pick-up slip.** On the card is recorded the scores of all the boards played for the round, then it is taken at the end of the round by the individual in charge of the event. **Scores are approved by East or West.** North is in charge of the table - scoring, moving boards, etc. Tip: North is the only player who can see the numbers on the boards right-side-up.

More about the cards: there are four suits in a deck. Two of the suits are red, two are black, and the suits are represented on the cards by symbols. The suits are ***spades*** (abbreviated Ss - they look like a black shovel), ***hearts*** (Hs - you can figure that one out), ***diamonds*** (Ds - a girl's best friend), and ***clubs*** (Cs - a.k.a. "puppy feet"). The suits are not equal. There are two **Major** (M) suits, spades and hearts, and two **minor** (m) suits, diamonds and clubs, their order from highest to lowest.

Every card has symbols and either letters, numbers and/or people on it. The highest card in each suit is the ace (A), followed by the king (K), queen (Q), jack (J), and ten. These cards are called the ***honor cards,*** or ***honors.*** The honors are colorful, so in general the prettier your cards, the better they are. The ten is followed by the nine, eight, seven, etc, down to the two, the lowest card in the suit.

MECHANICS AND ETIQUETTE

There are four suits in the fifty-two card deck, and there are thirteen cards in each suit. After the cards are shuffled together and dealt to the four players, guess what? Each player has thirteen cards for play, producing what is known as a **hand.**

When you remove your hand from the board, the first thing you do is to count your cards face down to ensure you have thirteen. If you do not have thirteen cards, you will immediately call the ***director*** of the game. The director is your mother, father, teacher, lawyer, policeman, politician, and computer geek all rolled into one person. It's nice to play the game with Big Brother watching over you...well...most of the time! He'll take care of any problem.

If you have the correct number of cards, pick up your hand and fan it out for organization. It's good to group the suits, alternating by color, to avoid accidentally mixing symbols. Check and recheck to be CERTAIN all cards within each group MATCH, a common error. You won't bid properly if you think you have an extra spade when you have a club instead. You'll see a mix of symbols and (hopefully) people, but what do they mean? Since an ace is the top card of a suit, it's great to have aces! Kings are really good too. Queens and jacks help you have a nice hand, and you love to see them with their corresponding aces and kings.

The next thing you look for is a *long suit*. In bridge, a long suit is **FIVE** or more cards. If you have aces, fancy faces, and a long suit, you are fortunate. A bridge hand is like a Christmas present - *you can't wait to open it up and see what's in there!* Some hands you'll adore, like a huge diamond ring or a Porsche, while other hands you may somewhat less enthusiastically accept, similar to getting the annual white thermal underwear from your grandmother.

The goal of each pair is to be in charge of the show, meaning in charge of the play of the fifty-two cards. A pair may be in control, IF TOGETHER they have a long suit, aces, and fancy face cards. For example, if you and your partner have several hearts, including honors, your team will want hearts to be known as the **"top suit."** If your opponents have several diamonds, they will want diamonds to be the top suit. How is this dilemma settled?

In bridge we have an ***auction***, battling it out between the pairs to determine which suit is the top suit for the board. During the auction, each pair describes the cards they have (via bids) in order to make the best decisions for the team.

The language used in the auction is the language of bridge. The language fits neatly into the bid box at your table. We do not use body language at the bridge table - it is ILLEGAL in the bridge world, so put on your poker face. Do not approach the bid box until you have considered your options and are ready to bid, keeping in tempo and not taking *too* long to bid. Never pull out a bid and put it back. Never reach out and touch or rummage in the box, then hesitate. Contemplate briefly, *without handling the box*, make your decision, then pull out your bid. Glance at it to make sure it is the correct bid you want to make, and place it on the table. DO NOT MAKE ANY COMMENTS, nor exhibit any dramatics like eye-rolling. Don't even make any eye contact. *(The same rules apply when you detach a card from your hand for play - make the selection of which card you want to play **before** you remove one - **all deliberation is internal.** Once the card is close to the table, it is considered a played card and cannot be retracted because you changed your mind.)*

How does an auction begin? The first player to have the option of bidding is the **dealer.** In duplicate bridge, he/she is the person with the word "DEALER" printed on the board in front of him or her. The dealer either makes a bid or ***passes***, shown by removing a green PASS card from the front of the bid box and putting it on the table. If the dealer can make a numbered bid, he becomes the ***opener***. An opening bid says that he meets certain requirements. *Pass* means he cannot make a bid at the moment. Perhaps later, but not now. A pass is not an opening bid.

How do we do this in an orderly way to avoid hair-pulling and fistfights? We use a **bidding ladder**, representing the **hierarchy of the suits** (see page 5). The lowest rung on the ladder is one club (1C), followed by one diamond (1D), *the minors*, then one heart (1H), and one spade (1S), *the Majors*. After one spade comes one no trump (1NT).

Although it is improper grammar, from this point forward number symbols will often be used in the text.

No trump? What's that? The no trump bidder does NOT want a top suit because he has honor cards in every suit. He wants to play the game "WAR" in which the highest card in the suit first put on the table wins the entire set of cards presented by all players. What does "trump" mean? If the spade, heart, diamond or club suit wins the auction, then that suit is the top suit, which becomes known as the _**trump**_ or _**trump suit.**_ The trump suit is the **most powerful suit** for that board. It will _**ruff**_ (overtake) any other suit, and may only be defeated by a higher trump. The smallest trump will beat aces, kings, and queens of the non-trump suits. *Carpe diem!*

But don't get so excited about ruffing that you forget something important: everyone must _**follow suit**_ until he runs out. If you are playing a game in which Ss, Hs, Ds, or Cs are the trump and you don't have the suit initially led, you may ruff or throw off a loser, usually a low card. If you are playing No Trump, you will throw away a card that doesn't seem like a future winner. Bridge etiquette requires that you ask your partner, **"No spades, partner?"** (or hearts, diamonds or clubs) when your partner doesn't follow suit. Why? To prevent a _**revoke or renege**_, a misplay in which a player doesn't follow suit when he should. This is done in order to keep the game going smoothly. Your team may get a penalty or an adjusted score if one of you revokes, so help out partner who has gone to sleep on the job. Will you feel weird questioning your partner at first? Yes, but don't worry - you'll get used to it. Social: you'll negate and reshuffle.

Back to the bidding ladder - after 1NT, we climb the bidding ladder to level two and see that the next rung is 2 clubs (2C), then 2 diamonds (2D), 2 hearts (2H), 2 spades (2S) and 2NT. The next steps are in the same order all the way to the top level, level seven. **We only go UP the ladder as we bid in the auction, NEVER DOWN the ladder.**

To illustrate, suppose the dealer opens 1D. A suit higher than diamonds or NT may be bid at the **same level** as the diamond bid: 1D-1H, 1D-1S, or 1D-1NT. If someone wants to bid the **lower-ranked** suit, Cs, he must rise to the **next level:** 1D-**2C**. If a player wants to bid the **same suit,** he must bid it at the **next level:** 1D-**2D**. If the dealer opens 1H, another player may bid 1S or 1NT, but must bid **2Cs** or **2Ds** since those suits are lower than Hs, or he must bid **2H** if he wants to bid the H suit. If the dealer opens 1NT, then any suit or NT must bid at the two level or higher: 1NT-2C; 1N-2D; 1N-2H; 1NT-2S; or 1NT-2NT. Examples of proper bidding between partners (opponents pass throughout): 1C-1S; 1H-2H; 1D-1NT; 1S-2C; 1H-2D; 1NT-2C-2S; 1NT-2H-2S; 1S-2D-3C-4D; 1S-2H-2S-4S; or 1H-1S-3H-4NT.

 Important: No Trump and the Majors SCORE MORE POINTS than the minors, so we prefer to play in a Major suit or in NT.

How do you know if your hand is worthy of bidding? There is a simple **high card point** (HCP) counting system used to evaluate your hand, giving you an idea of how high you'll be able to climb the ladder. Add together the points of your top four honor cards in every suit:

Aces	=	**4 HCP**
Kings	=	**3 HCP**
Queens	=	**2 HCP**
Jacks	=	**1 HCP**

Tip: 10s & 9s = 0 HCP, but it's very helpful to have mid-range cards, especially when they are with their matching honor cards.

How good is your hand? Each suit has an A, K, Q and J, so each suit has a maximum of 10 HCP (A+K+Q+J). If you calculate, you will discover the entire deck has 40 HCP (10 points in each suit x 4 suits = 40). If all the points are divided among the players, the average hand is 10 HCP. Do you have a below-average, average, or above-average hand?

YOUR HCP IMPACT YOUR CAPACITY TO BID.

If the average hand is 10 HCP, it makes sense that an opening hand should be a little bit superior, so we open the bidding with **12 HCP.** You may think that 12 is not much above average, but you have a partner sitting across from you who also holds 13 cards. What does he have that might help you? You'll find out.

The Bidding Ladder

_____7NT_____
_____7S_____
_____7H_____
_____7D_____
_____7C_____
_____6NT_____
_____6S_____
_____6H_____
_____6D_____
_____6C_____
_____5NT_____
_____5S_____
_____5H_____
_____5D_____
_____5C_____
_____4NT_____
_____4S_____
_____4H_____
_____4D_____
_____4C_____
_____3NT_____
_____3S_____
_____3H_____
_____3D_____
_____3C_____
_____2NT_____
_____2S_____
_____2H_____
_____2D_____
_____2C_____
_____1NT_____
_____1S_____
_____1H_____
_____1D_____
_____1C_____

You have this hand. Each x is a small card, the 10 or lower.

Spades: AKxxx
Hearts: QJx
Diamonds: KJx
Clubs: xx

What are your HCP?
A+K+Q+J+K+J = **14** HCP
Can you open the auction? Yes, if it's your turn.

MECHANICS AND ETIQUETTE

The auction begins. The dealer may open if he meets the **minimum requirement of 12 HCP.** If that requirement is not met, he passes and the opportunity to open goes to the person on the dealer's **left.** He must meet the same requirement or pass, then the auction moves to the next player, etc. When one of the players makes a numbered bid, the auction is *open* and usually proceeds with more bidding until a *contract* is reached. **After three consecutive passes, the last numbered bid becomes the contract**. Every now and then the HCP are evenly divided among the players and there are **four** passes in a row. If that happens, the cards are returned to their slots and the next board is played.

> You have this hand...
> Spades: Axxxx
> Hearts: Kxx
> Diamonds: Qxx
> Clubs: xx
> What are your HCP?
> A+K+Q = **9** HCP.
> Can you open? No, but you may have a *future* bid.

It's your turn and you meet the minimum requirement of 12 HCP. If you have a 5+ card Major, bid it by placing 1H or 1S on the table. Lucky you! But that doesn't happen all the time. What do you do if you have 12 HCP and no 5 card Major? Go to Plan B - you'll open a minor (1C or 1D). Bid your longest minor, promising 3-4, or more, in the suit. **You don't have to have 5.** You'll say, "But I don't want to be in a minor - they're bad!" No, they're only "bad" as the final contract. The honors in minor suits win as often as the honors in major suits - they're the icing on the cake - but you want to score the maximum points possible, so primarily seek a major or NT contract. You have a PARTNER - perhaps he or she has a long major suit if you don't. At least let your partner know the good news - you have 12 or more HCP, a strong hand. The auction will continue, probably with other bids, until there are **three passes in a row.** How **HIGH** can you bid? *The number of points you have will guide you.* Think of points as money to enable you to bid in the auction. Just as in any auction - the more money you and your partner have, the higher you'll be able to bid.

What happens at the conclusion of the auction? Of the pair who won the auction, the one who named the suit or bid NT **FIRST** is now the *declarer*. He'll play the hand and take the correct number of "tricks" he needs to fulfill his contract, or more. Taking a *trick* means **one player wins ALL the cards in the group of four cards placed on the table in play.** There are a total of **13 tricks** in a hand. How does the declarer know how many tricks to take? **The first six tricks** he wins are known as a *book*, required of all declarers, and ADDITIONAL tricks are needed to complete the contract, which is the **number on the final bid card.** If the bidding ends in **2H**, the pair must take **8 tricks** (6+2=8). If the bidding ends in **4S**, the pair must take **10 tricks** (6+4=10). If the bidding ends in **6NT**, the pair must take **12 tricks** (6+6=12). You'll see, as one climbs the bidding ladder during the auction, *each new level means another trick must be won.* Any tricks taken in excess of the contract number add extra points to the team score.

If the declarer fails to fulfill his contract, he gets *set,* or "goes down" the missing number of tricks. Each trick the declarer is set counts 50 points, unless one is **vulnerable** (a handicap, usually shown by red in or above the card slot), then each one counts **100 points**, a heavy penalty. **All of those points go to the opponents.** Each player must be careful to evaluate his hand properly and to pay attention to his partner's bids. Each pair should bid as precisely as possible, as no one wants to give away points.

Once the declarer is identified, his partner becomes the *dummy*, supposedly a French word that is no reflection on the intelligence of the player. The person who gets to play the first card of the hand is the opponent to the left of the declarer. He is now the *leader* and the card he plays is the *lead*. He will select a card that seems likely to win a trick or is from a good suit. The top of a sequence or the 4th card down from an honor are often good leads. This is the first strike the opponents, now called the *defenders*, can make to defeat the contract, their goal.

After the lead is selected, it is placed **face down** on the table and the leader asks, "Any questions, partner?" At that time, the partner can make certain the right person is on lead and he may ask questions about the bidding, if any. When all players are ready, the card is turned over and the competition begins. **The dummy's entire hand now goes face up on the table** in vertical rows of suits ordered from high to low. The dummy will play the cards the declarer tells him to play: he **never** reaches for any card without a directive, nor does he ask the declarer which card he wants. The declarer does not touch the dummy's cards. In fact, **no one touches anyone else's cards**. The trump suit will be placed on the dummy's far right, to the declarer's left. In a NT contract, clubs go on the dummy's right. The other suits are usually alternated by color or are placed according to declarer preference.

Play continues clockwise around the table until everyone has put down the card he has chosen from his hand. **Each player must follow suit.** If a player runs out of the suit led, he'll throw away a losing card, typically a small card, or he'll ruff in a suit contract if he has some trump cards and his partner can't take the trick. He shouldn't trump partner's winning card! There will be one winner who takes the trick. **The winner of the current trick decides what to lead next.**

Building Bridges © 2022 Jeanne R. Wamack   May not be reproduced in any form.

MECHANICS AND ETIQUETTE

After use, each spent card is placed face down on the table directly in front of the player. The card will be **vertical** if a winner or **horizontal** if a loser, NOT gathered up by the victor. The overlapping line of vertical and horizontal cards **is a record of the playing order of the hand.** There is no looking back at previously played cards, *but as long as any player's card remains **face up** on the table, he may request to see what cards were played on the current round.* Once all cards are turned over, the trick is closed. Once the trick is closed, each player is allowed to privately look back only at the last card played, perhaps to check and see if the right person is on lead. After all thirteen cards have been played and **EVERYONE AGREES ON THE OUTCOME,** the cards are scooped up, mixed up, then put back into the slot from which they were pulled, face down. **All players MUST AGREE on the results before the clean up.** If there is an error, it may be found and resolved.

The score is recorded, and the next board is played. After all the boards on the table are played, the ***round*** is over. The boards are moved to another table, and pairs either move to the next higher-numbered table or move to the table designated on the guide card, depending on how many tables are in play. Sometimes the method of change has it's own lingo:

The boards get younger and the players get older.

Winning scores are determined by either pulling the ***contract card*** from the bid box, which has all the scores on the back, or calculating the math. Losing (set) scores are on the back of the pass card. Soon everyone will have a special piece of paper on which to record scores, known as a ***convention card***. Never leave a card turned sideways in the bidding box or on the table to remind yourself of the contract. Why? Other players may see the card and know what to expect on that set of boards. Look at the dummy's **far left** column of cards if you've forgotten the contract. **Why the proper etiquette?** *To create as fair and impartial a game as possible for everyone.*

After all the boards have been played, thank the opponents for the round. Always be polite and courteous. Take all your belongings with you and throw away your trash.

More improper grammar to come...

Building Bridges shorthand *is defined here*

KEY:

A=ace	**M**=Major	**st**=suit	**h/hs**=honor	**V**=vulnerable
K=king	**m**=minor	**tr**=trick	**pts.**=points	**NV**=not vulnerable
Q=queen				
J=jack		o = opener	**<** = fewer than; **>** = more than	**c**=card(s)
T=10 (used both ways)				**conv**=convention
			HCP=high card points	**x**=small card (10 or lower)
NT=No Trump			**SA**=Standard American	**X**=double
S/Ss=spades				**XX**=redouble
H/Hs=hearts			**LHO**=left hand opponent	
D/Ds=diamonds			**RHO**=right hand opponent	**bal**=balanced
C/Cs=clubs				**dist**=distributional
			PIG=**P**ass, **I**nvite, **G**ame	
P= pass			**TOX**=takeout double	**open, opr**=opener
part=partner				**resp, rsp**=responder
PA, part. agree.= partnership agreement			**NF**=non-forcing	**over**=overcaller
			F=forcing	**adv**=advancer
min=minimum/minimal hand			**med**=medium hand	**max**=maximum hand

Bridge definitions, such as "Golden Fit" or "singleton", are briefly explained as they appear in the text. If the term is bold, italicized, and underlined, it will be found in Appendix A, starting on page 83. There definitions are listed by chapter in the order presented, and many definitions will be explained in greater detail.

The numbers 4333, 4432, 5332, 5530, etc. show the number of cards held by a player in each of the four suits. They are often, but not always, in order from the left starting with Ss, then Hs, Ds, and Cs. If the player has zero cards in a suit, the suit is termed **void**.

Bidding examples in the text assume neither partner has previously passed. Any changes or ***interference***, as bidding by the opposition is called, will be noted for you.

THE OPPONENT'S BIDS ARE SHOWN IN BRACKETS [ ] THROUGHOUT THIS MANUAL.

Practice & Application Lesson I: Building brick by brick by brick...

Housekeeping.   Cover the answers.

1.	Which suits are the major suits?	Spades and hearts
2.	Which suits are the minor suits?	Diamonds and clubs
3.	What is the total number of points in a deck?	40
4.	What is the average number of points?	10
5.	How many points do you need to open the auction?	12
6.	Who officiates the game?	The director (at a club)
7.	Who runs the table and sees the numbers on the boards face up?	North
8.	What are the honors in a suit?	The A, K, Q, J and 10
9.	Who has the first opportunity to open the auction or pass?	The dealer
10.	First choice to open?	A five card major suit
11.	Second choice to open?	Your longer minor suit
12.	How does the auction **stop**?	After three passes in a row, it's over.
13.	What is the lowest rung on the bidding ladder?	1C (club)
14.	What is the highest rung on the ladder?	7NT (No Trump)
15.	What is the point count of each honor?	A=4, K=3, Q=2, J=1 (10=0).
16.	What is a "book" in bridge?	The first 6 tricks taken by the declarer.
17.	If you bid 2 spades, for how many tricks have you contracted?	8 Book + 2
18.	If you bid 4 hearts, for how many tricks have you contracted?	10 Book + 4
19.	If you bid 5 clubs, for how many tricks have you contracted?	11 Book + 5
20.	If you bid 3 No Trump, for how many tricks have you contracted?	9 Book + 3
21.	After the play is over, when do you gather up your hand and put it away?	**After everyone agrees** on the final outcome of the hand.

Which are correct bidding sequences? If incorrect, what is the correct bid? Cover the answers.

1.	1 club - 1 spade? (1C-1S)		1.	Y	
2.	1 No Trump - 1 diamond? (1NT-1D)		2.	N	2Ds
3.	1 club - 1 heart - 1 spade? (1C-1H-1S)		3.	Y	
4.	1 club - 1 spade - 3 clubs? (1C-1S-3C)		4.	Y	
5.	1 spade - 2 hearts? (1S-2H)		5.	Y	
6.	1 club - 1 diamond - 1 spade - 1 heart? (1C-1D-1S-1H)		6.	N	2Hs
7.	1 club - [1 spade] - 2 hearts - [pass] - 3 clubs? (1C-[1S]-2H-[P]-3C)		7.	Y	
	The opponents entered the auction , shown by bids in [ ].				
8.	1 heart - 2 spades? (1H-2S)		8.	Y	
9.	1 spade - 2 hearts - 2 diamonds? (1S-2H-2D)		9.	N	3Ds
10.	1 No Trump - 1 spade? (1NT-1S)		10.	N	2Ss
11.	1 No Trump - 2 diamonds - 2 clubs? (1NT-2D-2C)		11.	N	3Cs
12.	1 club - 1 No Trump? (1C-1NT)		12.	Y	

As long as you climb the bidding ladder, "jump bids" also known as "skip bids" may be made as seen in 4 and 8.

If a bid is too low or **"insufficient,"** such as 1S - 1C, or for any other irregularities, call the director for options. This is **NOT** rude or mean, so **DO NOT GET UPSET by a director call!** Director calls are **commonplace** in the bridge world and do not mean the offender is in trouble. *Director calls are made to **restore equity** after an error.*

As you learn this exciting game, you may feel overwhelmed by the guidelines of play. Take "heart" and realize just about everyone feels uncertain at first. There IS a lot to learn, but it all blends together as you attend lessons each week. That is what makes this game so intriguing - it is not a game learned in five minutes, like UNO. There is no national UNO organization, and there are no UNO tournaments! UNO is fun, but **bridge is a game that will always interest and challenge you.** Just because you may be a beginner, *it does not mean you should feel inadequate.* Everyone starts **somewhere.** It's like two adults and two children playing checkers. The adults are trying to outwit each other and the children are only trying to earn crowns! **Everyone is having a good time,** though the levels of play are different. You will start by playing cards, perhaps in a fog, unsure of what you are supposed to be doing, then you will rise to the occasion with a little practice and suddenly become a player! We ALL start out the same - even the highest level of players. Just ask them. They persevered and so will you. Repeat classes if necessary to gain further understanding, and ask questions if you are not clear on a topic. We're all **glad** to help you.

Building Bridges © 2022 Jeanne R. Wamack May not be reproduced in any form.

Lesson II - Bidding the M and m's, Part One

Let's get down to business in the Standard American (SA) system...

OPENING THE AUCTION

Add together all of your HCP. If you meet the minimum requirement of **12 HCP** and you're the dealer, you should open the auction. You will **first** check your Major suits to see if you have at least one 5 card (or longer) suit. If so, bid 1H or 1S. If you have **two** 5 card Ms, bid the higher ranked M suit, Ss. If you have a 4 card M and a 5 card M, bid the 5 card M first. If you like the 4 card M better, you may be able to find a 4/4 fit later. If you have a 4 card M do not bid it, *no matter how pretty it is*, because your partner will expect you to have 5, and he'll base all of his responses on the fact that your bid **guarantees 5**.

If you have 12+ HCP and no 5 card M, open a minor suit. You'll bid your longer minor, promising at least 3 or 4 in the suit - not every hand has a 5 card suit. When you are the first bidder, you become the opener. The opener may have anywhere from **12-21 HCP**, a wide range of points.

What are your goals? Your first objective is to find the *Golden Fit* in a M suit, meaning you and your partner have at least 8 together of the 13 available, a supermajority. The 8 cards will be divided between you in one of several ways: 8/0, 7/1, 6/2, 5/3, or 4/4, the most *"elusive"* fit. We begin searching with a 5 card M to find that fit, because you may get left in 1H or 1S and that is safest minimum amount for you to have. Your second objective is to find the **best contract** for your team... Is it game?

Now you'll wait and see what your partner does...

RESPONDING TO THE OPENING BID

Your partner, the opener, wants to know what's in *your* 13 cards: your HCP, possible fit, and the length of your suits. Since he has a new name, you do too - you are now the *responder*. You should answer your partner with **at least 6 HCP**. With fewer than 6 HCP, you'll pass.

It's IMPORTANT for you to bid if you have enough points. Do not pass in confusion - *bid something.* You need to keep your partner informed: **it builds trust.** You know he has at least 12 HCP, a 5 card or longer suit (if he bid a M), and if your pair can compete, *but he knows nothing about your hand or your team's potential*. Your responses clarify your strength, whether minimum (6-9 HCP), medium (10-12 HCP) or maximum (13+ HCP), and whether you have an 8 card fit in one of the suits. We'll start with **Major** opening bids and responses.

MAJOR SUIT OPENING BIDS & MINIMUM RESPONSES:

Opener:	Responder:	Meaning:	(Minimal holding - "either/or")
1S	2S	I have 3-4 Ss & 6-9 HCP	Minimum hand. We have a fit!
1S	1NT	I have < 3 Ss & 6-9 HCP	Minimum hand. No 8 card S fit.
1H	2H	I have 3-4 Hs & 6-9 HCP	Minimum hand. We have a fit!
1H	1NT	I have < 3 Hs & 6-9 HCP	Minimum hand. No 8 card H fit.

> The weak 1NT response promises 6-9 (or 10-) HCP, and denies 3 of the M.
>
> What the rest of the hand is like, it's "shape," (the length he has in the other suits) is **unknown**.

How can you tell these are the minimum responses to a M opening bid? The **repeat** of a partner's suit at the **lowest level** is somewhat of a "stop" bid for the responder, saying, "Don't expect a lot. I'm in the weak category (below the average count of 10), but I do have some points." Bidding NT at the **lowest level** is also a "stop" bid. One response indicates you have the sought after **Golden Fit**, while the other indicates you do not. If the opener also has a minimal hand (12-15 HCP), "That's all Folks!" A game level contract is not expected, and the opener isn't required to make further calls. This is communication - *what the bidding is all about.*

When responding over 1S, these two bids are the **ONLY CHOICES** that show a minimum hand. While similar bids show a minimum hand over 1H, since Hs are lower on the bidding ladder than Ss, **you have an additional bid should partner open 1H...**

Building Bridges © 2022 Jeanne R. Wamack May not be reproduced in any form.

BIDDING THE MAJORS

ANOTHER POSSIBLE RESPONSE OVER 1H:

| 1H | 1S | **I have 4+ Ss & 6+ HCP, no limit on Ss OR points for now.** Seeking a 4/4 SPADE fit; may or may not have 3H. This is a **NORMAL RESPONSE** with 4 or more Ss. The 1H-1S bid is one way to show 4 (or more) Ss, seeking a 4/4 fit, the most *elusive* fit. |

NOT YET A MINIMUM RESPONSE - <u>ACTUAL STRENGTH UNKNOWN, SO THE OPENER MUST BID AGAIN.</u>

Tip: If you have 3 Hs and 6-7 HCP, **bid 2Hs**, even with 4 Ss. Bridge lore says that if one pair has a fit, the other pair has a fit too. The 2H bid will make it difficult for the opponents to enter the auction with a minor suit because they have to gamble at the **three level**. If they have a S fit, who is going to cause the opponents trouble? You!

What if your hand is BETTER than the minimum of 6-9 HCP? That happens quite often.

MAJOR SUIT OPENING BIDS & MEDIUM+ RESPONSES:

Open:	Resp:	Meaning: (Medium+ holding: 10 HCP, *or more*)
1H/1S	2C	**I have 10+ HCP & 4+ Cs.** H or S fit unknown as yet.
1H/1S	2D	**I have 10+ HCP & 4+ Ds.** H or S fit unknown as yet.
1S	2H	**I have 10+ HCP & <u>5</u> Hs.** A possible S fit: more later, partner.
1H/1S	2NT	**I have 11-12 HCP, a balanced hand & no M support (< 3).** If 1H is the opening bid, **< 4 Ss.** Opener will bid game with 6+ of the M, top honors & 14+ HCP, 3NT with 5 of the M & 14+ HCP, make a guess with 13 HCP, or pass with 12 HCP. An uncommon response. Why? *You'll have a 4+ card m suit with no M fit or M bid, and you'd usually show the suit.*
1H/1S	3NT	**I have 13-15 HCP & a balanced hand with no M support.** Over 1H, resp has < 4 Ss.

> Suit responses to a M opening bid should ideally be a source of tricks, as a NT contract is a possibility with no M fit.

The responder's SUIT bids **DO NOT DENY AN 8 CARD M FIT.** If you have the Golden Fit, why would you bid a different suit? *TO SHOW YOUR HCP.* This is good news for your partner: **the two level bid of a "new" (heretofore unbid) suit always shows 10 or more HCP.** If you don't have 10+ HCP, you CAN'T make a two level bid in a new suit, you must find another bid. *Pay attention to this rule because it is often broken by newer players, leading to an unfortunate outcome.* Your subsequent bid will show your M support, if any.

Regarding the Ms: bidding 1H-1S is different than bidding 1S-2H. Since you are still on the one level when you bid 1H-1S, showing 4 or more Ss, you may safely seek a **4/4** fit in Ss and be able to bail out of a misfit in 1NT. The 1S-2H bid always shows **5** or more Hs, never 4. **The MINOR SUITS give you the option of showing 10+ HCP with a FOUR card suit.** You will NOT bid 2M or 1NT, the minimum bids, with 10+ HCP because you have TOO MANY POINTS.

THE OPENER MUST BID AGAIN <u>*(REBID)*</u>...
...if the responder bids a new suit. Then the responder will continue or conclude the auction.

1. If he has **6+** of his M, he will bid his M again. *He shouldn't with only 5.** Example: 1S - 2C - **2S.** His first bid shows **5.** A rebid (without support) means **more** cards in his suit. Partner will <u>expect</u> at least 6 Ss.   *On the <u>rare</u> occasion, with no other option, the opener might have to rebid a strong 5 card suit.*
2. If he doesn't have 6 of his M, he will bid his next best suit: a 4+ holding in his second longest, lower-ranked suit. Example: 1S - 2C - **2D.** *The opener has exactly 5 Ss and 4 or more Ds.*
3. He may raise partner's suit with 3+. If responder bids a m, opener will assume he has at least 4. Ex: 1S - 2C - **3C.** Over a H response showing 5 Hs, he'll raise with 3 Hs. Ex: 1S - 2H - **3H.**
4. He may bid the lowest available NT if he is <u>balanced</u> & <u>minimal</u>, meaning he has some of every suit and only 12-15 HCP. Ex: 1H - 1S - **1NT.** Shows 5Hs & **< 4 Ss.** With 4 Ss, he'd raise partner's Ss.

Both bidders now have several options to describe their hands. Make the bid that BEST tells your points and distribution, and do not make a bid that misleads partner. **IF YOUR CALL DOESN'T FIT IT, YOU MUSTN'T BID IT:** make a *better* bid. For example, as responder, if partner opens 1S and you have 4 Ss and 11+ HCP, you would NEVER bid 2S because you are **too strong**. The bid of 2S doesn't **FIT** what you hold in your hand - spades yes, but points, NO!

Perhaps the next bid will help you...

THE LIMIT RAISE

If the responder has **FOUR** of partner's M suit and a **medium strength** hand (10-12 HCP), there is a special bid to show these two features known as a *__Limit Raise__*. The responder *__jump bids__* in the opener's suit. A limit raise is a game invitation. If the opener has "EXTRA PIZZAZZ" in his hand - **extra points, extra trumps, an extra long outside suit** (outside the trump suit), a __singleton__ (one card in a suit) or a **void** (0), he'll bid game.

    1H - 3H   I have 4 H and 10-12 HCP   or   **1S - 3S**   I have 4 S and 10-12 HCP.

The two hands combined are very close and...

He who knows...goes!

FYI - not everyone concurs that a limit raise requires **4** trumps. A few programs teach that you only need **3**. But since you show 10+ HCP by bidding a different suit and coming back to the M suit to show 3 card support, it is helpful to immediately make the **distinction** between having **3** trumps and **4** trumps in addition to a medium-strength hand. *That extra trump may be the pivotal bit of information needed to tip the scales into game for your side.*

GAME

What is game, deemed so important in bridge? A *__Major game__* is **4H or 4S**, based on the points per trick (see __Scoring__ on page 19). Most boards are played in a *__partscore__*, which is any contract below game, but you want to bid game if you have the points. It usually takes **25-26 combined HCP** to win ten tricks. Bid your M game if you can, because there is a **SIGNIFICANT BONUS** built into the score. If you do NOT bid game, you do NOT get the bonus, *even if you take more tricks than anyone else in the room*, **because you didn't take the risk.** If you open with 12 HCP, you can do the math and see that your partner's limit raise or two level response brings you very close. Bid game with EXTRA PIZZAZZ in your hand. What if you have opening count and your partner opens the auction?

Opening Count + Opening Count = Game
If game is possible - **bid 4H or 4S.** *Don't miss that high score!*

Summary/Pointers:

• After you sort your hand, add your HCP and assess what you may be able to do: whether open the auction, respond to your partner, bid game, or pass. You'll search for the "Golden Fit" and hope for a game contract.

• If you can open the auction, you will first look to your M suits to see if you have a 5 card M to bid. Then you will observe your partner's bids to see what he communicates to you.

Assuming your partner opens a major suit...

• If you are the responder, you show a **minimal hand** (limited to 6-9 HCP) by bidding 2M or 1NT (1H-2H; 1H-1NT; 1S-2S; or 1S-1NT), based on the number of cards you have in partner's M. The opener DOES NOT have to rebid over a minimal response. If you have 10+ HCP, you WILL NOT make one of these minimal bids.

• Sometimes you will respond 1S because you have 4 Ss and that is the correct response (1H-1S). Your **second bid** will show your minimal hand by either supporting partner's M suit at the lowest level, by bidding your S suit again at the lowest level (with 6 in the suit, rarely 5), by passing partner's second suit if he rebids at the two level, or by passing partner's S or NT rebid. The opener MUST BID AGAIN because of your NEW SUIT. Examples of minimal responder hands: 1H-1S-2C-**2H**, 1H-1S-2C-**2S**, 1H-1S-1NT-**2S**, 1H-1S-2C-**Pass** (no H fit, but the responder does have 4+ Cs), 1H-1S-2S-**Pass**, or 1H-1S-1NT-**Pass**. A 2NT bid by an unpassed responder is considered invitational (showing 11-12 HCP), so you should choose the best of the other options if you are minimal.

• If you are the responder, you may show a **medium or greater hand** (10+ HCP) by bidding a **new suit** over partner's M opening bid, OR by jumping in his suit - a limit raise. These bids include the 1H-1S bid, which could show **EITHER** a weak or strong hand. You may also bid 2NT or 3NT to show a medium+ hand and no M fit.

• **If you bid a __new__ suit at the two level, you MUST have 10+ HCP.** If you don't have 10+ HCP, you have to make a minimal bid even if you have a long suit you'd like to show. *You do not have enough HCP and do not want to **deceive** your partner.* You may or may not be able to show your long suit in the future. Follow the principles of your system.

• **The opener must bid again** if the responder bids a new suit. Such bids are forcing, *as long as the responder has never passed,* since the responder has not yet limited his hand. The opener will 1) Rebid his M with 6+, 2) Show his second 4+ card suit, 3) Bid NT if otherwise balanced (5332 in the suits), or 4) He will support partner's suit.

• NT bids are not forcing: they are limited (known range) bids whether made by opener or responder: 1H-1S-1NT= a minimum *opening* hand, and 1S-1NT= a minimum *responding* hand. The NT bids "put the brakes on" for the bidder.

• If the team has **25+** HCP, they should bid **game** (4H/4S). It is often the responder's job to place the final contract.

Practice and Application Lesson II: The M and m's - a major treat
Study guide p. 88

Suits left to right, in order, spades to clubs. A dash is a void, and an x is any card under (and often including) the 10.
Your hand below: **A.** Points? **B.** Can you open? If yes, what suit? **C.** If you can't/didn't open, can you respond?

	♠	♥	♦	♣	A. HCP?	B. Open?	C. Respond?
1.	KQxxx	Ax	Jxx	QJx	1. 13	Yes, 1S	Yes, and you should bid game.
2.	xxxxx	AKxx	KQx	x	2. 12	Yes, 1S - *really!*	Yes, and bid game somewhere.
3.	KQx	Qxx	xxx	Jxxx	3. 8	No	Yes, and you can support either M.
4.	-----	AJxxx	Kxx	KQxxx	4. 13	Yes, 1H	Yes - bid game.
5.	Jxxxx	AKQJ	Kx	xx	5. 14	Yes, **1S**, NOT 1H.	Yes - bid game.
6.	KQx	AQJxxxx	Kx	x	6. 15	Yes, 1H only, **not 2H.**	Yes
7.	Jxxxxx	Kx	Qx	Jxx	7. 7	No	Yes

Responding to partner. No one else is bidding.
Partner opens 1 Spade. What would you bid?
1.	xxx	Kxxx	Qx	Axxx	1.	2S
2.	xx	Kxxx	Qxx	Axxx	2.	1NT
3.	-----	KQxxx	Axxx	Jxxx	3.	2H
4.	x	KQJx	Qxxx	Kxxx	4.	2C: you're too unbalanced for 2NT.
5.	xx	QJ10xx	Axx	xxx	5.	1NT: you can't bid 2Hs with < 10 HCP.

Partner opens 1 Heart. What would you bid?
1.	AKx	QJxx	Jxx	xxx	1.	3H: a limit raise. You have a nice fit. Show it.
2.	AJx	xxx	xx	QJxxx	2.	2H
3.	KQxx	Jx	xx	Kxxxx	3.	1S
4.	KQx	QJ	Kxxx	Qxxx	4.	3NT: 13 HCP, balanced, < 4 Ss and no support for Hs
5.	Kxxx	AQx	Kxxx	xx	5.	1S, intending a game contract in Hs.

A few more questions...

1. What is the point range for a minimum response? — 6-9 HCP
2. If partner opens a M & you have 10 points and 3 card support, what do you do? — Bid a new suit at the two level, or bid 1S over 1H, if appropriate. You will not bid 2M as it shows a weak hand.
3. If partner opens 1H and you hold 2 Hs, 8 points, and 6 nice Ds, what do you bid? — 1NT. You do not have enough points to show the Ds.
4. If partner opens 1S and you have 3 cards in each major with 15 points, what do you bid? — A 4+ minor suit at the 2 level, anticipating game in Ss.
5. What are two "stop" bids if partner opens 1 of a major? — Two of the same M, or 1NT.
6. How may the responder show a medium hand? — He should bid a new suit or 2NT, based on his HCP.
7. What bid is a forcing bid? — Generally, a new **suit** bid by an unpassed hand.
8. What is **EXTRA PIZZAZZ**? — A hand with additional HCP, additional trumps, a two-suited hand, or a hand with a singleton or void. These concepts may be intertwined, as a a two-suited hand will often have a singleton or void. EACH of the above, or ANY COMBINATION of the above **increase your hand's value.** Look for "extra pizzazz" whenever you are considering bidding higher in the auction. *We'll learn more about EXTRA PIZZAZZ later.*

Lesson III - Bidding the M and m's, Part Two

In the last chapter we learned the Major opening bids and responses. What if you don't have a 5 card M, but do have 12 HCP? Then you should open your longer minor. To clarify minor opening bids: **we typically show 4+ Ds with a 1D opening bid and 3+ Cs with a 1C opening bid.** For complete information on minor opening bids, see the lower half of page 16.

Can you find a **M fit** if you bid a minor first? Yes, you can - it's your primary objective - so do not fail to open the auction: DON'T PASS with 12+ HCP because you DON'T have a 5 card M. If you refuse to show partner your points **now,** he will never believe you have 12 or more HCP later... **and you never lie to your partner.** The responder could have a long (5) or extra long (6+) M and you need only a few cards in his M to have a fit. YOU might have a 4 card M and partner has 4 of the same M: the Golden Fit could be one bid away.

MINOR SUIT OPENING BIDS & FIRST PRIORITY RESPONSES:

Opener	Resp:	Meaning:
1C	**1H**	I have <u>at least</u> 4 Hs and <u>at least</u> 6 HCP.

Do you have 4 Hs? **I may also have 4Ss, but NOT 5 or I would have have bid Ss first.** Opener should support Hs with 4, bid 1S with 4 Ss, or bid 1NT with a minimum balanced hand. Opener <u>must</u> rebid. His last choice would be to rebid the Cs with 6, or 5 if desperate for a rebid. *Responder could have* **more than** *4 Hs and* **more than** *6 HCP.*

| **1C** | **1S** | I have <u>at least</u> 4 Ss and <u>at least</u> 6 HCP. |

I might not have 4 Hs because I skipped over Hs, BUT if I have 5 Ss, I could have 4 OR 5 HIDDEN Hs. *Do you have 4 Ss?* Opener <u>must</u> rebid with some of the same choices - support Ss, rebid Cs, or bid NT.

| **1D** | **1H** | I have <u>at least</u> 4 Hs and <u>at least</u> 6 HCP. |

I <u>may</u> also have 4 Ss (but not 5). Opener should support the Hs with 4 Hs (his first priority), bid 1S with 4, bid NT, etc.

| **1D** | **1S** | I have <u>at least</u> 4 Ss and <u>at least</u> 6 HCP. |

I might not have 4 Hs because I skipped them, BUT if I have 5 Ss, I *could* have 4 OR 5 HIDDEN Hs, etc. The opener must rebid.

> When your partner opens 1C or 1D, you want to find a Major suit fit. If you, the responder, have a 4+ card M, bid it even with a nice minor suit.
>
> Keep reading to find out what to do with *two* 4 c Ms.

A major bid over an opening minor bid is ambiguous. **All you know for the moment** is that the responder has **4** of the M and **6** HCP. He could have **several** of the M and **20** HCP. *THE TRUE LENGTH OF EITHER OF HIS MAJORS OR HIS POINT COUNT IS <u>UNKNOWN</u>.* The opener must continue the auction as no "stop" or other limited bid has been made. Since the opener promises only 3-4 of his m, *his true minor suit length is unknown as well.* That is why these bids **force for one round** - to allow further description.

MEMORIZE - THIS IS A BIDDING IMPERATIVE TO DESCRIBE YOUR HAND:

If you have two 4 card Ms, bid them *"up the hill!"* (Hs, then Ss).
If you have two 5 card Ms, bid them *"down the mountain"* (Ss, then Hs).
If you have a 4 card AND a 5 card M, always bid the 5 card M first.

Why bid the Ms this way? The order in which you bid the Ms may tell partner how many you have in the suit and/or keeps the bidding low for ease in communication as you search for a M fit.

If the opener has **4** of the your M, you have the Golden Fit. Great news! The opener may rebid **1S** (showing 4) **over the 1C/1D - 1H bids,** searching for the *elusive 4/4 SPADE fit* in case the responder has both Ms. If you still have no fit, **bid NT for a higher score,** rather than staying in the minor suit. *Read that again!* The opener may tell more about his hand and/or fit at his next bid, or pass.

Tip: If you end up in a 4/4 trump fit, is just as good as, or better, than a 5/3 trump holding. Why? If you have a 3/2 trump split between the opponents, the odds-on split, a 4/4 holding leaves a trump in **both** the declarer's and the dummy's hands, while a 5/3 holding **removes** the trumps in the dummy's hand as the outstanding trumps are pulled. Hmmm...

OTHER RESPONSES OVER A MINOR SUIT OPENING BID

1C - 1NT **I do not have a 4+ card M,** I do not have 5 of your suit, and I only have 6-9 (10-) **HCP.**
1D - 1NT Ugh - often a difficult contract. Pass with a bare opener (12-15 HCP), OR rebid 2C/2D with **5**, another exception to the 6 card rebid rule, allowable because, if partner doesn't have the Ms (fewer than 4 in each one), he should have cards in the minor suits, but know that **a fit is not guaranteed.** If you open 1D, your partner may have a long C suit.

1C - 2C **I do not have a 4 card M,** but I do have 5 Cs or 5 Ds & 6-9 HCP.
1D - 2D A minimum raise showing the Golden Fit in a m. The score for 1NT or 2m is the same, but any overtricks you earn will make a difference in your score in NT, so determine if NT is feasible. *If you have 4 Ds and expect partner to have 4, 2D would be a reasonable contract if NT isn't possible.*

1C - 3C **I do not have a 4 card M,** but I do have 5-6+ Cs or Ds & 10-12 HCP.
1D - 3D A **limit raise** - the pair should consider a **NT** contract with that nice minor fit.

1C - 1D * **I do not have a 4 card M,** but I do have 4+ Ds and 6+ HCP.
Opener must bid again since no "stop" bid has been made. **NT** anyone?

1D - 2C * **I do not have a 4 card M,** but I do have 5+ Cs & 10+ HCP.
Where do you go from here? Try NT with M suit stoppers.

** These bids may be redefined in the future. We'll keep things **simple**.*

MINOR CONTRACT OR NO TRUMP CONTRACT?

If you are considering **GAME** in a **minor**, you need **28-29 HCP** and you must take **ELEVEN tricks.** Are you *SURE* you don't want that minor suit fit to help you make a **NINE trick, 25-26 HCP, 3NT** game contract for the **same score** (or better) instead? Hmmm...

(Important)

NO TRUMP RESPONSES OVER MAJORS OR MINORS:

We have seen 1NT as a weak response to any opening bid, M or m, but a NT response is not always weak. If 1NT shows 6-9 (10-), then it follows that 2NT or 3NT show greater HCP.

- **1 of any suit - 1NT = 6-9** HCP,** *no fit* — Fit: **3** of a major or **5** of a minor - the resp denies either fit. Over a minor opening suit, **resp first choice is to bid a 4+ card M.**

- **1 of any suit - 2NT = 11-12 HCP,** *no fit* — Fit: **3** of a M. Resp could have a m fit. Over a M opener, resp shows a balanced hand rather than bid a suit, possibly implying stoppers in both unbid minors. If open bids 1H, resp has fewer than 4 Ss and fewer than 3 Hs. If opener bids 1S, responder has fewer than 5 Hs. **Tip:** 2NT over 1S expect a 2443, 2434, or 2344 hand, & 2NT over 1H a 3244 hand. Over a m opener, **no 4+ card M.** Your team has a lot of HCP. Seek a NT contract, even with *(or especially with)* a m fit.

- **1 of any suit - 3NT = 13-15 HCP,** *game* — If a minor suit was bid, **no 4+ card M,** but may have a m fit. Opener stops with minimum HCP. Why? Your team has bid a **game contract.**

*** The **10** is missing. What is the reason?* **THE TRUE VALUE OF 10 HCP,** the break between a minimum and medium responding hand, is uncertain when answering in **NO TRUMP.** You must evaluate the 10 as a "rich" 10, or a "poor" 10. If the HCP are together: AKQJx(x) in one suit, KQxx, KQxx in two suits, or the HCP are concentrated in partner's suit, it is a rich 10 because it **yields tricks in a NT contract,** an 11-12 HCP holding in disguise. If the HCP are in **short suits,** or are spread out in Qs & Js (the "Quacks"), then you have a poor 10 that might not deliver enough tricks to make your contract because your low and/or unprotected honors will lose to the opponent's higher honors. Though your hand *appears* rich, it is deceptively weak. Most 10s are rich, but a NT contract **CANNOT COUNT ON RUFFING FOR EXTRA TRICKS,** so if the opener is minimal you won't encourage game with a poor 10 HCP. Think of 10 HCP as the dividing line between "hopeless" and "hopeful," from the responder's point-of-view.

If you bid at the two level in a SUIT to show points, ANY 10 HCP WILL DO.

UNLIMITED BIDS

You will hear or read about *1-over-1* bids, also noted as **1/1** (1C-1H, 1H-1S), or *2-over-1* bids, also noted as **2/1** (1H-2C, 1S-2D), terms used to describe some of the bids you've learned in the major and minor chapters. They may also be referred to as *unlimited bids*. They're forcing as long as partner has not previously passed. You may wonder if there are **limited bids.** Yes, they are: bids that show a specific range of points (1S-**2S**, 1S-**1NT**, 1S-**2NT**, 1S-**3NT**); the low NT rebids by opener (1C-1S-**1NT**); a simple rebid of a suit by either partner (1S-1NT-**2S**, 1C-1S-1NT-**2S**); or a limit raise (1S-**3S**).

A FEW MORE TIPS...

- **What if partner has previously passed?** He has from 0-11 HCP. If you open 3rd or 4th seat with bare bones, you won't expect a game contract with a partner who's already passed, but partner could surprise you with a hand that changes **dramatically** with your M bid if he holds **5 trumps and around 8-11 HCP**. If he has that type of hand, he will **BID GAME IMMEDIATELY**. More often, a previously passed hand is nothing to brag about.
- If partner has previously passed, and later responds to your opening bid with a **2NT** bid of his own, he shows **10-11 HCP**, not 11-12 HCP. If he had 12 HCP, he would have opened the auction when he had the opportunity:

BRIDGE IS A GAME OF SUBTLETIES

- Think **"at least"** about bids during the auction. The first bid you display may neither show the entire length of your suit, nor your total points. Don't worry if your hand isn't completely revealed after only one bid: a rebid may further "tell your story" - the story about your cards. **Your story changes with each bid you make, and your partner's story changes with each bid he makes.**

Whew! Responding, though it seems overwhelming at the moment, is not hard if you are aware of the basics: **DO NOT PASS when you can bid, and DO NOT promise GREATER or FEWER points than you have.** Partner is counting on you! I have witnessed unbid **games**: the responder had 6 HCP, 3 Hs, and *passed*. The 1H opener (me) had **20 HCP,** and tried not to cry. Never pass because you "don't like the look of your hand" (that's a classic), because you are "scared" (we're all terrified at first), or because you "couldn't think of what to do" (that means you aren't studying). Partner has 13 cards too, and your hands may dovetail beautifully. If your responding partner has **denied** 4 Hs, as in 1C - 1S or 1D - 1S, do not feel compelled to mention your 4 card H suit now with a minimal hand. Bridge is neither "Dear Abby," nor confession to your priest! Go with the information you have from what has been bid, adding any information you can deduct from what has **not** been bid. Partner may be able to show Hs later, **IF** he has them. *And don't be embarrassed in front of your teacher if you make mistakes.* What makes someone an expert? Mistakes! An expert is experienced at what NOT to do. *I've made EVERY mistake in my bridge career.* **So will you.** Your current mistakes will teach you correct bidding, and will prevent you from repeating the same mistakes in the future. Regard them as "educational encounters," or "opportunities for improvement." *To prevent basic errors, read/review this book often.*

When I quit making mistakes, I'll let you know, but don't expect to hear from me until I'm 168 - it could take 150 years of bridge!

Summary/Pointers:

- If partner opens a m suit, he shows 12+ HCP, 3-4+ in the m, **no 5 card M.** Your pair's **first priority** is to find a M suit fit. If you cannot find a M fit, you should investigate a NT contract. A minor suit contract would be your last choice.

- If the responder has a 4 card M, he bids it even if it's weak. With two 4 card Ms, he bids them "up the hill" (Hs then Ss) to keep the bidding low as the pair searches for a M fit. With a 5 card and a 4 card M, he bids the 5 card M first. He may be able to show the 4 card M later in the auction. With 5/5 in the Ms, he bids Ss first ("down the mountain"). Minor or NT responses indicate partner **HAS NO 4+ CARD M.**

- The team should remember that 1/1 bids and 2/1 bids are **forcing.** Neither side should pass until one partner has **limited** his hand. Ex: 1C-1H-1S-1NT; the responder limits his hand with 1NT. Ex: 1C-1H-2C; the opener limits his hand with a low 2C rebid. Bidding 1C-1H-1S-2D, the opener must bid again as **neither** partner has limited his hand.

- If the pair cannot find an 8 card fit in a M or m, they should get out of the auction ASAP. Partners should not "rescue" each other, as this may lead to an out-of-control auction, too high for safety. The contract may have to be in a lesser seven card fit, which may be quite successful, *especially if the contract is kept at a low level,* or in NT.

- When considering NT, a 10 HCP hand should be **upgraded** or **downgraded** based on its **trick-taking ability.**

- The rebid of a suit, M or m, **should show 6** in the suit, unless the player has no other bidding option. If a player must rebid a 5 card suit, it should be strong enough (additional honors) to safely pull trumps and maintain control.

BIDDING THE MINORS

Practice & Application Lesson III: The M and m's - one last taste   *Study guide p. 88*

Suits left to right, in order, spades to clubs. A dash is a **void**, and an **x** is any card under (& often including) the 10.
Responding to partner: partner opens 1 Diamond. No one else bids. What would you bid?

	♠	♥	♦	♣	
1.	xxx	Kxxx	Qx	Axxx	1. 1H
2.	AKQx	Kxxx	xxx	xx	2. 1H
3.	-----	Axxxx	KQxxx	Jxx	3. 1H - Yes, all hands in 1-3 respond 1H.
4.	KQJx	Qxx	Kxxx	xx	4. 1S
5.	Kx	QJ10	Axx	AJxx	5. 3NT: 15 HCP, balanced, no 4 card M.

Partner opens 1 Club. What would you bid?

	♠	♥	♦	♣	
1.	AKxx	Qxxx	Jxx	xx	1. 1H (up the hill)
2.	AJx	Jxx	xx	Qxxxx	2. 2C: no 4 c M, 5 Cs, weak Ds (can't bid 1NT), min hand.
3.	KQxx	Jx	xx	Kxxxx	3. 1S: a Major contract is your priority
4.	KQx	QJx	Kxxx	Qxx	4. 3NT: 13 HCP, balanced, no 4 card M.
5.	Kxxxx	AQxxx	Jx	x	5. 1S (down the mountain)

Your hand below. What would be the correct auction?   Partner opens: You: P's rebid: You:

	♠	♥	♦	♣				
1.	KQxx	Ax	Jxx	QJxx?	1. 1C	1S	2S	4S - maximum
2.	xxxx	AJxx	Kxx	xx?	2. 1D	1H	1S (NF)	2S - minimum
3.	Kx	AQxx	xxxx	AQJx?	3. 1D	1H	1S	3NT - maximum
4.	x	AJxx	Kxx	KQxxx?	4. 1C	1H	2H	4H - maximum
5.	QJx	KJx	KJxx	xxx?	5. 1C	2NT	Pass	Medium
6.	xx	AKxx	xxxxx	QJ?	6. 1D	1H	1S	2D - minimum (10-)
7.	Qxxx	AKxx	Axxx	x?	7. 1D	1H	1S	4S - pizzazz (sing C)
8.	Jxxxxx	Kx	Qx	Jxx?	8. 1C	1S	1NT	2S - minimum (~~NT~~)
9.	Jxx	Qxxx	Jxxx	Jxx?	9. 1D	Pass		< 6 HCP

➤ *See page 26 for further notes about M and m bids.*

OPENING A MINOR SUIT: With 12+ HCP, you will open the auction. If you have no 5 card Major, you will bid your <u>longer minor</u> promising **3 or 4** in the suit. There is more to opening minors though, so study the information below.

D	*Open the higher-ranked suit of EQUAL LENGTH minor suits down to FOUR/FOUR holdings:*
I	• With two 6 card minors, open 1D.
A	• With two 5 card minors, open 1D.
M	• With two 4 card minors, open 1D.
O	*With MORE Ds than Cs, open 1D:*
N	• 6 Ds and 5 or fewer Cs, or
D	• 5 Ds and 4 or fewer Cs, or
S	• 4 Ds and 3 or fewer Cs.

This means if you open 1D, partner will expect 4+ Ds.

C L U B S: *With a THREE/THREE holding in the minors, OR with MORE clubs than diamonds, OPEN 1C.*

Two exceptions (1) If the two minors are nearly the same length (4/5) but the shorter Ds are **much** stronger than the Cs, the opener has the *option* of opening the better D suit, then he may rebid Cs. This avoids rebid issues. Not a favorite option among bridge experts, but it's suggested as a standard option in ACBL literature. (2) When the opener has the somewhat rare holding (3%) of two **4 card Ms, 3 Ds & 2 Cs,** he'll open 1D, *even without 4 Ds.* Why? He logically anticipates the final contract to be in a M or NT. If his partner doesn't have a 4 card M, he'll have a balanced hand or a long minor. If he chooses to open 1C, he must **forever** announce that 1C opening bids "could be short." Bridge players prefer to open their longer minor, *not a doubleton*, and they'd rather not make an announcement.

Why the specific requirements about opening a minor suit? The groundwork is set for bidding certain difficult-to-bid hands.

Summary: You'll expect an opener who bids 1D to have 4+ Ds, and an opener who bids 1C to have 3+ Cs. The lone exception for a 1D opening bid having only 3 Ds, would be a 4432 holding - standard procedure.

Lesson IV The Rule of 20 and Very Offensive Bidding

THE RULE OF 20 OPENING BID

There is an opening bid which does not meet the minimum requirement of 12 HCP. It is known as the "Rule of 20." Why do we disregard our newly established bridge protocol to make this bid? We bend the rules because of the **power of length**. If you have a hand with 10-11 HCP, and **two** long suits where all your points are found, you know your hand has something good about it, but what is it? You figure your two reasonably strong, very long suits will pay off in tricks, so you'll open the auction as if you held 12 HCP. What takes tricks? **High cards**, **long suits,** and **ruffing.** You have the keys to success in your hand.

Your suits will be likely be 5/5 or 5/4, but could be 6/5 or 6/4. Open your longer suit. If your suits are 5/5, open the higher-ranked suit. *Then pray for a fit with your partner.*

The Rule of 20   =   Your HCP + The number of cards you hold in your 2 longest suits.
If that number equals at least 20, open the auction.

You should never waste an opportunity to learn a bridge adage. Even if your suits are 5/5, the tip still applies...

Six, five - *COME ALIVE!*

Bridge author, and generally good player Mel Colchamiro, author of the book How You Can Play Like an Expert (Without Having to Be One), recommends that you also have two ***quick tricks***: AA, AK (same suit), A - KQ or KQ - KQ. This is good advice because what will your partner think when you open? That you have 12+ HCP. If he has 12-13+ HCP, he will bid game. You must have a decent Rule of 20 hand, with two immediate wins for early control, to make that game partner so confidently bid. Mel calls this...

The Rule of 20 + TWO (2 quick tricks). *Some call it the Rule of 22. It works.*

THE PREEMPTIVE BID - OFFENSIVE & DEFENSIVE & OFFENSIVE

Do you think you've learned all you need to know about opening bids? Let me tell you a bridge secret... THERE'S ALWAYS MORE TO COME! We emphasized the value of length when we learned the Rule of 20, showing a two-suited hand. Partner picks one of your suits, or does his own thing. There is also a bid for a hand with ONE long suit. A suit in which you almost have the "Golden Fit" all by yourself. Hands with *fewer* points than opening count may make as good a score as hands with *greater* points because of that looong suit. And where there is length, there is shortness...for ruffing.

There's another distinction about these hands: they are virtually worthless if you DON'T get the contract. How do you proceed? You make an offensive and defensive bid at the same time by preempting. A ***preemptive bid*** tells partner you're weak (< 11 HCP), but have an extra long suit. You show this type of hand by **opening above the one level**. The level at which you bid corresponds to the number of cards you hold in your suit. *In the Standard American bridge world, a one level opening bid is stronger than than a two, three or four level opening bid.*

Preempt at the 2 level with 6 cards in your suit.
Preempt at the 3 level with 7 cards in your suit.
Preempt at the 4 level with 8 cards in your suit.

Do not preempt at the two level with 7 or more cards. It doesn't work - I've tried it. Preempt correctly.

You should have **5-10** HCP to preempt. If you have only 5 HCP, they'd better **all** be in that trump suit. If you have less than 5 HCP, forget it. This is not a wondrous, miraculous cure for a worthless, miserable hand.

Tip: if you have 11 HCP, open a good suit at the one level, then rebid it to show 6 cards in your suit. You are too strong for a weak bid. A 6 card suit gives you an <u>automatic rebid</u>. Hmmm...

Vulnerability is a factor too. If you are **non-vulnerable,** you may open with fewer HCP because the penalties are lower. That's when those 5-7 HCP suits may be bid preemptively. *They may be bid, but they do not HAVE to be bid. Nobody is making you do it!*

If you are **vulnerable**, you should have **8-10 HCP** *AND* **two of the top three,** *OR* **three of the top five honors**: AK, AQ, KQ, AKJ, AQJ, AJ10, KQJ, or QJ10. Protect yourself from the "Terrible Two Hundred", which is getting set two tricks vulnerable. Most preemptors follow the rules at the **two level**. Above that, it's a free-for-all,

THE RULE OF 20+2 AND PREEMPTIVE BIDDING

within reason of course. Time for a soon-to-be-famous bridge saying I made up...

CHECK & RESPECT: KNOW YOUR VULNERABILITY

The **offensive** element of this bid you can easily see: you will jump into the auction in an aggressive way with a long suit. The **defensive** element means that you open at such a high level you **take bidding space away from the opponents.** They don't have much room to interact before they are at game level, perhaps without a fit. We don't even need to point out how *offensive* this bid is to the opponents, who planned to open the auction. They will often grit their teeth and pass. Congratulations! You and your bid performed your crime well. Grand larceny!

However, bridge wisdom indicates to put the brakes on with certain distributions. If you'd like to preempt a minor, you should not have a 4 card M. Why? Your partner may have 4+ in the same M suit and, unless you are preempting the other M, you may end up in a minor contract for **fewer points**, thus a bad score. Some bridge gurus say not to preempt with a void. I would preempt regardless, especially if I was preempting a M and did not have 4 of the other M. Try the preempt on and see how it fits. I predict you're going to LIKE being a bit NAUGHTY as you meddle with the opponent's communication. Remember, at the **two level**...

Non-Vulnerable: 5-10 HCP and some honors; the fewer the HCP, the more honors in the preempt suit.
Vulnerable: 8-10 HCP and two of the top three OR three of the top five honors

Thats's your story and you should stick to it - especially when you're vulnerable.

When should you preempt? *You may preempt at any time during the auction.* If your first bid is a jump bid, it is a WEAK bid in a basic auction, unless it is a limit raise, 2NT, or 3NT. As opener, preempting makes life difficult for your opponents, especially if you have a M suit - obstruct! Second seat is okay, but the "cat is out of the bag" if RHO opens and his responder adds together their HCP: you may not intimidate them at all. Try it anyway **NV**; it might not be as effective because they have a lot of information, but perhaps you'll frighten them out of a makable NT contract, or make them miss their **SLAM** (12/13 level bid with a BIG bonus). Ex: Your suit - QJxxxx. If one opponent has the A and the other opponent has the K, they won't know they have **TWO** stoppers. They'll place you with an unstoppable AQJ1098 or KQJ1098 and miss their high score! *It happens all the time.*

After two passes to you, third seat is imperative! Where are all the points? In the next hand? Mess 'em up! It's okay even in 4th seat as an opener, **but only if you have spades or a 3 level minor**. *Why open the auction for them to find their M fit?* Some players will jump bid with a minimum hand (12-13 HCP) and a long suit in the 4th seat to *prevent* interference.

NON-OPENING PREEMPTIVE BIDS

You may **respond** to your partner with a preempt after the auction opens. This shows a weak holding (fewer than **6 HCP**, or you would bid as usual) and a long suit - a **"drop dead"** bid. You may also enter the auction holding a weak suit to "rain on their parade." The following are non-opening weak preempts:

1C (part) - [P] - **3S** (you: < 6 HCP & 7 Ss)   or   [1C by RHO] - **2H** (you): < 8 or so HCP & 6 Hs)

• **Now you have TWO MORE OPENING BIDS at your disposal to start the auction** •

For Future Study: _____

<u>The Rule of 17:</u> Your partner preempts at the two level in a major suit, you have a beautiful hand with lots of HCP, and you have two or more cards in partner's suit - a fit. You know he will make his bid with flying colors, but is there more to be made, like **game**? Especially when you're vulnerable and your partner is a **disciplined** bidder?

Some smart bridge player somewhere noticed this predicament too, and came up with the "Rule of 17". This rule means that you should add your HCP together with the number of trumps you hold, and if that number equals 17 or greater, you should bid game in a M. If partner preempts a <u>minor</u>, you could bid **NT** with a strong hand, IF you have other three the suits and some of partner's minor to serve as a source of tricks and/or transportation.

Rule of 17 (or 18): If your number of trumps + the number of your HCP = 17, bid GAME

Why 18 (or even 19)? As a new bridge player, sometimes I found it difficult to make game because my play-of-the-hand skills were not good yet, so my partner and I played this as "Rule of 18" until we were better players. Like Frank Sinatra, I had to do it "My Way."

<u>Continuing partner's preempt if you are weak</u>: the FEWER points you and your partner have, the MORE points the opponents have. It may be advantageous to your side to create confusion on the other side by raising your partner's suit or bidding game with FEW HCP and a fit. They'll be unsure of your exact holding and might not bid their game or slam. Don't make life easy for the opponents, and **don't worry about getting set NV**- they have game or better!

THE RULE OF 20+2 AND PREEMPTIVE BIDDING

Practice & Application Lesson IV: The Rule of 20 & Preemptive, Interfering, Nosy Bidding *Summary p. 89*

Open these hands, if you dare.

	♠	♥	♦	♣	
1.	Kxxxxxx	xx	Jxx	x	Pass; < 5 HCP
2.	Jxx	AKQxxx	xxx	x	Preempt 2H, V or NV: a strong preemptive hand.
3.	AJxxx	KQxxx	xx	x	Open 1S. The classic Rule of 20 opening hand.
4.	xx	Kx	Axxxxx	xxx	Preempt 2D NV, Pass V
5.	xx	xx	KQxxxx	KQx	Preempt 2D - NV or V.
6.	xxxxxx	Qx	Kx	Kxx	Pass. Poor Ss & an unprotected QH. Strength in short suits.
7.	AQTxxx	Kx	Qxx	xx	Open **1S**. Good S suit, protected honors, automatic rebid (2S).
8.	KQxxx	Axxx	Jx	xx	Pass. Your count is 19 instead of 20.
9.	AQJx	Axxxx	x	xxx	Open 1H using the Rule of 20. Your spades are prettier, but you only have 4. **Partner will bid Ss if he has 4.** If partner has 4 Ss, you will find your spade fit, don't worry.
10.	xxxxx	Jxxxx	AQ	K	Pass. Your HCP are not in your long suits and your K is a singleton. Your AQ will **depend** on the lead coming from the LHO for the Q to win. Ewww!

A few more questions...

1. If you preempt VUL, what will partner expect you to have? — Two of the top three OR three of the top five honors and 8-10 HCP.
2. Will you bid again if you preempt? — No! You have told your story. If you have a strong hand, strong enough to bid again, **you won't preempt.**
3. How many cards are in your suit if you preempt @ the three level? — 7
4. Does it mean a stronger hand if you don't open at the two or three level, but open at the ONE level? — YES!

FYI: You'll often see two level preempts referred to as "Weak Twos" in bridge literature. I put all preempts under the same umbrella. Why the different labels among the weak bids? In previous bidding systems, two level bids were strong, taking up a lot of auction space. Methods have changed through the years, but you will still find players who prefer strong two level opening bids.

In the next chapters, you will see the card table we use in bridge represented by a square. The directions are typical, with South at the bottom. South is usually **you** - answer questions from your point of view based on the diagram. The presentation should look more like the auction you see at the table. Further instructions, if necessary, will be in the text.

```
    N
W  □  E
    S (You)
```

SCORING:

Major tricks: Each trick=30 pts.   **Minor tricks:** Each trick=20 pts.   **NT:** 1st trick=**40** pts, subsequent tricks=**30** pts.
Game=100 pts. **Majors: 4** tricks x 30 pts.=120 pts; **Minors: 5** tricks x 20 pts=100 pts; **NT: 3** tricks-40+30+30=100 pts.
Game level contracts = Book + required tricks. Ms: 4H/4S (10 tricks); minors: 5C/5D (11 tricks); NT: 3NT (9 tricks)
Corresponding HCP value: 25-26+ = NT/M game   **28-29+** = m game   **33+** = Small slam   **37+** = Grand slam

Partscore (below game) bonus: +50 pts   **Game bonus:** +300 NV, +500 V   *Larger bonuses for slam level contracts.*
Set Contracts: *Each undertrick is -50 NonVul, or -100 Vulnerable   Penalties are higher if the contract is doubled.*

- A partscore is any score below game. Typically, 18-24 HCP will only be enough points for a partscore.
- Major partscores: 1H/S, 2H/S, or 3H/S. Minor partscores: 1C/D, 2C/D, 3C/D, or 4C/D. NT partscores: 1 or 2 NT
- A **three level** bid (not including 3NT) generally requires **22-24** HCP to be successful, a **two level** bid **20-22** HCP, and a **one level** bid **18-20** HCP. A suit contract, due to ruffing, may gain extra tricks with FEWER points, especially with extra trumps. Distributional (two-suited) hands are powerful - often much more so than their points indicate. You will adjust the value of your hand positively with extra trumps and/or long suits: that EXTRA PIZZAZZ.
- NT contracts require **slightly more HCP** than suit contracts because there will not be **extra tricks from ruffing.**

Lesson V   1NT Opening Bids and Conventional Responses, Part One

You learned all about the M and m's in chapters two and three. If you have 12+ HCP and a 5 card M, you will open that M, even if it has neither an honor nor any mid-range cards and you're mortified to bid it. If you have 12+ HCP without a 5 card M, you will bid your longer minor. You learned two more opening bids in chapter four - bids that STRETCH the standard opening requirements with good reason. There is yet another opening bid you can make: 1NT.

What if you meet the requirements to open a **minor,** but have between **15 and 17 HCP?** Your points create the need for a **special** opening bid, a bid that allows you to immediately convey to your partner that you have an unusually strong hand. If you have no voids, no singletons**, and no 5 card major,*** **open 1NT** instead of opening a minor. You promise a ***balanced hand***, meaning that you have at least two cards in every suit, and at most only one doubleton. It is an imposing bid, revealing a lot of information to your partner, while intimidating your opponents. *With 18+ HCP, open a minor, NOT 1NT. You will miss games if you fudge even a little bit.*

The NT opener's PARTNER ***announces*** "**15 to 17**" when the bid is placed on the table. The responder will feel somewhat absurd at first, but will soon become accustomed to the seemingly strange habits of bridge. When the opener shows such a strong hand, the responder knows his side has game if he holds 10+ HCP - not possible with a minor opening bid. A "rich" or "poor" 10 doesn't matter. *All 10s are rich when partner opens 1NT.*

Now that we understand the nuances of the 1NT* opening bid, let's examine the responses. The responses we will learn are noteworthy bids known as *conventions*. What is a ***convention?*** It is an artificial bid prompted by a specific auction, in this case the 1NT* opening bid. A convention, agreed to by both partners, helps a team learn more about each other's hands with minimal or low level bidding. Two conventions, *Stayman* and *Jacoby Transfers*, were developed for communication over 1NT* and are the most commonly used conventions today. If you employ them, **suit responses over 1NT* no longer have their usual meaning of length in the suit that was bid.** You'll find the use of these conventions well worth the loss of the "natural" bids. Why? They allow the pair to discuss their **suits** and **points** in detail. The natural bids do not. These conventions also allow the strong hand (the 15 to 17 hand) to remain hidden, no matter the contract, so that it's secrets cannot be seen. *Every hand has a secret!* The strong hand playing the contract is usually advantageous to the declaring side. The declaring side may even get a extra trick, known as a ***free finesse,*** with a lead into the big hand. Think about the opening lead coming *into* the AQxx in the declarer's hand. No worries about the location of the K!

However, before we learn these specialty bids, there is another system to learn we'll call the "PIG." The responder uses it to tell his number of HCP. It may be used alone over 1NT,* or in conjunction with NT conventions. This allows the NT opener and the responder to determine their optimum contract.

THE PIG RESPONSES OVER A 1NT OPENING BID

PASS	shows **0-7** HCP	(Poor hand)	The "P"
2NT	shows **8-9** HCP	(Invitational hand)	The "I"
3NT	shows **10+** HCP	(Game going hand)	The "G"

You will use the PIG over every 1NT opening bid by your partner. Memorize the point ranges.*

If the opener bids 1NT* and the responder has short Ms (< 4 Hs or < 4 Ss), responder goes directly to the PIG:

Opener:	Responder:	Meaning:	Final result:
1NT*	PASS	0-7 HCP	The opener will play 1NT unless the opponents intervene. No game.
1NT*	2NT	8-9 HCP	The opener will pass with 15 HCP. The opener will consider game with 16 HCP. The opener will bid game with 17 HCP.
1NT*	3NT	10+ HCP	Game is established. Opener passes.

*   *The responder says "15-17." He will always announce the point count for 1NT because the range may vary among pro teams.*
** *ACBL standards for opening 1NT bids allow a singleton A,K or Q, but a singleton may endanger a NT contract, rendering the declarer defenseless in that suit. I recommend the traditional method of no singletons, which fits best with the conventional responses to and expectations of 1NT.*
*** *Some pairs will bid 1NT with 15-17 HCP & a 5 card M, a semi-balanced hand. It's a partnership agreement (PA).*

OUR FIRST CONVENTION: THE JACOBY TRANSFER

Your partner opens 1NT.* You have a five card M suit you'd like to tell your partner about in case he has three or four cards in the same M suit. After all, you know he has at least two cards in your suit because he opened 1NT. How can you tell him about your long M, together decide the final contract, and let him play the hand whether the contract is in NT or the M suit? Enter the Jacoby Transfer. The Jacoby Transfer, bid by the responder says, *"Partner, I have a FIVE CARD MAJOR."* The clever part of this bid is that **the responder doesn't bid his own suit:** he coerces partner into bidding it. The big hand remains hidden whether the contract is in the responder's long M suit or NT. How does he do this? ***Referring to the bidding ladder, he bids the suit one rung below his actual suit.*** The opener says aloud, "Hearts" or "Spades," then bids responder's **true suit** at his next opportunity. This is called ***completing the transfer.*** Next, the responder bids the PIG to show his points, usually keeping the auction open another round so that the NT opener may have the option of placing the final contract. The NT bidder could have only two cards in his partner's suit and knows there is no Golden Fit, so he may prefer a NT contract. He will be glad to know about the responder's long holding, because it will help the opener win tricks in his short suit. The opener may favor the responder's M (holding 3 or 4 cards in the suit), and make the M suit the final contract. Transfers require **zero** HCP.

The Jacoby Transfer: Responder **shifts** his 5 card M bid to the opener; NO HCP requirement.

Opener:	Responder:	Meaning:	Opener:
1NT*	2D	I have **5 Hs.**	Says "Hearts" as soon as the 2D bid is made, then bids **2H** at his next turn.
1NT*	2H	I have **5 Ss.**	Says "Spades" as soon as the 2H bid is made, then bids **2S** at his next turn.

(Another public speaking opportunity, this one for the NT opener.)

After the transfer is accepted, locking the contract into the opener's hand, the responder shows his HCP (PIG).

Let's see a more complete auction. No one else bids in the following examples:

	Opener:	Responder:	Opener's rebid:	Responder shows his HCP:	
PASS:	1NT*	2D ("Hearts" by NT hand)	2H	*Pass.*	Bidding over.
	1NT*	2H ("Spades" by NT hand)	2S	*Pass.*	Good luck.

Responder shows a 5 card M suit & 0-7 HCP. The opener will play 2Hs or 2S, even with a 7 card fit. The responder hopes his long suit will help his partner make the contract because of its ruffing value. He's giving all he has to give to the team. These contracts are usually successful, especially if the responder has at least 3-4 HCP. *See top of p. 22.*

	Opener:	Responder:	Opener's rebid:	Responder shows his HCP:	
INVITE:	1NT*	2D ("Hearts")	2H	**2NT**	The opener sets final contract at his next bid.
	1NT*	2H ("Spades")	2S	**2NT**	Invitational strength.

The responder first shows his 5 card M suit, then 8-9 HCP with his 2NT rebid. The opener will pass 2NT, bid 3NT, or correct to 3 or 4 of the M, depending on his M holding and HCP. Opener may have just two of the M - his *worst* suit. He will be glad the transfer and subsequent bidding allow him to have a choice of contracts.

- With **15 HCP**, he'll make his best bid at the **lowest level** by passing or bidding **3** of the M.
- With **16 HCP**, he will consider his distribution and how many of the M (2, 3 or 4) he holds. He will pass, bid 3NT, or 3/4 of the M.
- With **17 HCP**, he will bid game: 3NT or 4 of the M, if he holds 3 or 4 cards in responder's M.

	Opener:	Responder:	Opener's rebid:	Responder shows his HCP:	
GAME:	1NT*	2D ("Hearts")	2H	**3NT**	Opener will pass OR bid 4Hs.
	1NT*	2H ("Spades")	2S	**3NT**	Opener will pass OR bid 4Ss.

The responder first shows a 5 card M suit, then 10+ HCP with his 3NT rebid. The NT opener is given the **option** of a NT or Major game contract. If he has at least 3 of the M, he will probably bid the M game.

1NT OPENING BIDS AND CONVENTIONAL RESPONSES, PART ONE: THE JACOBY TRANSFER

Why would you transfer then pass with few HCP? Why not pass as usual? Your HCP are important to find game, but it is also important to be in the safest contract for your side if you are **weak**. In fact, the weaker you are, the more important it is to be in a **suit** contract because of your ability to **ruff**. Desperate times call for desperate measures. If you have a 5 c suit, you WILL have a doubleton (or shorter suit) somewhere in your hand. Let your partner use the good in your pitiful hand - your length and shortness - to get the best possible score. With the traditional balanced NT hand, he should have at least two cards in each suit, a reasonable fit, AND don't forget the opener has a big hand to cover the responder's deficiencies, so DO NOT PASS with a long suit, even with **0 HCP**.

Is this a concept that takes some getting used to? Yes, and expect mistakes in the early days.

Practice & Application Lesson V: Jacoby Transfers (with this little PIGGY)   *Study guide p. 89*

1NT* - ?   You are the responder.   What do you bid with each of these hands?   No one else bids.

	♠	♥	♦	♣	
1.	Kxx	Kxxxx	Qxx	xx	Bid 2D, transferring to Hs, then 2NT (8-9 HCP) inviting game.
2.	KQxxx	Jxx	Ax	xxx	Bid 2H, transferring to Ss, then 3NT. Opener will bid 4S if he has 4 Ss.
3.	Kxx	AQJ	xxx	Kxxx	Bid 3NT, game. You have no 5 card M to transfer.
4.	Qxx	Kxx	Axxx	xxx	Bid 2NT, inviting game. You have no 5 card suit to transfer.
5.	xxxx	xxxx	Ax	Qxx	Pass. You don't have 8 HCP to invite game by bidding 2NT.

1NT* - 2H - 2S - ?   What do you bid after the transfer?

	♠	♥	♦	♣	
1.	Kxxxx	Kxx	xxx	xx	Pass. You have 0-7 HCP.
2.	Kxxxx	Axx	QJx	xx	3NT. If partner prefers S, he'll bid 4S.
3.	Qxxxx	Axx	Qxx	xx	2NT. You have told partner that you have 5 S and 8-9 HCP. He may pass, bid 3NT, or 4S. Perfect!
4.	Kxxxx	Jxx	xxx	xx	Pass. You have 0-7 HCP.

For Future Study:

Get comfortable with transfers, then learn how to bid these hands. Make sure partner knows these methods of bidding too. If the responder has "extra pizzazz" in his hand, increasing its value, he may bid game with as few as 7-9 HCP.

"I have a 6 c M."

Transfer as usual, then **rebid** your suit (3M) to invite with **7-9 HCP**, or bid game directly at your next bid (4M) with **8-10+ HCP**. What would give greater value to a 5-7 HCP hand? A singleton or void. The more distributional the hand, the fewer HCP needed for game. You already **know** you have a fit. That is why you insist on your suit by bidding it *"twice."*

Ex: 1NT*   2D   2H   **3H**   Resp has **6 Hs** & 7-9 HCP. The 1NT opener may bid game.
      1NT*   2H   2S   **4S**   Resp. has **6 Ss** & 8-10+ HCP. He knows there is a fit and game.

"I have TWO 5 c Ms."

Transfer to Hs, then bid Ss. This unexpected auction can mean only one thing - a second five card suit. The opener will select the M suit with the Golden Fit. If the responder has 9+ HCP, he will bid game and with fewer HCP, he will pass.

Ex: 1NT*   2D   2H (transfer accepted)   2S (Completely unexpected turn of events!) This shows **both Ms.**

For those who are addicted to bridge and want to better themselves, there is another method to show two 5 card suits. If you hand is very weak (< 5 HCP) transfer LOW with LOW points, if your hand is strong, transfer HIGH with HIGH points. **When you are willing to bid at the three level over a 1NT opening bid, you say you are interested in game.**

Ex: 1NT*   2D   2H   2S   Weak - pass or bid 3H if you have more Hs than Ss.
      1NT*   2H   2S   3H   Strong - bid game. A M game is expected because opener wouldn't bid 1NT* with two weak doubletons.

Building Bridges © 2022 Jeanne R. Wamack May not be reproduced in any form.

Lesson VI   1NT Opening Bids and Conventional Responses, Part Two

The Jacoby Transfer, showing a 5 card M, and the PIG are easy to incorporate into your bridge repertoire with a little practice. But what if you have a FOUR card M? You can't use the Jacoby Transfer because it is reserved expressly for **five card suits.** Again, that *elusive* 4/4 fit causes trouble - or does it? You're in luck since someone in the world of bridge developed a convention to find a 4/4 M fit if partner opens 1NT.* It is known as Stayman.

Stayman works similarly to transfers. After a 1NT* opening bid, responder's **2C** bid initiates Stayman, then Stayman is followed by the PIG. However, there are significant differences between the two systems. Besides the suit length difference, the responder must have **eight or more HCP** to use Stayman. Without 8+ HCP, the responder will pass. Following Stayman, the PIG has some alterations. **These alterations tell whether or not you have a fit in the same M suit.** Let's see how it works.

OUR SECOND CONVENTION: STAYMAN

Using Stayman (1NT - **2C**), the responder says, *"Partner, I have a FOUR card major."* He hopes the opener has one too, and that they MATCH. After the test for a fit (the opener's response), the team will discuss details about HCP. The requirements for the responder to launch Stayman are **at least one 4 card M** and **at least 8 HCP**. When the NT opener rebids, he must remember the usual caveat: two 4 card Ms are bid "up the hill" (Hs first, then Ss.)

Stayman: Seeking a 4/4 Major suit fit: The responder must have a minimum of **8 HCP**

The opener will make one of only three responses over Stayman...**2D, 2H, or 2S.**

Opener:	Responder:	Opener:	Meaning:	Responder bids a version of the PIG:
1NT*	2C	**2D**	I have NO 4 c M	**2NT** with 8 or 9 HCP (invites game) **3NT** with 10+ HCP (game)
1NT*	2C	**2H**	I have 4H *(& maybe 4S)*	**3H** with 4 Hs & 8 or 9 HCP ** **4H** with 4 Hs & 10+ HCP ** **2NT** with <u>4 Ss</u> & 8 or 9 HCP *** **3NT** with <u>4 Ss</u> & 10+ HCP ***

** If you get a **"hit"** on your suit, show your HCP <u>WITH YOUR SUIT</u> by bidding 3 or 4 of the M.
  If you DON'T get a "hit" on your suit, **respond in NT.** This shows you have **THE OTHER MAJOR SUIT.**

*** The opener can **CORRECT** to 3 or 4 Ss holding 4 Ss in addition to 4 Hs because your NT bid shows Ss.
  He already knows how high to bid **because your NT bid showed your HCP.** Hmmm...

1NT*	2C	**2S**	I have 4Ss, **but not 4 Hs**. Opener **skipped** Hs - he would bid 4 c Ms "up the hill"	**3S** with 4 Ss & 8 or 9 HCP * **4S** with 4 Ss & 10+ HCP * **2NT** with <u>4 Hs</u> & 8 or 9 HCP **** **3NT** with <u>4 Hs</u> & 10+ HCP ****

**** In case of confusion, there will be **no** correction to the other M in this auction. Why? Because the opener **denied** having Hs by bidding Ss. If you, the opener, have a H suit, *always bid it regardless of whether the S suit is better.*

IF EITHER THE OPENER OR RESPONDER HAS TWO 4 CARD MAJORS AND THEY FIND A FIT IN ONE M, THERE IS NO NEED TO "MENTION" (BID) THE OTHER M - GO WITH THE **KNOWN FIT.**

Over any **2NT** or **3M** invitational bid: with **15 HCP,** the opener will PASS.
                                              with **16 HCP,** the opener will CONSIDER game - will pass if too balanced.
                                              with **17 HCP,** the opener will BID GAME.

1NT OPENING BIDS AND CONVENTIONAL RESPONSES, PART TWO: STAYMAN

QUICK STUDY CHART OF 1NT* - STAYMAN 2C - PIG (INCLUDING VARIATIONS THAT INDICATE A FIT OR LACK THEREOF)

Opener:	Responder:			Meaning:	Final result:
1. 1NT*	2. **2C**				
3. 2D, 2H, 2S	4. **2NT** (no M fit)	**3H** (fit)	**3S** (fit)	**8-9 HCP**	The opener will pass with 15 HCP.
	"The Three Little PIGs"				The opener will <u>consider</u> game with 16 HCP.
					The opener will bid game with 17 HCP.
					If the opener is 4/4 in the Ms, he'll correct to Ss.
1. 1NT*	2. **2C**				
3. 2D, 2H, 2S	4. **3NT** (no M fit)	**4H** (fit)	**4S** (fit)	**10+ HCP**	Game. If the opener is 4/4 in the Ms, he'll bid 4S
	"The Three Little PIGs"				over 3NT.

Responder's rebids in **NT** show **NO FIT** and his HCP. Responder's rebids in a **suit** show a **FIT** (same suit) and HCP. Since the responder must have 8+ HCP to use Stayman, he will not pass, skipping the first bid of the PIG system.

Practice & Application Lesson VI: Stayman (and the Three Little PIGs)   *Study guide p. 89*

No one else bids...
1NT* - 2C - 2H - ?   You are the responder. What do you bid with each of these hands?

	♠	♥	♦	♣	
1.	Kxxx	Kxxx	Qxx	xx	Bid 3H, inviting game. The 3H bid shows a **H fit.** *Do not bid Ss.*
2.	KQxx	Jxx	Axx	xxx	Bid 3NT, showing your suit is Ss. Opener will bid 4S if he has 4 Ss.
3.	Kxx	AQJx	xx	Kxxx	Bid 4H. You have game values and a H fit.
4.	Qxxx	Kx	Axxx	xxx	Bid 2NT. This rebid tells the opener you have 4 Ss and 8-9 HCP.
5.	xxxx	xxxx	Ax	Qxx	Pass from the beginning. You don't have 8 HCP.
6.	KQJx	xxxx	Ax	Qxx	Bid 4H. You have 12 HCP. That your Hs are lousy doesn't matter.

1NT* - 2C - 2D -?   You are responder. What do you bid with each of these hands?

1.	AKxx	Qxxx	xx	Kxx	3NT
2.	AKxx	Jxxx	xx	xxx	2NT
3.	Axxx	xxxx	Qx	Kxx	2NT

4. What are the requirements to open 1NT*?   15-17 HCP inclusively. Not 14, not 18 (open a m).
5. With **one** worthless doubleton and 17 HCP, what do you open?   1NT*
6. With **two** worthless doubletons and 17 HCP, what do you open?   A minor suit.
7. What doe this auction mean? 1NT* - **2C** - 2H - 2NT - 4S?   The opener is 4/4 in the Ms and has 17 HCP.
8. What does this auction mean? 1NT* - **2C** - 2S - 3NT?   The open has 4Ss. The resp has 4 Hs & 10 HCP.
9. What does this auction mean? 1NT* - **2C** - 2S - 3S?   The partners have a S fit & resp shows 8-9 HCP.

Tip: How can you remember whether it's Stayman or a Jacoby Transfer? Think of Stayman 2♣ as a FOUR leaf clover showing a FOUR card M.

Tip: Bridge lore says you don't have to use Stayman if your hand is completely balanced (4333), you may choose to bid the **PIG** instead. The theory is that you won't be able to ruff until so late in the play that sometimes there is little benefit in having trumps. Your partner is balanced, so he can't ruff early either. Balanced hands usually play best in NT, but it's your choice.

The first time I didn't bid Stayman with a 4333 hand (to test the theory), we were set for a **zero** score - the worst outcome in the room. I was chagrined, expecting to have a good result. But don't let my unfortunate experience prohibit you from following expert advice. Experiment for yourself.

- **Most conventions are OFF with interference.** If the opponents interfere with your Stayman or Jacoby Transfer bids, you will make Standard American (natural) responses, OR
- **With a partner who doesn't play Stayman or Jacoby Transfers,** you will make Standard American responses.

Standard American responses are explained on the following page...

Some players with whom you'll play bridge, especially in a social game setting, do not know Stayman and Jacoby Transfers. These players can only bid their five card suit, have no means to show a four card suit, nor do they have a means to convey a range of HCP. Their method to deny game interest is to bid their long suit as low as possible, and to show game interest by making a jump bid. This is the Standard American style of responding to a 1NT* opening bid, employed before conventions were invented. You need to know Standard responses because Stayman and transfers are **off** with interference.

STANDARD AMERICAN: USE WITH INTERFERENCE OR AN "UNCONVENTIONAL" PARTNER:

If your partner doesn't play conventions, any low level response is weak and "to play."

- Interference: If the responder bids at the lowest possible level, it shows a weak hand (0-7 HCP) and a long suit. If the responder bids at the two level, the suit may be five cards long. If the bid must be made at the three level, the suit needs to be six cards long OR the responder must have more HCP (5-7). All these responses are known as **"drop dead"** bids. The opener will not rebid.

If your partner doesn't play conventions, a jump bid shows a 5+ card suit and forces game.

- Interference: If the responder **jumps**, it forces game and shows 10 HCP, or a 8-9 HCP hand with an extra long M suit. A S overcall is a problem. The pair must decide under what conditions the responder should bid 4H: should the responder bid 4H with 5 Hs & 10 HCP regardless of whether partner may have only two? The pair may decide that 4NT by the opener is "to play" without a 3-4 card H suit.

- Standard American responses **do not** provide a means to show a **four card M.** You may only bid 5+ card suits.

- Interference crowds the auction, making it difficult to bid suits with **8-9** HCP since the responder is unsure of the opener's exact point count. The NT responses are difficult too: if the responder bids 2-3NT to show his HCP, does it also show a stopper in the interfering suit? Does he expect the NT opener to have a stopper? The team must decide the answers to questions like these BEFORE the game begins and must establish a defense that both players understand. The purpose of **their** interference is to disrupt **your** auction, and they often succeed.

- Yet another issue: the bids above are useful over **natural** suit interfering bids, but the bridge world is full of conventional bids used to interfere with a 1NT opening hand. Many conventions show **two-suited** hands. **You need to know which suits the opponents have before you can ascertain whether to play or defend.** Ask the partner of the bidder what the bid means **when it is your turn in the auction,** then perhaps you will know how to proceed. You may get more information as the auction continues.

** *Prefer a 3NT contract to a D contract.*

For Future Study:

Get comfortable with Stayman and Transfers FIRST, then learn how to bid these hands. Make sure partner plays Stayman and Transfers and learns these too. Look for/ask for classes at your club.

"I have a 4 card M AND a 5 c M. I also have 8+ HCP."

Start with Stayman to see if you get a hit on EITHER suit. If not, **bid the 5 c M,** showing an extra card in that suit. The big hand will be the dummy if the opener has 3 of your longer M suit. Oh well. Another option: taking in all your information, he might bid NT.

Without at least 8 HCP, transfer your FIVE card suit and PASS.

Ex:	1NT*	2C	2D	<u>2S</u>	Partner is showing an extra S. He has 5 S & he also has 4 H.
	1NT*	2C	2D	<u>2H</u>	Partner is showing an extra H. He has 5 H & he also has 4 S.

Transferring to a minor:

There are several complicated ways to transfer to a m, but I prefer to bid **2S** for a transfer to Clubs, and I **jump to 3 Clubs** for a transfer to Diamonds. The strong hand remains hidden. You must be weak with **SIX** in the minor because you will be at the **three level.** If you are weak with a **5** card minor, **pass.** ALERT this non-standard transfer.

If you have a strong hand you do not want to play in a m. Bid the PIG.

Once you play Stayman and Transfers, a jump to 3C has nothing to do with SA bids unless there is interference.

1NT OPENING BIDS AND CONVENTIONAL RESPONSES, PART TWO: STAYMAN

- Using a convention means you give a bid. The benefit should outweigh the loss. If it doesn't, don't use the convention. Stayman and Jacoby Transfers are popular, evidence of their value.
- You may now use the Stayman and Jacoby Transfers Study Guides in Appendix A on pages 89 and 104.
- Mr. Jacoby authored a second well-known convention. To distinguish a Jacoby Transfer from Jacoby 2NT, say *"Transfers"* when referring to the Jacoby Transfer. Many players will say they play Stayman and Jacoby, which could lead to confusion in the future when you learn the other Jacoby bid. Instead, say you play "Stayman and transfers," or "Stayman and Jacoby Transfers."
- A tip: in the later lesson on defense, it is stated that the dummy usually has the short holding of trumps. When would the short holding NOT be in the dummy? *After a Jacoby Transfer.*

Summary/Pointers concluding our M, m, and NT opening bid chapters...

M and m notes

If you're overwhelmed by the M and m auctions, perhaps it will help you to think of the **common patterns.** These bids share the same values (Golden fit, no fit, HCP, non-forcing) whether bid over a M suit *OR* a m suit. Any other bid will be a forcing 1/1 or 2/1 response. In the forcing 2/1 response, the 2 level bid must be a NEW suit.

Opening bid	Minimum response	Medium response	Maximum response
1S/1H or 1C/1D	2S/2H or 2C/2D Golden fit & 6-9 HCP, NF		
1S/1H or 1C/1D		3S/3H or 3C/3D A jump bid = a Limit Raise Golden fit & 10-12 HCP, NF	
1S/1H or 1C/1D	1NT No M fit & 6-9 HCP, NF	2NT No M fit & 10-12 HCP, NF	3NT No M fit & 13+ HCP, NF

- If you or your partner open the auction, your goal is to play in a **Major or NT contract**. With a minor suit fit, take a chance and bid **NT.** *Do not be overly concerned about getting set in NT unless you have a void, singleton, or very weak doubleton in an unbid suit.* Try for the **best** score. The more NT contracts you play, the better your skills will be. Start practicing now.
- Research has shown that Major suit contracts are consistently the better contracts for bridge games because ruffing will stop the opponent's strong suit and usually provide extra tricks for a higher score.
- **Each hand tells a story.** Some are thank you notes (thanks for trying), some are short stories, and some are an epic tome like Lord of the Rings. Tell your story and stop. Do not repeat the **same** story over and over after it is completely told in one tidy bid UNLESS you are forced to rebid. Partner can see your bids on the table.
- Remember, each of your bids **change your story,** and each of your partner's bids **change his story.** *Look at your bids from your partner's point-of-view: what would you think your bids mean if you were in your partner's position? What are you conveying with each bid you make?*
- Anticipate what partner could bid, then think and plan before you bid.
- **Stop bids** are bids of an "old" suit at the lowest possible level, or NT bids at the lowest possible level.
- The bidding ladder is a "spiral staircase" for some - **spiral out of control.** Pay attention to "Stop, partner" bids and **end the auction.** You might end the auction **before** reaching game if you are in a terrible misfit, even if you have game values.
- Observe the auction to figure out how you and your partner fit together. If the sum of your HCP is at least 25-26, bid game with a fit. Trust your HCP. If game is not possible, *win the contract as cheaply as you can.*
- So far, we've concentrated solely on the responder's HCP, shown by minimum, medium, or maximum responses. **We will whittle down the opener's 12-21 HCP into a minimum, medium, or maximum range in the future.**

Lesson VII   Overcalls

It looks as if the opener and his partner have all the fun in bridge, but that is not the case. As we move around the table, an opponent who enters the auction (a.k.a. the **_overcaller_**) has an important job: to create trials, trouble, and tribulation. Just because the "bad guys" open doesn't mean the other side can't have a partscore or even game.

A LONG SUIT

If you sit behind (immediately follow) the opener, you may bid with certain restrictions. If the auction begins at the ONE LEVEL, you may overcall at the ONE LEVEL with as few as **8 HCP and a good 5+ card suit**, as in [1C]-1H. The suit needs to be **lead-worthy** (AK, KQ, AQJ, no less) because either you will be on lead, or your partner will lead that suit to you expecting good things to happen, like winning a trick or two. With only an eight point hand, you are NOT planning to take the contract, **you are making a defensive move to win tricks.** If your suit is poor, pass. If you are able to bid, perhaps your partner will have some points too. If he has support for your suit, he may raise your suit, continuing the auction. You will bid no further.

What if you must bid at the **two level**, as in [1S] - 2D, or [1S] - P - [P] - 2D? Then you should have a **full opening count with a reasonably good 5+ card suit,** especially if you are vulnerable. If you're non-vulnerable, 12+ HCP is preferred, though you might overcall with 11 HCP and a good **6+** card suit IF you have EXTRA PIZZAZZ in your hand, known as **_distributional value_** - 1 or 2 long suits (7/4, 6/5, 6/4, 5/5, or a good 5/4) and/or shortness, one of which, in theory, should be a singleton or void. *If you bid at the two level with fewer than 12 HCP you MUST COMPENSATE with safety features that enable you to gain control, pull trumps, and win tricks.* Vulnerability is shown by a red card pocket and/or "vul" on the top of the board. You want to let your partner know you have a lead-worthy, trump-worthy suit. Someone has the remaining points - could it be your partner?*

The reason for caution should be obvious: there is already a bid on the table showing 12+ HCP. The opposing side has a lot of information and can use it **against you,** if they have the remaining points. It may be good to step out and bid, or it may be a very dangerous step to take - a gamble on the outcome.

Some sources encourage two level overcalls with as few as 10 HCP. *Be very careful when challenging a bigger hand.* What if they leave you there, or double you for a high penalty? Overcalling at the two level is DIFFERENT than RESPONDING at the two level. When responding, there is the protection of partner's opening bid on the table promising 12+ HCP, so the responder may comfortably bid higher. That is why you must have more HCP to overcall at the two level, especially vulnerable - *you are taking a chance on the whereabouts of the remainder of the points.* Be consistent with overcalls so partner will know how high he can bid.

THE TAKEOUT DOUBLE

What if you have several HCP (12+), but are without a long suit? If your **_distribution_** (the number of cards in each suit) is correct, you may make a **_takeout double_** (TOX). You're asking partner for his best suit saying, *"My hand will make a great dummy for you. I can support anything you bid."* What is the correct distribution? Perfect distribution is 4441, with one card in the opener's suit. However, we don't live in a perfect bridge world, so TOX with **0-2** in the opener's suit as long as you have AT LEAST **Jxx** in all the unbid suits. If you break the rules and TOX with three cards in the opener's suit, two four card suits, and a doubleton, you can bet your partner will bid your doubleton. What then? **Be disciplined,** and rewards will come your way. How do you bid a TOX? Pull out the red card with the white X on it and place it on the table. A TOX may be bid in the 4th seat after two passes, showing opening or near-opening count and the unbid suits. You'll primarily seek a **M fit.**

After a **_direct seat_** (the bidder right after the opener) takeout double, your partner (the advancer) will bid his longest suit. He MUST bid unless the responder bids. If there is no intervening bid, the advancer has some responsibilities. If he has fewer than 10 HCP, he will bid his suit at the lowest available level. If he has 10 or more HCP, he will **jump** to show extra HCP. This is **invitational,** or if he has **opening count**, he will **bid game.** With **9 HCP** and a very long suit (6+), he may push the envelope and jump bid. His long suit creates shortness elsewhere in his hand for ruffing. The partnership has to have at least nine trumps between them - a powerful fit. If partner's best suit is *their* opening suit - he'll bid NT.

---

* *Vulnerability originated in rubber bridge. One side wins 100 points (a game) creating "vulnerability" which raises the stakes for that team. They are penalized greater (a handicap) for getting set, but the rewards are greater for bidding and making game or slam with the threat of a high penalty for failure. Vulnerability rotates among the boards in duplicate bridge. Players should privately check each new board to see who's vulnerable. VULNERABILITY IS NEVER ANNOUNCED AT THE TABLE.*

There is even more to this story. Assume the opponent to your right (RHO) opens the auction. You perform a TOX, but this time the other opponent responds. If your partner bids, he has to have some points because his bid is a ***free bid*** (not *Free Bird*, though some crazy bids a partner puts down may make you wonder if he's experimented with a mind-altering substance). He didn't have to bid because the opponent's bid frees him. He must have some HCP, a long suit, distributional values, or *something* that enables him to continue. It may be that the *contenders* have few HCP and wants to steal the contract. Trust your partner, not the opponents. *See why you never lie to your partner?*

OVERCALLING NT

What if you are balanced with 15-17 HCP sitting in the direct seat? You may overcall **1NT**, promising the same hand as if you had opened 1NT. Since a TOX **denies** the opener's suit, the 1NT overcall **implies** high cards in the opener's suit since you would have bid a TOX without his suit. If there is no interference from the responder, your partner may bid as usual over 1NT, known as "***systems on***" to seek the right contract. **Your systems are PIG, Stayman, and Jacoby Transfers.**

In the ***pass-out seat*** - also called the ***balancing seat*** - when your pass will become the third pass ending the auction, a bid of 1NT may show as few as **10 - 11 HCP** because bridge is more forgiving when you are in the fourth seat. You'll show a balanced hand with implied ***stoppers*** (high cards) in the opener's suit. **Don't let them have a one level contract if you have some points**. Without their suit, you would TOX in the fourth seat or bid your own long suit. *At times you'll make a fourth seat NT bid without the best of stoppers to join the auction (10983, J742) when you have several points.*

THE MOST PAINFUL NON-OVERCALL OF ALL

What do you do in the direct seat if you have a balanced hand with **12-14 HCP** and **3-4 or more cards in the opener's suit?** *YOU DO NOTHING BUT PASS.* You do not have a long suit (except for the opponent's suit, and you can't bid that - they'll destroy you), do not fit the requirements for a TOX, nor do you have enough HCP to overcall 1NT. You'll just sit, stew, and suffer through the auction to see what your partner does. The good news...you're in a great defensive position. You'd bid NT in the pass-out seat, NOT in the direct seat. *But 12-14 HCP?!!! Yeah, I know, I know...*

WHAT IF THEY PREEMPT?

If the opener preempts, there could be trouble brewing on the horizon for someone. If you are in the direct seat and have a good opening hand (better than the lowest minimum count - have 14-15**+** HCP), with a **very good 5+ card suit**, bid your suit if you can at the **two level**. You may have even more than five cards, because a long suit in one player's hand often creates long suits in at least two other hands. Sometimes the fourth bidder has a boring, balanced hand with no clue about the long suits everywhere else and is shocked at the seemingly reckless auction. (I've had the fourth hand several times.) Why must you have such a good hand? Because you are stepping out at a **high level** with no promise that partner holds **any** help for you at all - suit wise OR point wise.

Do not preempt over a preempt because you are too weak. Let partner bid his own suit or double for you to bid yours, if he has enough points. It's difficult to pass, but do it anyway.

Facing a three level preempt made by the opponents, unless you have a very big hand (18+ HCP) with an extra long suit, good grades, and fancy faces, defend. Same with the four level - you'd better have close to game in your own hand through length and distribution. *These holdings do occur because after all, a preempt shows a weak, obstructive hand. They are concerned about what YOU have!*

What do you do if they preempt, you don't have a long suit, but you do have a lot of HCP and the other three suits, each one with at least three cards and at least one honor? Sound familiar? With **16+ HCP**, make a TOX. Why do you need so many HCP? Partner may have **ZERO HCP,** and might have to bid at the three or four level if there is no intervening bid. After you force him to bid, you might discover you have an imperfect fit at a high level without enough points to compete and get set. You could be better off defending with fewer than 16 HCP: set THEM. Partner needs to know if you make a TOX with 16 HCP because he is supposed to jump with 10 HCP or more and if you have 16, your combined points are enough for a game level bid. Always tell the truth, and make sure your partner understands you. How can you make sure he understands you? **Take the time to discuss how each of you bid and play before the game begins.** Forge those partnership agreements - you'll be glad you did.

OVERCALLS

OVERCALL SUMMARY

A long suit level one   V or NV   A good, **lead-directing** (2+ honors, no less) **5+** card suit and **8+** HCP.

A long suit level two   V   A lead-directing, 5+ suit with 2+ honors and 12+ HCP.
                         NV   A lead-directing, 5+ suit with 2+ honors and 12+ HCP OR
                                     A good **6+** suit w/ honors and at least one short suit with 10-11 HCP.

Partner **MUST** be able to rely on these bids as accurate: your side may have game and he will bid game **based on your overcall.**

Takeout Double (TOX)   May be bid in either the direct seat or the fourth seat.

Promises opening count (or slightly less fourth seat) with at least **Jxx** in all unbid suits.

Advancer MUST bid unless there is an intervening bid by the opponent.

Advancer will bid at the lowest level with < 10 HCP, and he will jump with 10+ HCP. Expect 4 cards in his suit. *If advancer has an extra long (6+), strong M, he may jump with **9 HCP.***

If the responder intervenes after the TOX, and the advancer bids over the responder, he has to have a good hand or something special about his hand (a void or a very long suit) because his bid is a "free bid."

A TOX (in the direct seat) over a **preempt** requires a strong hand - at least 15-16+ HCP.

1NT Overcall   Direct seat: 15-17 HCP and stopper(s) in the opener's suit.
                    Fourth seat: 11+ HCP   and stopper(s) in the opener's suit.

Overcalling a preempt   The overcaller may bid at the two level with a 14-15+ HCP hand and a long (5+) suit.

The overcaller may bid at the three level with 18+ HCP and a long (5+) suit. If the overcaller is very distributional (he has a 2-suited hand), he may bid with 16-17+ HCP.

These bids may be dangerous, but the rewards may be high!

Special note: If the opponent bids a M and you TOX, it is a PARTNERSHIP AGREEMENT whether you promise FOUR of the other M. You will ALWAYS have at least **Jxx**, but it is up to you and your partner to decide specifics. I suggest that you not strictly limit yourself, but join the auction to at least let partner know you have opening count.
Frank Stewart writes, "Many a hand may compel you to enter the auction, though the hand may be imperfect in some way."

```
        N              You sit South. What do the following bids tell you about your partner's hand or your hand?
    W [ ] E            The opener is shown by o.
        S
```

1H?	1NT	2H	P	X	P
o1C ☐	o1D ☐	o1S ☐	o1C ☐ P	o1S ☐	o2H ☐ P
(you)	(you)	(you)	1NT	(you)	X (you)
Partner:	Partner:	Partner:	You show:	Partner:	You show:
8+ HCP	15-17 HCP	12+ HCP	11+ HCP	12+ HCP	15-16+ HCP &
& 5+ Hs	& D stoppers	& 5 Hs	& C stoppers	0-2 Ss & at	at least Jxx+ in Ss/Ds/Cs.
				least Jxx+ in H/D/Cs	

For Future Study:

If partner makes a TOX and you hold a LOT of high cards in the opener's suit (it's your best suit), and you KNOW that your **vulnerable** opponents will get set badly, you may pass and leave the X "in" for **penalty.** Your score will be higher if they are vulnerable and fail to make their contract than if you bid your next best suit for a partscore (+200 for you if they are set only one trick, and it gets worse after that). Hmmm...

Your other option would be to bid **NT**.

Building Bridges © 2022 Jeanne R. Wamack   May not be reproduced in any form.

OVERCALLS

Practice & Application Lesson VII: Overcalls of all sorts - Get your head in the game! *Summary p. 88*

Which of these can you overcall? RHO opens the auction.

	RHO:	You: ♠	♥	♦	♣	
1.	1S	x	AKxx	Kxxx	QJxx	Double. You have a perfect takeout double (TOX).
2.	1S	x	AKx	Kxxx	Axxxx	TOX. The Hs are good enough to first seek a **M fit.**
3.	1S	xx	Ax	Kxxx	AQxxx	Not enough Hs for a TOX. Overcall 2Cs.
4.	1S	xxxx	AJxx	Axx	Ax	You have no bid - too many Ss and too few Cs. Wait and see what develops.
5.	1S	AKxx	Qxx	Axx	Kxx	Bid 1NT. You have S stoppers and 15-17 HCP.
6.	1S	Kxx	AKxxx	Jx	Qxx	Bid 2Hs. Full opener.
7.	1C	Kxxx	QJxx	AJxx	x	TOX. Your distribution is too good to pass.
8.	1C	KQxxx	Axx	Jxx	xx	Overcall 1S because it's a level one bid.
9.	1D	xxx	AQJxxx	xx	xx	Bid 2H if NV, a preempt, and good luck!
10.	1D	xx	AKJxx	xxx	xxx	Overcall 1H. If the responder bids Ss & they end up playing in Ss, **you've given partner a great lead.**
11.	1H	KQxxx	xx	Axxx	xx	Overcall 1S. If they play in Hs, you'll lead the KS.

What is your bid?   ○ = opening bid

1. ○1C X P You?
♠ Kxx
♥ Qxxxx
♦ Kx
♣ xxx

2. ○1D X P You?
♠ Kxx
♥ Kxxx
♦ Qxxx
♣ xx

3. ○1S X P You?
♠ AJx
♥ Qxx
♦ xxx
♣ xxxx

4. ○1S 2H P You?
♠ Ax
♥ Kxx
♦ KJxx
♣ QJxx

5. ○1S 2H P You?
♠ xxxx
♥ Ax
♦ xxxx
♣ Kxx

6. ○1H 1S P You?
♠ Qxx
♥ Axxx
♦ xx
♣ Jxxx

7. ○2H X P You?
♠ Kxxx
♥ Ax
♦ QJxx
♣ QJx

8. 2H○ You?
♠ AKxxxx
♥ Kx
♦ QJx
♣ Qx

9. 1S○ You?
♠ AKxx
♥ Qxx
♦ QJx
♣ xxx

10. 1C○ You?
♠ AQxx
♥ Qxx
♦ Qxx
♣ AKx

11. 1C○ You?
♠ KQxx
♥ QJxx
♦ Axx
♣ xx

12. 2S○ You?
♠ Ax
♥ KQxx
♦ Axx
♣ Axxx

1. 1H   2. 1H   3. 1NT (for a higher score)   4. 4H (Partner promises a full opener)   5. Pass
6. 2S (Weak raise as usual)   7. 4S   8. 2S   9. Pass   10. 1NT   11. X (TOX)   12. X (TOX)

Building Bridges © 2022 Jeanne R. Wamack May not be reproduced in any form.

Lesson VIII Bidding after Interference

Back to the original opener (you), and your partner (who hasn't bid yet),...those diabolic adversaries dared overcall your opening bid! However, did you know your partner can **bounce valuable information off their interference?** The opponents thought they were pulling a heist, *but their bid can be used AGAINST them in two ways ...*

THE NEGATIVE DOUBLE

The *elusive* **4/4** fit is often hard to find. If partner opens, can you tell partner for certain how many you have in a M suit? Sometimes you can. You'll perform a ***negative double,*** the bid that sounds like an Olympic dive.

Opener	Opponent	Responder	Meaning
1C	[1D]	X	I have **4/4** in the M suits. With only one 4 c M, bid it AS USUAL: 1H or 1S. *
1C or 1D	[1S]	X	I have **4** Hs and **4** of the unbid minor. **
1C or 1D	**[1H]**	**X**	I have **4S** and 4 of the unbid m. *Partner, do you have 4S?*
1C or 1D	**[1H]**	**1S**	You KNOW partner has **5+** Ss since he DIDN'T NEGATIVE X.
1S	[2C]	X	4H/4D: shows Hs, Ds, < 3 Ss, and **8+** HCP. Two suits revealed. With 5 Hs and **10+** HCP, **you would bid 2H as usual.**
1H	[2D]	X	4S/4C: two bids in one. The X shows **8+** HCP since it's a 2 level bid. **With 5 Ss & 10+ HCP, bid 2S.** The responder has < 3 Hs or he'd support Hs.

The minimum point requirement for a negative double: ***

Level 1 = 6 HCP (1C - [<u>1</u>H]- X);   **Level 2 = 8 HCP** (1S - [<u>2</u>C] - X);   **Level 3 = 10 HCP** (1C - [<u>3</u>D] - X)

• The negative X is a **response** to your partner's opening bid. You cannot X partner's bid if he is the overcaller, the other opponent passes**,** and you have the other two suits. You will have doubled your partner, **an illegal bid.**
• if your partner opens and there is an intervening bid, could it be **weak** & **lead directing** for the opponents? You must try to respond with 6+ HCP. *Let your partner know you have points.* You may not have to negative X - you may be able to raise partner's suit. Don't forget the basic opening bids and responses. If you can't raise, can you bid NT? A new suit?
• And remember... a H overcall allows for a MORE PRECISE **S** COUNT. Internalize the bracketed info above.
• Experts state that if you are showing a major and a minor you may have merely a "tolerance" for the minor. A ***tolerance*** means you don't have four, but do have three reasonably good ones, such as QJx. This is to protect your contract if you end up in NT and need stoppers in the m you indicate you have.

1C - [1S] - X (by you) could mean any of the following:

1. xx AJxx Kxxx xxx   The classic holding of 4/4 in the unbid suits, *promising 4 in the M.*
2. xx KQxx QJx Kxxx   You hope partner supports your Hs, but if the opener has Ss, shown by a NT rebid, you will be satisfied that you are in the right contract.
3. xx KJxxx QJx Qxx**   Since you can't bid 2H directly (< 10 HCP), *you show your Hs by doubling.*

---

*   Auction: 1C (partner) - [1D] - 1H or 1S (you): you **PROMISE FOUR** of the M, essentially disregarding the D overcall. A negative X would show **four of EACH M.** With a 4 card and a 5 card M, **bid the 5 card M first.**
** Your partner opens 1D. You plan to bid 1H to show that you have 4 Hs. The auction goes 1D - [1S] - *you?* You DON'T have **10+** HCP so you could bid at the two level, but you DO have 6-9 HCP, 4-5+ Hs and some good Ds - NEGATIVE X. Your partner may have 3-4 Hs: you'll find your fit. Depending on your HCP and the rest of the auction, you will pass at your next bidding opportunity OR you'll bid 2H with 6+ Hs.
*** **If your X forces your partner to a higher level,** you should have the points to compete at that level. Example: 1H - [1S] - X = <u>8</u>+ HCP. If partner bows out in NT, he will be glad you have extra HCP for his NT contract.

For Future Study

Players will try to show a 4 card M, even if they don't have <u>anything</u> in the **unbid** suit (no length OR strength). If your hand fits this category, *you **must** have support for your partner's suit* **in case he doesn't have your M,** OR you can bid NT because you also have the overcaller's suit and enough HCP. You've got to have SOMEWHERE TO RUN: A LANDING PLACE, AN ESCAPE ROUTE - in case of a **M misfit.** Auction: **1C - [1S] - X (by you**) could mean...

1. xxx QJxx x KQxxx   **You will rebid Cs** if there's no H support from your opening partner.
2. xx KQxx QJx Kxxx   You hope partner supports your Hs, but if the opener has Ss, shown by a NT rebid, you will be content. If he has no H support or S stoppers, **you'll rebid Cs next round**.
3. KJ9x QJxx AJxx x   **You plan to rebid NT** if partner has no H support, since **you** have S stoppers and HCP.

- What if the opponents **double** the opening bid? Be thankful for the information and bid as if they had passed, depending on your hand and HCP of course. Be aware that they should have an opening point count and **the three unbid suits,** making them the more "dangerous" hand should your team end up winning the contract.

A tip: Think of the **negative double** as a relative of the **takeout double** - except that you have the **two** unbid suits.

Tip two: On page 10, it says that 2NT is rarely used as a response. If 2NT is the responding bid after an overcall, it shows 10+ -12 HCP, no M fit, and stoppers in the overcalled suit: 1S-[2H]-2NT= < 3 Ss, medium HCP, and H defense.

Another tip: Your partner has told you two suits he holds. *A lead, perhaps?*

THE CUEBID

A second way to give information to your partner after interference is a *cuebid*. A cuebid is **the bid of the opponent's suit**. Yes, *his suit!* If your partner has **opened OR overcalled,** a cuebid shows support (3+) and 10+ HCP (unlimited, unless you've previously passed). You don't have to worry if it is a rich 10 or a poor 10. Cuebids force a rebid on your partner - he can't leave you in *their* suit. **The cuebid is an extremely important bidding tool to know.** Showing 10+ HCP with support may be difficult because of interference, and it is urgent for your partner to know your hand is not hopeless but is actually quite strong. Your partner also needs to know whether your side has the majority of the points so he may comfortably continue to compete in the auction. Use the cuebid with interference to show a medium+ hand over Ms *or* ms.

○ = opener	LHO	Partner	RHO	You	Means:	
1.		○1H	[2C]	**3C**	I have 3+ **Hs** and 10+ HCP	
2.	○[1C]	1S	[P]	**2C**	I have 3+ **Ss** and 10+ HCP	(For my overcalling partner)
3.			P (dealer)			
	○[1D]	1H	[P]	**2D**	I have 3+ **Hs** and 10-11 HCP	(I've previously passed, but I have 10-11 HCP and H support)
4.	○[1C]	1H	[1S]	**2C**	I have 3+ **Hs** and 10+ HCP	(Cuebid their lowest suit)
5.	○[1S]	2H	[P]	**2S**	I have 3+ **Hs** and **10-12-** HCP	
				~ or ~		
				4H	*If I have 12+ -13+ HCP, I will go straight to game.* Partners don't lie. You promise an opening hand if we're V and you overcall at the two level. *(Right, partner?)*	

A **cuebid** is better than a **limit raise** over interference because it **forces a rebid** on your opening partner. Why is that good? He could pass a limit raise with 12-13 HCP (fearing that you have only 10 HCP) and miss game, but you'd have another bid because you cuebid. He might have a big hand and can safely show you, knowing you also have more than minimum points and won't pass. *You* might have a big hand and want to bid again to tell more about your hand. You might have three of his M and 10 HCP and can't make a limit raise, which requires four of the M in standard bridge.

Cuebidding creates a dilemma with your jump bid to the three level. What was a limit raise has now been **replaced** by the cuebid due to interference. So what does a jump to the three level now show? Many partnerships make the agreement that a jump bid in partner's suit becomes **preemptive** (weak: < 10 HCP) over interference, a good strategy because those preempts cause a heap o' trouble for the opponents. They can't happily park at a low level because you took away their simple raise. How annoying! This defensive bid works especially well if they're vulnerable and you're not vulnerable. If you adopt this treatment for **weakness,** remember to always use the cuebid to **show strength.**

Without interference, you and your partner may agree the limit raise is in effect as usual - four card support and 10-12 HCP.

Therefore, if you have 10+ HCP with support and can't figure out how to tell partner your better than minimal count over interference - remember to use the CUEBID. For your partner, the surprise of seeing you bid the opponent's suit should be a **reminder** that this is a CUEBID and **he can't pass.** *After all, you wouldn't want to play in their suit.* Perhaps he has extra values and your side has game. At the very least, if partner opened, your side has enough points to compete at the three level (22-24 combined HCP). You'll find that you use the cuebid quite often.

- **Negative doubles** and **"positive" cuebids** - two great weapons for your bidding arsenal •

BIDDING AFTER INTERFERENCE

Practice & Application Lesson VIII: Bidding after they cut in: the nerve!   *Summary p. 93*

Part.	RHO	You ♠	♥	♦	♣	Bid?	Hide the answers!
1. 1H	[1S]	KQxx	Kxx	xxx	xxx	?	2H: 8 HCP and 3 H support. Your Ss will be handy.
2. 1C	[1H]	Kxxx	Kxx	Kxxx	xx	?	X: negative double - you show 4Ss and 4Ds.
3. 1H	[2D]	Kxx	xx	Kxxx	Jxxx	?	Pass: no H support, can't X, can't bid 1NT & HCP are too low to bid 2NT. Partner will have another bid.
4. 1C	[1D]	Kxxx	Kxxx	Qxx	xx	?	X: a perfect negative X.
5. 1D	[1S]	xxxx	AKJx	xx	QJ10	?	X: You have 4 Hs and a tolerance for Cs. If they continue bidding Ss, they will have trouble.
6. 1C	[1D]	KJxx	KJTxx	Kxx	x	?	1H: There is room for partner to rebid 1S.

LHO	Part.	RHO	You ♠	♥	♦	♣	Bid?	Hide the answers!
1. [1H]	1S	[P]	Kxx	xx	KQxx	Qxxx	?	2H: Cuebid - 3 c support and 10+ HCP.
2. [1C]	1H	[2C]	KQx	Qxxx	Axxx	xx	?	3C: Cuebid - 4 c support and 10+ HCP.
3. [1D]	1S	[P]	Kxx	Qxx	Jxxxx	xx	?	2S: You can make a simple raise.
4. [1C]	1S	[P]	Kx	QJxx	Kxxx	Qxx	?	1NT - you cannot bid a negative X or cuebid.
5. [1C]	1S	[P]	Kxxx	AQx	xxx	xxx	?	2S: Shows minimum holding as usual.
6. [1S]	2H	[P]	Kxx	AQxx	x	Kxxxx	?	4H: Does partner tell the truth?!

What is your bid?

	1. 1S / ○1H □ 2H You?	2. ○1S □ 2C You?	3. ○1H □ 2D You?	4. ○1H □ 2D You?	5. 1H / ○1C □ P You?	6. 1S / ○1C □ P You?
♠	xx	Kxx	Axx	Jxxx	Kxxxx	Kxx
♥	x	xxxx	Kxxx	Qxxx	xx	Axxx
♦	KQxxx	AKx	xx	x	KQJx	QJxx
♣	AQxxx	xxx	QJxx	Qxxx	Kx	xx

Answers: Don't Peek!
1. X: X to show at least 4/4 in the minors & at least 8 HCP. Partner will have now have another bid. This is not a penalty double of 2H. It looks like a negative X, but is actually a TOX. The point is the same. You'd support partner's Ss if you could. If he rebids Ss to show 6, you'll be happy to pass.
2. 3C: Cuebid to show 3+ support and 10+ HCP.
3. 3D: Cuebid. A simple raise of 2H doesn't show your true HCP.
4. 3H: Weak and preemptive.
5. 1S: You cannot negative X because it is illegal! Partner would be barred from bidding again! BTW- you are too strong to bid 1NT, just in case you were considering it.
   *It's a partnership agreement whether or not a **new suit** forces one round after an overcall.*
6. 2C: Cuebid. Partner overcalled; he has at least 8 HCP - total unknown. You should succeed in 2S if he is minimal.

MINI REVIEW: At times new players have a moment of confusion - *When do I bid a 4 card suit?* You may open a **4** card **minor** suit, NOT a 4 card **M** suit. You may RESPOND in a **4** card **Major** suit OVER partner's opening m, in an effort to find a 4/4 M fit (1C-1H/1S). You may bid 1S over partner's 1H opening bid showing **4** (or more) Ss (1H-1S). You may REBID 1S over partner's 1H response to show **4** Ss (1C/D-1H-**1S**). *If you'd had 5 Ss, you'd have opened 1S.* You may choose to REBID partner's m, holding **4** with no M fit, instead of passing NT (1D-1H-1NT-**2D**). Open's rebid shows a **4+** card suit (1S-2C-**2D**), and a TOX or neg X shows **4(+)** in a M suit.
Suit OVERCALLS should be at least **FIVE** cards long, since you are saying with your bid you'd like for your suit to be the trump suit. It could be deadly to overcall with fewer cards: you won't be able to **draw AND ruff**. Ex: [1H] - 1S = 5+ Ss, [1S] - 2D = 5+ Ds, etc.

Lesson IX   Leads

You've exerted much effort learning how to bid, *but half your time is devoted to playing against their contract*. It's time to learn some **defense**. The opening lead is your **first defensive move.** Do not dismiss this important opportunity and table just any card.

GOOD LEADS

What is a good lead? First of all, did the auction give you any clues? Did partner bid a suit? If so...

Lead partner's suit

You'll make your partner happy by helping him set up his suit, and it's good to make your partner happy when you can. Lead his A if you have it, lead a doubleton in his suit **high/low,** or lead low from 3-4 with a **lone** honor (Kx$\underline{x}$, Kxx$\underline{x}$). If you have **two** honors, lead the higher honor, the lower honor, then lead the small card: Q$\underline{J}$x. Finally, lead the middle then top of junk (9$\underline{7}$2) a.k.a. MUD (p. 37). You'll lead a middle card then a higher card so partner won't think you have a doubleton OR an honor. Was he an overcaller? You hope he told you the truth and bid a lead-worthy suit.

When you lead a high or low card in his suit, you are giving him specific information about *your* holding. If you lead his A, partner may not know much about what else you have, but he'll love the fact that you have his A. (If you ever supported his suit in the auction, he'll know you have at least **3**, and if you responded NT, he'll expect **2 or fewer**). If you play a doubleton high/low, he'll know you can ruff the third round - and maybe win the Q they have. If you lead low showing an honor, he'll try to trap a high card in an opponent's hand. If you play two honors then your lowest card, he'll know where all the "goodies" are in his suit. Not all these leads may be considered standard leads, but they are *REVEALING*. Develop an understanding with your partner about your team's leads. What if partner didn't bid? Do you have a promising suit? Your lead reveals information about your hand. The best lead is to...

Lead the top of a sequence.

A sequence vs. their suit contract may be as few as **two touching cards** because the third round is likely to be ruffed. Lead the top of AK(Q), KQ(J), QJ10, or QJ9. Versus a NT contract, lead the top of **three touching honors.** Sometimes you don't have a ***perfect sequence***, but a ***broken sequence***. Defending a suit contract lead the top card from $\underline{A}$KJx. If you have the AQJx, try to **wait** for the suit to be led to you, so you can trap the declarer's K, if he has it. With an ***interior sequence*** such as K$\underline{J}$10x(x), defending a NT contract, lead the **top of touching honors,** here the J. Your intent is to drive out the opponents winner(s) so that you control the suit. Versus a suit contract, if you can wait, you may trap multiple honors, OR your suit may cause problems in the end. What if you don't have a sequence?

Lead fourth from your longest and strongest suit,
NOT headed by the Axxx or Jxxx.

You may lead a small card from Kxx$\underline{x}$(x), Qxx$\underline{x}$(x), or from non-consecutive honors such as the KJx$\underline{x}$. This tells your partner that you have a **lone** high honor somewhere in that suit and he should lead it back to you, but occasionally it is your longest suit (xxxx$\underline{x}$x) without honor cards and you have no better lead. Do not lead an "Ace from space" (Axxx) and hand over the suit for free (costing them only small cards that will lose anyway), and do not lead from Jxxx. The opponents always seem to have the 10, so your lead killed your J and gave them a **free trick.** Let your "four to the Jack" (a description of what you hold) be a troublemaker, not a gift. What if your partner leads a J? He did not follow the usual "good lead" suggestions, so he must be leading from a interior sequence (KJ10xx), OR from J1098 in a desperate attempt to set up a future winner. *He sent a boy to do a man's job!* He's telling you what he holds in the suit - help him set up his suit. If you are defending a NT contract and he leads a M, even if it's weak, he'll try to win the 4th and/or 5th trick. Down one! Any other possibilities? Perhaps you could...

Lead the unbid suit...

if the opponents bid three suits, especially if they end up in a NT contract. If all else fails, lead a trump.

Lead a trump

...if they limped to a partscore, settled for second choice, seem to be in a misfit, or sacrificed to get the contract, shown by a hotly contested auction. If they debate (via their bidding) over the trump suit, each hand is probably showing a long suit. The declarer may plan to throw all his losers on partner's suit to succeed. Shorten his trump stack, which may be his entries to the board, OR could be the trumps he uses to ruff *your* winners. Perhaps the dummy has few trumps. If so, get rid of them. If they have two suits and your side has the other two suits, prevent a deadly cross-ruff or cross-trump which will hold you helpless as they take your winners. *However, don't keep leading trumps once the dummy is void because it will be a two-for-one sale for the declarer.*

Building Bridges © 2022 Jeanne R. Wamack   May not be reproduced in any form.

Lead partner's negative X suit

During the auction, did partner negative X? Maybe he has strength in those suits. Lead one with no better option.

If things are really bleak, lead the dummy's suit.

Did the dummy to your left bid a suit the opener didn't like? Do you not like it either? If so, *your partner may have length in that suit.* Some experts say to lead the dummy's first bid suit while others say to lead the second suit.

Did they end up in a NT contract? Did they bid 1NT-2NT-Pass or 1NT-3NT? Perhaps they don't have much in the majors, so...

Lead a major against a No Trump contract, if they opened NT and stayed in NT.

If you're weak, lead your shortest M, hoping to tap partner's M. If you are strong, lead your longest M (4+).

NOT SUCH GOOD LEADS, BUT NONETHELESS, THEY'RE LEADS
...because you may lead anything you want to, even if it's an awful lead.

You've learned to lead an A when you have the K. If you don't follow that rule, you may set up the opponents' suit for them by leading an **_unsupported_** ace (an ace with no other honors). If you lead that beautiful A, what will the opponents play on it? They'll happily throw their smallest cards in the suit. So, be patient and...

Do not lead an Ace from space.

If THEY have the honors in a suit in which you hold the A**,** YOU control the suit until the A has been played... *and control is what defense is all about.* Never lead the A without the K (A J54), or lead away from an A in a suit contract (A43 2). You may lead an A, or lead away from an A vs. their NT contract IF you have a scattering of high cards and length in your suit, such as AQ9xx or AJ97x. Let the A be worthy of his rank because...

...Aces catch faces...

not worthless trash. Make them pay for taking the contract by forcing them to **use an honor card to dig out your ace** so they LOSE A TRICK they were depending on. Another lead that is not especially a favorite is...

The top of nothing.

If you don't have anything in the suit, partner might. If you lead it, he will have to play a high card if he has one. His best card will **die** under the declarer's higher card and you'll have accomplished nothing for your side, but you will have given the bad guys a **free finesse.** If partner doesn't have a high card, you've given the bad guys a **free trick.** ARGH! Partner doesn't want to know what you DON'T have, partner wants to know what you DO have. In spite of everything, if you have to lead from a forlorn suit, lead an **8 or 9,** telling partner **NOT** to return the suit. **A low card usually indicates an honor and asks for a return,** as in Kxx x or Qxx x. A high card is **discouraging.** The good news? You've told partner to return a different suit, which is helpful information for him...if he notices your card.

Do not lead a doubleton...

planning to clear the suit in time for **third round ruffing.** Why? Because by then, someone else will be out as well. Forget it, unless it is the AK doubleton, partner bid a suit, you lead the third trick to partner, he actually has the A of his suit, he remembers to lead your suit back to you, you can beat the declarer's trump, the opponents are in a game contract, *and all urban legends are true.* Then maybe you'll set them.

More often than not, leading a doubleton is a useless shot in the dark. I should know...I've beat my head against that brick wall enough. Do you believe in miracles? If you lead doubletons you must. And how often do miracles happen? Not very often - that's why they're miracles. I believe in them, but not at the bridge table when you lead a doubleton.

Do not lead a RANDOM singleton either...

because you will likely hand control to the opponents and they'll take it all. How do I know? I've tried that too - many times, I shamefacedly admit. My team would get low scores, and it would be all my fault because I led poorly. I would sit quietly during the **_post-mortem_** (after play discussion) and hope no one noticed me. If it dawned on my partner that my lead was the problem and he gave me "the look," I'd run hide in the restroom!

FYI - I once undertook a casual poll of singleton leads at a tournament. Out of approximately 408 boards played during the week, the RANDOM lead of a singleton would have benefitted my team ONCE.

However, continue reading...

You may lead a doubleton or a singleton under certain circumstances

You should ALWAYS lead a doubleton or singleton if it is in your partner's suit. If you have a doubleton, play **high/low**. This shows you have only **two** in his suit to set up a 3rd round ruff, OR to tell him how many you have in his suit so he knows how many rounds he can safely continue playing his high honors. You may lead a singleton if you preempted, perhaps if you have several trumps including winners that regain control for your side, or if you have **a very weak hand** and expect your stronger partner to have entries to return your lead for ruffs. Another situation: perhaps you and your partner bid a suit together but didn't win the auction. Your first lead is a card from yet another suit: "**the unexpected lead.**" What did you tell partner with your lead? That your card is a singleton (NOT a doubleton), and he should return that suit for a ruff if he wins later. This is especially effective if you lead an unbid A, win, then lead your mutual suit: that A figuratively screams, "I am a singleton!" Hopefully partner wins in your mutual suit, then returns your original lead. Be prepared for declarer's glare. If partner doesn't have the A of his suit, perhaps one of you can get back in **immediately** with the A or K of trumps - allowing another ruff before you're out of trumps.

The problem with a **random** singleton lead is that all the other hands have that suit, *and two of the three hands belong to the opponents.* Will you be setting up their suit for them, or worse, giving them control to draw trumps? What if your trumps are the Qxx? You are likely to get ONE trump trick anyway, so what did you accomplish? If partner NEVER bid, what are the chances he has the A you seek? One day you'll figure out when a singleton lead might win, **based on the auction,** but don't automatically do it right now; search for the MOST beneficial lead. No random tosses because you have a singleton, please. However, never say never. Ever. *Especially in bridge!* On occasion, random singleton leads are good leads - 1 out of every 408 boards!

Don't lead an unsupported honor

There are few honor cards in each suit: only four out of thirteen cards have assigned points. If you have honors, play them in a way that benefits your side. You know not to lead an A from space. Try not to lead away from an **AQ** either. Declarer may have the **K**, so try to ***trap*** it (catch the opponent's high card with a higher card of your own), and establish other winners in that suit for yourself. Partner will wonder why you didn't lead your own suit. You'll hope that he is sharp enough to lead it to you, *through the declarer.* If the K is in the dummy...*oh well.*

Don't lead away from Jxxx

Yes, this may be your longest and strongest suit, sorry, *but don't lead it.* Don't lead the J OR the lowest card: "four to the jack" can be a "thorn in the flesh" to the declarer in any contract, because the J may keep a long suit from being established, and/or could be the setting trick. Grrrr! The J may not amount to a hill of beans, but you don't yet know his *True Hollywood Story.* Now might be the time to lead the unfortunate "top of nothing" from another suit. At least tell partner you don't like the suit you led.

If partner leads a J, consider why he would do that, especially facing a **NT** contract. He might be leading from an interior sequence - KJ10xx. *Depending on your holding,* (AQx, A4, Q6) you may need to play **high** so that you keep a **low** card to return to him at a later opportunity to avoid ***blocking*** his suit. If you keep your high cards in your partner's suit, you could "wall off" his suit. He'll be unable to continue running the rest of his long suit, because your **lone card is higher than any of his,** and he has no other entries to his hand. Don't worry about losing YOUR high cards - *get them out of partner's way.* Show partner what you have in his suit and help him set it up. *He has the length necessary for winning tricks.*

Sometimes the opening lead is a PROCESS OF ELIMINATION,

the lesser of evils...like voting for a politician. Lead the 8C from Axx Jxxx Kx 8643, because you can't lead anything else. Partner will be looking at both your lead AND the dummy to figure out information about your hand. If you lead the A, he will expect you to have the K. If you lead the K, he will expect you to have the Q. If you lead 4th, he will try to lead back to your hidden honor unless there is danger in the dummy. If he plays high/low **while on lead in your suit,** he is showing a doubleton. Time for a ruff. If you were unable to bid in the auction, partner cannot expect very many HCP in your hand, and vice versa if he didn't bid. Better luck next time.

These are guidelines to help you make a tough decision. The principles behind them are based on what works on average. As there will be times when what seems to be the best or proper lead fails miserably, you may console yourself with the thought that you made a "standard lead." For success, make sure you and your partner understand what each other's leads mean, and remember that many hands do not give a textbook lead. Discuss your leads with your partner and make your leads as **clear** as possible: *think clarity, not charity.*

Figuring out the best lead is an art form **nobody** has mastered.
Thoughtfully consider the auction and do your best.

LEADS

Practice and Application Lesson IX: Leading by a Nose *Lead table p 87*

Your partner bid 1S, but you didn't get the contract. What would you lead?

You				Lead	Cover the answers.
♠	♥	♦	♣		
1. Kxx	Qxxx	Jxxx	xx	?	Lead your smallest S to show a lone honor.
2. Kx	Qxxx	Jxxxx	xx	?	Lead the K of Ss, then a low S: shows a doubleton.
3. QJx	Kxxx	xxxx	xx	?	Lead the Q of Ss, then the J, then the low S.
4. xxx	AKxxx	Qxx	xx	?	Either the middle spade, then top (so partner doesn't expect an honor or doubleton), *or* the A of Hs. Partner must be weak if you didn't get the contract. See if he plays **high or low** in Hs. Can you get a third round ruff?

Partner never bid.				Lead?	Answers
1. AKQxx	xxx	Jxxx	x	?	Ace of Ss (top of a sequence).
2. xxxx	QJ10xx	Axx	x	?	Q of Hs (top of sequence)
3. xxx	QJ10xx	Ax	Axx	?	Great opportunity to set 3NT!!! Lead Q of Hs, then lead the J when you get in with an A. Finish playing the rest of the Hs when you get in with the 2nd A. **If you lead an A, you will NEVER set 3NT.**
4. KQxx	xx	AJxx	xxx	?	K of Ss. **Do not lead a D!** You may get **two** D tricks, depending on where the K and Q are located, if you **wait.**
5. Kxxxx	Jxx	Qxx	Ax	?	4th S
6. Jxx	Jxx	Kxxx	xxx	?	4th D
7. NT contract:					
Auction: 1NT - 3NT:				?	Lead a M. It's a toss up as to which one unless the auction gives you a clue, which it does not.
Qxxx Qxxx KJx xx					

Final bid is underlined. You are on lead - what do you lead?

	1. ○1S	2. P	3. ○1S	4. ○1C
	<u>3H</u> 2H	P ○<u>2H</u>	P <u>2H</u>	<u>2H</u> 1H
	2S	P	P	2C
	You	You	You	You
♠	KQx	QJ10xx	Qxx	AK
♥	Ax	xx	xx	xx
♦	xxxx	Kxx	xxxx	xxxx
♣	xxxx	Axx	xxxx	xxxxx

1. K of S, then the Q.   2. Q of S   3. Lead lowest S   4. AK of S, THEN a C. Partner may return your original lead for a ruff. Why else would you lead this way?   *FYI: some partnerships lead **KA** to show a doubleton.*

* **MUD** stands for "Middle, Up, Down," a lead used to better describe your holding than simply leading a low card from three in partner's suit, as a low lead should show an honor. If you play a doubleton high/low, MUD helps partner distinguish that your lead is from three cards rather than two cards. You give **count** with your lead. Hmmm...

Building Bridges © 2022 Jeanne R. Wamack   May not be reproduced in any form.

Lesson X   The Finesse

When you are the declarer, you'll find that you don't usually have all of the top cards in each of the 4 suits. There will be missing honors to which you may lose tricks, and all those lost tricks put together could set your contract. How can you make the most of what you have? You learn to *finesse*. **A finesse is an attempt to make a low card (lower than an A), possibly a losing card, a winner.** You've seen the word previously in this book - in the NT chapter and in the lead chapter. Now you will learn the meaning of the finesse, its purpose, and how to do it.

Let's say you have the AQ10x in a suit and xxx in your hand. If you lead the A, what will everyone put on it? His lowest card in the suit. Will an adversary **donate his K** to help you make your contract? Would you? Of course not! Now the A is gone, and you play the Q. What will happen to the Q? The K will carry her off. Later, you lead the 10. If the J hasn't fallen yet, you'd better believe he will fall now. How many tricks have you taken in the suit? ONE LOUSY TRICK! The suit is a reasonably decent suit with multiple honors and should have **yielded more tricks.** How can you possibly hope to take additional tricks with a holding like this? *You must play it differently.* You should...

Lead low to the card you want to win a trick.

In our example (AQ10x), you are missing the K and J. Let's say you first choose to finesse the Q instead of playing the A. The missing K is located either in front of or behind (follows) your Q. **You have a 50/50 chance to make the Q win IF you finesse, instead of a near 100% chance for her to lose if you DON'T finesse.** You will finesse by **leading low to the Q from the OPPOSITE hand.** If the K shows, win with the A. Now your Q is the top card in the suit (she has been *promoted)*. If you don't see the K, play the Q. Maybe she will win. If she loses to the K, you have made **the best play** for what you have in the suit. Some comfort - if the K is held by the RHO, **the Q was never going to win anyway.** *But if the K is on the left...!* Don't despair if your finesse loses - you still have a second finesse waiting in the wings - the finesse of the 10 for the missing J.

Finessing is the heart of play-of-the-hand skills. With finesses, you may trap honors, gain tricks, set up long suits, succeed in risky contracts, and use cards as transportation to the other side. There are many types of finesses in bridge and the topic is worth study. We will explore some common finesses.

You are South. North is the dummy. Remembering the instructions above, how would you finesse? Answers are on the next page.

1.	2.	3.	4.	5.	6.
A	A	K	A	A	A
Q	x	Q	Q	J	x
x	x	x	10	10	x
x	x	x	x	x	x
☐	☐	☐	☐	☐	☐
x	Q	x	x	x	Q
x	x	x	x	x	J
x	x	x	x	x	10
					x

THE FINESSE

1. & 2. Lead low toward the Q from the opposite side. In #1, you hope the K is on the **left,** in #2, you hope the K is on the **right.** If the K is where you hope he is, you will get at least 2 tricks. It doesn't matter if the A and Q are together or separated - **the method of finessing is the same - lead low toward the card you want to win.** In 2, DON'T lead the Q toward the A. If she is covered by the K, you must play the A and won't have next round control.

3. Lead low to the K or Q, it doesn't matter which one, because they are <u>touching</u> (consecutive) honors - essentially the SAME CARD to you since you hold both of them. You hope the A is on your **left.** If the finesse works, **come back to your hand** and lead low to the other honor. Remember...

If a finesse works, repeat it the same way if you need to finesse again.

You would **never** lead low to the K and when it wins, **play the Q.** You must finesse **the same way again,** or the Q will fall under the A when she shouldn't. *I once made that mistake...*

Sometimes there are 2 missing honors, as in our original example...

4. If you need three tricks, or want to take as many tricks as you can and are not worried about losing control, **lead low to the 10** and hope both the **K and J** are to your **left**. If you led low to the 10 and the **K** wins, the **J should be on your left.** The Q is safe now. If you also have the 9, *use it in a future finesse against the J!* Their honors may be <u>*split*</u> - one honor on each side, so you may lose only one of your high cards.

The two missing cards will be divided one of four ways - each a 25% chance with no clues from the auction.

They could both be on the left, both on the right, the K on the left and the J on the right, or the J on the left and the K on the right. Regardless, **finessing is the best play for what you hold in the suit.** If you lead to the 10, and the J takes it instead of the K, it's a guess as to where the K is located. **Finesse the same way** and hope for an honor split. See the box on the right.

5. Same as #4, finesse the same way twice (to the 10, then the J) and hope the honors are split or both on the left. Don't faint if the finesse works. *It's worked for me!*

6. Now you have some honors in each hand, so your approach is different. You may lead low from the A holding towards the Q, recommended by experts, perhaps cashing the A first, OR you may **lead the Q** and if the K covers her, play the **A.** If the K doesn't show, **let her ride.** If the **Q wins**, lead the **J.** The K should be on the left since it didn't cover the Q the first time, so it is *trapped.* If the K covers the J this time, play the A. The 10 will now have been promoted and you own the suit. If the K doesn't show, let the 10 ride as usual and you'll win the entire suit! Remember this caveat...

If you lead an honor in a finesse, you want it to be covered. If you DON'T want it to be covered, *DON'T LEAD THE HONOR!*

What are clues that a finesse won't work? The auction is the first clue. If an opponent bid the suit you are trying to finesse, can you guess where the missing honors are? If your LHO leads **low** in this suit, is he showing an honor? Perhaps that is a clue.

In Ex. 6, if your RHO bid that suit, *lead low to the Q in your hand, BUT ONLY AFTER pulling trumps.* You must pull trumps because his partner is likely void and will ruff. You won't lose much anyway, as he bid a K high suit. YOU'LL NEVER FINESSE AND CAPTURE THE KING, if it **follows** (sits behind) the A. Now <u>you</u> own the suit.

Another clue is how many points each opponent holds. If one opponent bids and the other one never bids, chances are the missing honors are in the bidding hand. Not a guarantee, but it's a clue. If no one bids, initially it's a guess. If the opening opponent, who did not land the contract, plays two Ks and two As or the equivalent, he's probably exhausted everything he has. The remaining points **may** be in the other opponent's hand.

Learn to finesse, and you will find you do it quite often...and sometimes that little ole finesse *saves your big ole contract.*

---

4. Your dummy:
A
Q
10
x
☐
x
x
x
Your hand as declarer.

The missing K & J will be split one of four ways:

LHO	RHO	Odds
KJ	----	25%
K	J	25%
J	K	25%
----	KJ	25%

With no clues from the bidding, you have a 50% chance that the K is located to your left.

With no clues from the bidding, you have a 75% chance that both honors are to your left OR that they are split and at least one finesse will work if you plan to finesse the 10, then the Q.

You have a 25% chance that both honors are to your right - the worst outcome.

The odds are in your favor.

Practice & Application Lesson X: A Fine Finesse *Finesse chart p. 93*

1.	2.	3.	4.	5.	6.	7.	8.	9.	10.	11.
A	A	A	K	A	x	A	K	x	Q	A
Q	Q	x	x	Q	x	J	J	x	J	K
x	x	x	x	10	x	x	9	x	x	x
x	x	x		x			x			x
	x			x						x

☐ ☐ ☐ ☐ ☐ ☐ ☐ ☐ ☐ ☐ ☐

x	J	Q	x	x	A	K	x	Q	A	x
x	x	J	x	x	Q	10	x	J	10	x
	x	x	x	x	x	x		x	x	
		x						x	x	

<u>You are the declarer sitting south. How would you play each suit?</u>

1. Lead low to the Q from the south, and hope that the K is on the **left.** You may get two tricks.

2. Lead low from south to finesse the Q, then play the A. You hope that the K is doubleton on your **left** because you have 8 in the suit. Lead this way unless the bidding tells you the K is on the right; then lead low to the J.

3. If you don't know where the K is due to the auction, play the A and lead low to the Q. You will get at least two tricks, possibly more, if the suit breaks evenly.

4. If you *have* to play this suit, lead low to the K and hope the A is on your left.

5. If you need 3 tricks from this suit, lead low from south to the 10. Whether or not the 10 holds, go back to south and finesse the Q. You hope both honors are on the L, or that they are split. If you only need two tricks, finesse the Q, not the 10. *You may finesse the 10 later.*

6. Lead low from the dummy toward the Q to get two tricks.

7. You are missing the Q. Where is she? You hope that the **opponents** lead this suit for a **free finesse.** If you must lead it, have there been any clues from the bidding or play of the hand so far, indicating where she may be? If only one opponent bid, could she be in his hand? Do you remember how many points have fallen so far? If a non-bidding or weak opponent has already played an A and K, or the equivalent holding of only 6-7 HCP, perhaps the other opponent has her.

When playing a NT contract, if one opponent is "dangerous" because they have strength or a long suit in which you are weak, this is the type of hand that allows you to finesse *away* from the dangerous opponent.

8. Depending on how many tricks you need from the suit, you may want to finesse the 9 first, then the J.

9. If you have to lead this suit, lead low from the dummy to the Q or J, then repeat the finesse the same way.

10. You are missing the K. Where is he? Lead the Q toward the A and hope you trap the K on the right. If you're successful, lead the J, then lead the remaining low card to the 10. If the K is on the right and stays trapped, you'll win four tricks. *If this is not your trump suit, you'll get ruffed - draw trumps first. Beware!*

11. You have <u>**limited entries**.</u> From south, **play low and let it go!** *No matter what you see, do not play the A or K.* If the suit breaks 3-3, the last four tricks are yours with ONE entry to get there. This is not really a finesse, just a tip on how to play this holding correctly. It **would** be a finesse if you held the AKJxx opposite the xx. Finesse the J - he may win! Then play the rest of the suit from the A down. *One of my students, a fiery redhead, told me she "didn't believe this would work." She tried it, it worked, and she became a believer.*

If you want additional information on finessing, *The Encyclopedia of Bridge* has pages of finesses under the listing "Suit Combinations." If you sincerely want to improve your game, one day take the time to learn the various ways to finesse a suit. The finesses you will encounter most frequently are available on flash cards from bridge supply houses. According to professional player **Allison Howard Cappelletti,** once you know how to finesse correctly, you can play your hand more confidently, and spend your valuable time learning other aspects of play.

Lesson XI   Play of the Hand: Suits and NT

If the declarer doesn't pause to create a strategy for playing his hand, *he could jeopardize his contract on the opening lead.*

IN A NO TRUMP CONTRACT, COUNT YOUR WINNERS
...and see where you could make up for a shortfall.

How do you count winners? When the dummy is tabled, compare the two hands you'll play and count your **touching cards** in each suit **from the A down.** Every A you have is a winner. If a K is with the A of the **same suit,** the K is a winner too. To count a Q as a winner, she **must** be with the K and A of her suit. It is the same with the J. For the J to be a winner, the J must be with his A, K, Q, and so on. If a long suit is missing the A, but has the K and Q or better, it is a suit that might be *developed* for tricks, but no winners may be counted yet because you must **lose control of the entire hand** to create winners in that suit. **Winners cannot overlap** - the combined suits must be long enough, or one-sided enough for each winner to take a trick. The AKQJ opposite the xx will yield FOUR winners. The AK opposite the QJ will provide only TWO winners, even though the same four honors are present, because all the honors will fall together. Many times when playing a NT contract, you will be short of direct winners, and must work with your best or longest suits to turn your lower honors and mid-range cards into winners. What is your plan?

ESTABLISH YOUR LONG SUITS ASAP

Playing a NT contract, **"set up" your LONG suit(s) early to get all your tricks**. Rarely are they perfect: you usually have to flush out missing honors. You do this by finessing or *playing for the drop.* We've learned finessing. Playing for the drop means you have most or all of the top honors in a long shared suit. You'll play those cards in order from highest to lowest, hoping all outstanding cards will be captured. What's the best way to play long suits if the honors are divided between the declarer and the dummy?

PLAY HIGH FROM THE SHORT SIDE FIRST...

so **you do not block the suit.** In other words, you do not shut yourself off from the winners in your own suit. That would be agonizing, wouldn't it? Ex: AQx (dummy) KJxxx (declarer). Play the AQ **first**, then cross over to the KJx with the remaining small card to finish out the suit. Running a long suit forces discards from the opponents and destroys their hands, removing cards that protect honors and/or kills their long suits. They have to play something!

If you have a long combined suit, it will be the same as having "The Golden Fit" in a suit contract. You will be lucky to have 8 or more together in a suit. Often you'll have only 7. **The MAXIMUM number of tricks you can take is equal to the <u>COUNT</u> of the <u>LONGEST HOLDING</u>.** A **5/5, 5/4, 5/3 or 5/2** fit will yield at best **5 tricks**, no matter how many <u>total</u> cards are held in the single suit, while a **4/4** fit will yield at best **4 tricks.** You are not guaranteed that many, as you may lose a trick (or two) to a missing honor(s). Set up your long suits even if you lose control of the hand. **Give up your losers EARLY** - *before they know too much.*

You'll typically need to set up **TWO suits** to make your contract. Set them up to win **while you have stoppers in the OTHER TWO suits.** DO NOT play the winners in your shortest suits until you have run your long suit(s), because YOUR short suits are THEIR long suits. You'll need those winners for *transportation* or defense. If you play your beautiful AK doubleton right away, you'll have set up THEIR QJ1098, and they will take advantage of that as soon as they win a trick, or "get in." Time for a eulogy commemorating your once winning hand.

If you have a weak holding the defenders will attack to set you, take all your winners and don't do anything to endanger the contract, such as an unnecessary finesse. If you realize that one opponent is more "dangerous" than the other, because he can run a suit in which you are weak, try not to finesse into that hand, but finesse in the other direction if you can, and hope that side is out of partner's long suit, which leads to this concept...

THE "HOLD UP" PLAY

If you are weak and short in a suit, with only the A and space (Axx opposite xx), *don't play the suit yourself until the end of the hand.* If that suit is the opening lead, it is probably from the opponent's long holding. You **must keep your A until the opener's *PARTNER* is out of the suit,** often the third round. Your **"HOLD UP"** is intended to "ROB" the partner of the cards he has in the suit. If he wins a trick later and is on lead, he will be unable to return his partner's suit to set you. The "hold up" is officially known as *ducking.* It's a **crucial** play in NT.

Each side has the same strategy in NT: LET'S SET UP AND RUN OUR LONG SUIT(S)! That is why NT bidders **must have at least one stopper in every suit.** They need to get in control (or back in control) early.

My personal rule: if they bid a suit twice, I'd better have **at least two good stoppers.** *Something like the AK...*

PLAY OF THE HAND

IN A SUIT CONTRACT, COUNT YOUR LOSERS
...and see where you could get rid of them OR ruff them.

Once the dummy is tabled, you'll initially search for **losers** in each suit, focusing primarily on each AKQ, but also on the length in each suit. In theory, the AK opposite the xx has no losers. The AKx opposite the xxx, has one loser, the Q. The AKxx opposite the xxxx has two losers, the QJ. The AK opposite the xxx has no losers, due to the assumption that the remaining x will be ruffed or discarded after the AK has been played. If you have the AQx opposite the xxx, you must count two losers because you don't know where the KJ are located. What if you have the KJx opposite the xxx? You'll count three losers, because you don't know where the AQ10 are located. What if you have Kxx opposite Jxx? You have the same three losers, the AQ10. Think **"worst-case scenario"** when counting losers, and have a second plan-of-play ready.

How can you get rid of losers, especially if you have several that could defeat your contract?

Use your LENGTH and SHORTNESS

RUFF IN THE SHORTER HOLDING OF TRUMPS

Use the trumps on the short side, typically the dummy, to ruff your losers in a suit contract when the dummy is void or has a singleton. Each time you ruff, you **GAIN AN EXTRA TRICK.** It's true! Many poor contracts succeed this way. Why do you gain extra tricks? *The dummy's trumps don't cave in uselessly under the trumps in your long holding as you pull the trumps the opponents hold.* **They work independently, EACH trump you use for a ruff EARNING ITS OWN TRICK.** Go ahead and **lose** the singleton in the dummy or take it with your A, then ruff your other losers in that suit. Typically, the declarer pulls the opponent's trumps early: do not pull trumps if you need the dummy's trumps to ruff some losers. However, it DOES NOT HELP you to ruff early in your LONGER holding of trumps. You may be unable to maintain control of the hand and/or the trump suit.

USE A LONG SUIT TO YOUR ADVANTAGE

Throw your losers away on a long suit or on high cards (AKQ vs a singleton 2) that are in the other hand, and vice versa. If you have multiple losers, make certain you are throwing away the suit that will hurt you the most. For example, you are void in Cs in the dummy and you still have a trump in the dummy. You have a losing C in your hand. Since you can ruff the C in the dummy, it is not a loser like an x from the xxx opposite the AKx in Ds. **Toss the D loser**.

If you and the dummy together have a long suit, the opponents will be short in it, so you'll have to **clear most or all of the opponent's trumps** to safely play your long suit and toss your trash (your losers). You may need to _establish_ (set up) the long suit first. Sometimes you can use that long suit as a **bait suit,** tempting an opponent to play his final trump while retaining your own critically needed trumps. And don't forget to...

FINESSE

Finesse to create a winner, though it is an unnerving prospect at times. Hold your breath, steel yourself, and DO IT! It may be the winning move! If you know a K is in the opponent's hands, do not play your A right away, catching NOTHING BUT AIR, at least try a finesse. Don't knowingly give away a trick. If there's only one possible way to make your contract, summon your last bit of bravado and take the chance. Finesse!

THROW A LOSER ON A LOSER OR CROSS-RUFF

In a suit contract, you may get rid of a loser at any time by throwing it away (and not ruffing) if you are out of the suit they lead. Suppose you are down to the last few cards. When they lead, see if you can discard a **losing card** in yet another suit from either your hand or the dummy. Dump your doomed singleton and _clear_ that suit of any cards. Perhaps you can set up a _cross-ruff_. A cross-ruff or cross-trump is the ability to ruff losers in both declarer's and dummy's hands because each side has enough trumps *and is out of different suits.* Difficult contract made!

BUT IF YOU HAVE A MORE BALANCED DUMMY, DRAW TRUMPS

Beware of the opponent's lead: why did he lead that suit and what did he lead? Does he look for partner to ruff the third round of his suit? Most of the time the declarer pulls the opponent's trumps quickly to prevent a nasty surprise - *his own trump suit is being used against him.* Suddenly the contract is in peril! **Unless you need the trumps on the short side to ruff losers, to cross-ruff, or for transportation,** pull trumps early in the round. Your non-trump winners will STILL BE WINNERS after the opponent's trumps are gone - ***don't chance losing those tricks. Repeat - don't chance losing those crucial winners because you didn't draw trumps!***

FOR ALL DECLARERS: *WATCH YOUR TRANSPORTATION*. Some hands have few winners or secondary entries: safeguard them. Don't mindlessly play them while trying to decide your next move: they are confirmed winners. **Solve problems instead.** This is especially heartbreaking when you've misplayed a long suit by NOT playing high from the short side first, then find yourself stranded from your guaranteed winners due to a lack of transportation - transportation you just squandered. Plan ahead, be patient: maintain direction of the suits and the hand in general.

Tip: If you are fortunate enough to have an abundance of trumps in both hands - *use the trump suit for transportation if you have no entries.* **Keep a high trump on the weaker side.** Hmmm...

Recommended reading and a nice addition to your new bridge library: Louis Watson's **Play of the Hand at Bridge**.

For Future Study: How can you condense this information into something easy to recall? Think **ATAC**. (Attack)

A: AUCTION - Recall the bidding to gain clues to the location of their length and strength.

T: TRANSPORTATION* - Look for entries in both hands, and if there are few of them, see what you can do to preserve them until the right time. Unblock your suits properly: **AK932** opposite **J108(6)** wlll be a problem.

A: ANTICIPATE - Anticipate what the opening lead means and how it relates to your hand, anticipate what will happen if you lose the lead, anticipate where tricks can be developed, anticipate ruffs in the short holding of trumps, anticipate future finesses and **in which hand you need to be to make them**, etc. Anticipate=think ahead, mentally playing out the hand in advance - a skill that will improve through over time.

C: COUNT* - Count your WINNERS (NT contract) or count your LOSERS (suit contract). ALWAYS COUNT because it **FORCES you to see your strengths and/or weaknesses,** helping you visualize a strategy.

* These concepts are unique to the declarer.

WHAT ARE THE ODDS?

Any time you are the declarer, you will wonder how the outstanding cards are split between the opponents. Is one defender holding all your trumps? You will cringe (internally) if someone **shows out** (is void) when you pull the first round of trumps. You'll wonder the same thing if you are setting up a long suit in either a suit contract or a NT contract. Bridge players remember the odds and will "play the odds," hoping they are in their favor. The easiest way to remember how suits split is the saying that...

Even suits tend to split oddly, and odd suits tend to split evenly.

Have you ever noticed, in your play up to now, that if you have the Golden Fit, five trumps are out and they usually split 3-2? An odd number tends to split as evenly as possible. Have you ever agreed on a contract and found you have only 7 trumps? The opponents' trumps tend to split 4-2. Occasionally 3-3, but it seems like it is always 4-2 - unpleasant for you. The following table is a table of odds that you can think of when you are playing as declarer or as a defender.

If you have a fit of 7 cards between you & your partner and they have 6, expect a

3 - 3 break	36% of the time
4 - 2 break	48% of the time
5 - 1 break	15% of the time
6 - 0 break	1% of the time

If you have 8 cards between you & they have 5, expect a

3 - 2 break	68% of the time
4 - 1 break	28% of the time
5 - 0 break	4% of the time

If you have 9 cards between you & they have 4, expect a

2 - 2 break	40% of the time
3 - 1 break	50% of the time
4 - 0 break	10% of the time

If you have 10 cards between you & they have 3, expect a

2 - 1 break	78% of the time
3 - 0 break	22% of the time

PLAY OF THE HAND

Practice & Application Lesson XI: Play of the Hand - TWO pages full of fun!   *Chart p. 93*

First, review some bidding. No one has previously passed.

Partner	You	Describe everything you can about these responses, No interference by the opponents.
1. 1S	2S	Minimum raise: 3-4 card support expected with 6-9 HCP. Opener does not have to rebid.
2. 1S	2D	Invitational points (10+), an unlimited bid: 4+ D. Spade fit unknown. Opener must rebid.
3. 1H	3H	Limit raise: 4 c support and 10-12 HCP inclusive. Game invitational, not forcing.
4. 1NT	2NT	Invitational raise: 8-9 HCP and no 5 c M. Not forcing.
5. 1NT	2C	Stayman: The responder has at least 8 HCP and at least one 4 C M.
6. 1D	1S	Unlimited bid: 4+ S and **6+ HCP *(NOT 6-9!)***. True M holdings unknown. Opener must rebid.
7. 1NT	2H	A Jacoby Transfer to Ss: opener will bid Ss to accept the transfer, and partner will bid the PIG.

You're the declarer in a **suit** contract. Count your **losers**. The answers are at the bottom of the page.

1. KQxx	2. KQxx	3. xxx	4. KJxx	5. xxx	6. AKQxx	7. AK	8. KJ10	9. AKxxx
☐	☐	☐	☐	☐	☐	☐	☐	☐
x	xx	KQxx	xxx	QJx	xx	xx	AQx	QJxx

How many total tricks are possible? How should the suit be played?

1.	2.	3.	4.	5.	6.
A	Q	A	K	A	x
K	x	Q	x	K	x
x	x	x	x	x	
			x	x	
			x		
☐	☐	☐	☐	☐	☐
Q	A	J	A	Q	A
x	K	x	x	J	K
x	x	x		x	x
x	x	x		x	x
x	x	x			x

1. Five total tricks are possible with a 3-2 split. Play the AK, cross to the Q and finish the suit.

2. Five total tricks are possible with a 3-2 split. Play the Q, then cross to the AK and finish the suit.

3. Five total tricks are possible if the K falls. The best play is to lead low to the Q, and if she holds, play the A, and hope the K is doubleton on the left. If the K falls, in whichever hand you end up, the suit will not be blocked. Lead the low remaining card to the J and finish the suit.

4. Two tricks are possible right now. In a <u>NT</u> contract, do not play this suit early. The split is unknown and you do not want to set up the opponents QJ. If the cards are split favorably, you could get 4 tricks. In a <u>suit</u> contract, you have two winners and more winners if the suit splits nicely. Play the AK, and if everyone plays, you will trump the 3rd round and the last 2 cards will be winners for 5 total tricks. Good luck getting back to them!

5. Four total tricks. *A great suit to have for transportation if transportation is an issue.*

6. Four total tricks are possible with a 3-3 split. Lead <u>low</u> to the AK and let it ride no matter what pops out. When you have the chance, play from the A down to get the rest of the tricks. This is different from #4 because the AK are onside.

Answers to "Count your losers" above: 1) 1 loser - the A. The assumption is that you may ruff or discard your small losing cards. This suit may also set up to toss 1-2 losers from a *different* suit on the KQ, depending on where the A is. 2) 1 loser - the A. Assume the KQ will force out the A, creating a winner for the second small x on the remaining honor. 3) 2 losers - where are the A & J? 4) 3 losers - you don't know where the AQ10 are. 5) 3 losers - you don't know where the AK10 are. 6) 0 losers and one honor for the discard of a loser from another suit. 7) 0 losers 8) 0 losers 9) 0 losers IF you play the suit correctly. You must play the QJ first, then cross over to the A.

Building Bridges © 2022 Jeanne R. Wamack May not be reproduced in any form.

PLAY OF THE HAND

You're the declarer in a **NT** contract. Count your **winners.** The answers are at the bottom of the page.

1. AKxx	2. QJ10x	3. xxxx	4. AKQ	5. Qx	6. AK	7. QJx	8. AQ10x	9. xxxx	10. AKxx
☐	☐	☐	☐	☐	☐	☐	☐	☐	☐
xxx	xxxx	AKQJ	J109	AKx	Qx	AKx	xxxx	KJ109	QJxxx

How would you play these? Remember to count winners or losers and make a game plan. It would probably help you visualize the play if you set up a deck of cards just like the examples. The opponents never bid.

Bidding: 1NT - 3NT. Lead: 3H   **How would you get 9 tricks?**

```
K    Q    A    A
x    x    J    J
          x    x
          x    x
               x
          ☐
```

Make a plan right now.
First, count your <u>winners</u>.
You see 9 sure tricks - AKQ of Ss, A of Hs, A of Ds and AKQJ of Cs.
It appears you are home free, but what is the key to this hand?
You must play the Ss and Cs correctly by playing high from the short side first, then use the remaining small card to cross over to the other winners.

Since you are weak/short in the H suit, you need to take your winners and not endanger the contract by attempting to get extra tricks in the D suit.

```
A    A    10   K
Q    x    x    Q
x    x    x    x
x
```

The lead is a low H. Play the Q and **hope** leader led from the K. If she wins, you will make an extra trick.

Bidding: 1S - 2S - 4S. Lead: 4H   **How would you get 10 tricks?**

```
A    x    x    x
K    x    x    x
x    x    x    x
x    x    x    x
     ☐
```

You can see five <u>losers</u> in your hand - 3 Hs, 1 D, and 1 C. You may lose only *three* tricks to be successful. How can you get rid of your losers? **Use your length and shortness.** Whatever the 2nd lead is, you'll get control. Ruff your 2 small Hs in the dummy. This is a priority - do not play your As, use them for transportation back to your hand to ruff Hs.

You should make 10 tricks regardless of the trump split since there are only 4 trumps in the opponent's hands. You'll take 5 Ss, 2 H (ruffed in the dummy), 2 D, and 1 C.

```
Q    x    A    A
J    x    K    x
x    x    x
x
x
```

Answers to "Count your winners" from the top of the page: 1) 2 winners   2) 0 winners   3) 4 winners   4) 3 winners
5) 3 winners, if played correctly.   6) 2 winners - overlapping honors.   7) 3 winners - overlapping honors.
8) 1 winner 9) 0 winners - no A. 10) 5 winners - no matter how the 4 outstanding cards are split, you can win all for 5.

Which suits may be <u>established</u>? The suit in 1 could get as many as 3 tricks, with a favorable split of 3/3 between the opponents, setting up the 4th card to win. The suit in 2 will be established when the A and K are played. The suits in 8 and 9 should be finessed. The suit in 10 will play for the drop.

Building Bridges © 2022 Jeanne R. Wamack May not be reproduced in any form.

Lesson XII   Defense

When on defense, it is **vital** that you understand how to get all the winners you can, or to at least cause all the trouble you can. *Make the declarer anxious about the contract, and he will be more likely to err.*

THE OPENING LEAD

The opening lead is your first line of defense. Versus their suit contract, should partner have bid, lead his suit every chance you get UNLESS it will be won in the dummy or ruffed by the declarer in the SHORT holding of trumps. Don't give them extra tricks or THE DREADED RUFF AND SLUFF! A *sluff* (slough) is the tossing of one of the declarer's losers which is **your winner.** YOU, in turn, will feel like **tossing your cookies!** Making the declarer ruff in his LONG trump holding is often good for your side and bad for the declaring side. This means the dummy has several losers in your suit, but the declarer is void. The declarer could lose control of the trump suit, and perhaps the entire hand, if you force him to ruff before he can implement his strategy. Opposing their NT contract, keep leading your partner's suit as often as you can without fear of a ruff. If you must discard during play, keep at least one card in his suit for a return in case you get back in with a winner.

If partner didn't bid, you may have a good lead yourself, especially holding a *perfect sequence* (AKQ or KQJ). If you have a sequence of at least the QJ10 (or 9), you might set up a third round winner if the declarer and the dummy each have three cards in the suit. If not, you'll have established a winner that might cause difficulty for the declarer if he is short on trumps. Unfortunately, you will most likely have a *broken sequence* (AKJx or AQJx), or an *interior sequence* (KJ10xx). Defending a NT contract, lead the top of touching honors in the sequence, wherever it is within the suit. A broken sequence missing only the Q (AKJx) may be led vs. a suit contract, but a weaker holding should most likely be led only against their NT contract, IF you have a choice. If the suit is poor, but long, lead fourth down (J8753) in an effort to win the fourth and/or fifth trick vs. their NT contract. Here the interior sequence (the 87) is near worthless until it is promoted, which takes time and may never happen, *so show the honor by leading a low card.* If you lead the 8, it tells partner NOT to return your suit, as the lead appears to be from the top of nothing. If you don't have an honor, but do have a long suit, vs. NT you are showing *length* (10754 2), though it's ugly. Oh well - *c'est la vie.* Long suits take tricks: this suit may be your best shot to set them.

If leading fourth in your longest and strongest vs. their suit contract, partner will return your suit to you if he gets back in the lead UNLESS the dummy has high winners in your suit, such as the AQ which would finesse your K. Hopefully you'll be able to take a trick with your hidden honor facing a weak dummy. He WOULD return your suit opposing a NT contract to help you set up your long suit, even if you lose a few tricks along the way. Try to avoid "breaking" a new suit unless you have no better option, as this move often benefits the declarer the most.

Now you can see even better the importance of leads. They give your partner a **clue** of which card to play, or what suit to return to you. Remember to...

RETURN PARTNER'S OPENING LEAD

Make that hidden high card a winner, or perhaps your partner is void in the suit he led. This may happen if partner **preempts and doesn't lead his own suit** - he led his **singleton.** In either case, return his lead as soon as you can UNLESS you would help the declarer by leading it. When partner preempts, you may have the stronger hand since partner is weak, putting you in control more often, so it's up to you to "put the hurt on" the opponents by making good choices when leading back to your partner. Other strategies...

RETURN THE HIGHEST CARD IN PARTNER'S SUIT

Defending a NT contract, should partner lead low in a suit, you'll hope he is leading from an honor and at least some mid-range cards. If you win, **return the highest card you have in the suit**, hoping to **trap the declarer's honor.** If your second card wins, lead the suit AGAIN. This is extremely helpful setting the opponents. Why? Suppose partner leads low from his longest and strongest suit. His hidden honor is the K, but he also has the 10. The dummy plays low, so third hand - you - must go up with your highest card to try to win. You play the Q, which is taken by the declarer's A. When you win later, **you'll send your highest card in the originally led suit back to your partner.** He now knows **whether or not you have the J.** If the declarer is holding the J, it is **trapped.** If the declarer plays the J, partner's K will take it and his 10 is promoted. If he doesn't play the J, your partner will play the 10, then the K. Either way, the declarer is in distress. Don't worry if *your* high card is taken: **you are establishing your partner's winners.** Returning the highest card in partner's suit might work vs. their suit contract, but an honor card could get ruffed or taken by the declarer, so you must count cards and check the dummy's strength **before** you return the suit. **Avoid setting up winners for the opponents.**

DEFENSE

Now for a run of adages that will help you know what to do or lead at other times. *Put on your seatbelt...*

LEAD TO STRENGTH

You're on lead again. If the dummy is on your **left**, what do you lead? **Lead to the broken strength of the board** if you have no better choice. If you lead to a WEAK suit in dummy, who will have the points in the suit? The declarer! Partner will have to play high as a third seat player, and his high card will be covered by the declarer. Oh no! You finessed your partner! This may be a difficult position from which to choose a beneficial lead. "**Lead to the heft when the dummy's on the left.**"

LEAD THROUGH TO WEAKNESS

"**If the dummy's on your right, lead the weakest thing in sight,**" is the bridge adage that applies here. If you aren't able to return partner's suit and have no clue what to lead, lead the weakest suit in the dummy, *including trumps,* if the dummy is on your **right.** You may trap a high card in the declarer's hand, or the declarer may play low and partner only has to beat the dummy's card. This is a much easier position from which to lead. Your lead will be *through* the declarer's strong hand, perhaps forcing him to make a decision. You hope he makes the wrong decision.

SECOND HAND LOW, THIRD HAND HIGH

When a lead is made, it is often a low card. **The second hand usually plays low too**. It is up to the third hand to play high, *even if it hurts,* so that the opponents don't "**win cheaply**" (win with an unusually low card which gives them an extra trick), but play only as high as necessary, based on what you see before you. Suppose partner leads an 8, and you see the J1097 in dummy to your right. You hold the Q4. If the declarer plays the 7, you play your 4, *because partner's 8 will force out a higher card the same as your Q.* Keep the Q to cover the J, 10, or 9.

If you happen to have a **sequence in the third seat,** perhaps the QJ10, play the **LOWEST** card in the sequence, here the **10.** When the declarer's **K** takes the trick, your partner has a **clue** where to find the **Q and J.** This is the **OPPOSITE** of **LEADING a sequence**, when you would **lead the Q to show the J10 or J9.** Hmmm...

KEEP PAR WITH WHOM YOU FOLLOW

If the dummy is on your right, *keep par with what the dummy holds*. If you have a high card that will beat the dummy's high card, retain it as long as possible so that the declarer can never win a trick with the dummy's card. If the declarer is on your right, try to keep par with the declarer. His hand will be the stronger hand, but cause him whatever headaches you can.

WIN WITH THE LOWEST CARD POSSIBLE

The dummy is to your left. Partner leads **low**, declarer plays **low**, and you hold the **K** and **J** with other small cards in the suit. You see that the **10** is the highest card in the dummy. Which card would you play? All you have to do is beat the dummy, so play the JACK. Keep the K for more important jobs. This is common sense, but some players zone out as they think about the next trick, lunch, dinner, or traffic. Stay vigilant, even if your hand (or pair) seems too weak to be able to accomplish much - *you may be pleasantly surprised.* Down one!

THE RULE OF ELEVEN...

When partner makes a lead that is 4th down in his longest and strongest suit, there is a little "trick" that you may use to determine how many cards are out that are higher than partner's lead. **Subtract the number of the lead card from 11, and the result will tell you.** If partner leads the 7, do the math: 11-7 = 4. You see the 10983 in the dummy and you hold the K42. If the declarer plays the 3, you play small too. Why? There are four cards out that will beat the 7 and you can see **all of them** - three on the board and one in your hand. **The 7 will win!** If a higher card is played from the dummy, play your K! He will win and you can return your partner's suit. *This really works! I promise!* Remember though, **the lead must be the 4th card down in his longest suit.** If you and your partner make this standard lead, turn it into **information** for your side. *BTW, the lead of the 2 is always from 4 cards. Hmmm...*

WHEN YOU DON'T KNOW WHAT TO LEAD

I use the Physician's Rule in this case: **first, do no harm.** Do no harm to *your* side, that is. Would you return partner's lead if the dummy can ruff the suit? Not usually, unless you KNOW he led a singleton and can BEAT the dummy's low trumps. Otherwise, find a **safe** suit to return, even if you give the lead back to the declarer by **giving him a trick he's going to get anyway.** If you must change suits, called making a **_switch_**, it's usually done when a return of partner's suit is NOT beneficial to your side. Lead a weak suit in the dummy to gain tricks, if the dummy is on your right, or lead your own suit. Does the dummy have a long suit and few entries? Perhaps you should knock out the entries to the board. Declarer will throw his losers (your winners) on that suit. *Keep him away from that suit!*

DEFENSE

NOW FOR SIGNALING

Normally when you discard, you toss a card that seems useless. Why not make that first discard have meaning? *Standard signaling* is easy and is perfectly legal in the bridge world. Play a HIGH card to show that you LIKE this suit, or play a LOW card to say you DO NOT LIKE that suit. **High=like, low=NO.** Since a mid-range 6 is difficult to read, give it a unique job: you may agree that a **6 is neutral** - you are not asking for any suit. Don't worry that you won't have a 6 when you need it. I've noticed that my most wretched, ignominious hands always seem to have a 6. If you want to have two choices of neutral cards, some players allow that the 5 and 6 are signal-free. If you can't signal correctly, signal an improbable suit, such as the AKQ in the dummy - *lead something else, partner.*

My favorite signaling system is *Upside-down,* the opposite of standard: **High=hate, low=like.** This system preserves your high cards, *which could become winners,* **matches** the LEAD signals you already know, and is easy to remember due to alliteration. **U/D is overtaking standard as the favorite signaling system in bridge.**

Signals apply only on your FIRST DISCARD. Do not signal unless you have a winner, such as an A, a protected K (at least Kx) behind an A in the dummy, KQ(J)(x) for second/third round control, or high cards hovering over a weak dummy. If the dummy is to your right, sometimes you can easily beat the dummy's cards several times in the suit you are signaling: Dummy: AQ94 You: KJ1053. When you win, **do not play the suit yourself** as it will cost you tricks. Return a different suit for partner to lead the suit to you **again.** If the dummy is to your left, you'll signal for a certain suit if there is no card in the dummy that can defeat your high card. You: K1073 Dummy: 986. What if you have the QJx(x)? It takes time to promote Qs and Js, so do not signal your "slow" third round winners - you must lie in wait to win with your girls and boys. You and your partner will have to train yourselves to **look at each other's cards,** and you need to watch your opponent's signals too. You'll be able to figure out where those missing honors are - a very helpful bit of information. As I tell my students, "Take your nose out from behind your 13 cards and look at what is happening on the table!" *Learning how to signal will change your bridge life forever.*

IN CONCLUSION, read, reread, break and then read this chapter AGAIN. Make this defensive thinking effortless.

For Future Study: How can you remember all of this information? Think **ALAS:** *Alas, they won the auction.*

A: AUCTION - Remember what everyone bid. Who showed weakness, who showed strength, and in what suits?
L: LEADS* - All your pair's leads are important, from the opening lead to your final lead. The opening lead will be based on the auction, partner's bids, or on the leader's own holding: later leads will often come from signals.
A: ANTICIPATE - How do you think the declarer will play the hand? How would YOU play it, from what you observed in the auction and from what you see in the dummy? The two plans are usually similar. Anticipate what the declarer will do, *then plan your defense ahead of time.* **Play smoothly** to keep from giving away information - keep him guessing. Does he avoid a suit? Maybe it's because your side owns it. Does partner keep tossing the same suit in NT? You may need to keep that suit. Is there a long suit in an opponent's hand? If you have their long suit, maybe partner is short in it: can you create a ruffing situation? Did partner bid a suit? Where are the honors in his suit? Set traps if possible. Your job is to cause as much grief as you can.
S: SIGNAL* - Signal with your preferred system every chance you get: signal when you're leading, signal on partner's opening lead, when discarding, or if a high card (A or K) is led in a new suit.

* These concepts are unique to the defenders. The declarer also leads, but is not signaling with his leads. Deceiving, maybe...

_____**FYI:** A PUBLIC SERVICE ANNOUNCEMENT FOR DUMMIES_____
I have not discussed the dummy's role and there is space here.

The dummy's job is to play cards as directed: **he never touches a card without instruction,** even if he is certain which card the declarer wants. He'll ask his partner if he is out of a suit, help him remember in which hand he is, and he'll watch for revokes that the opponents make. He does not have to call attention to partner's revokes - that is the job of the opponents. When helping partner remember which side he is on, whether "in his hand" or "on the board," the dummy may privately check the last card he turned over, but may not reveal the card to the table. He'll keep an accurate record of winning tricks and **doesn't correct** declarer's incorrectly turned tricks during play.

The dummy **does not speak** during the round, unless it it to carry out his duties, and he does not normally call the director. He may summon the director AFTER the play is over for something everyone else overlooked. If the dummy misses seeing a card that was played, he cannot ask to see it after it's turned over. A dummy may use the time he has as dummy to practice counting points and suits, and he can help partner learn from his mistakes if something unfortunate happens and partner *requests* his opinion. **The dummy should not leave the table**, but if there is an emergency, he may call a director (or perhaps a caddy at a tournament) to pull his cards.

Building Bridges © 2022 Jeanne R. Wamack May not be reproduced in any form.

DEFENSE

Practice & Application Lesson XII: Defense, DEE-FENSE   *Chart p. 93*

1. Lead: 3H   Partner leads a low heart, dummy plays low and you win with the Q.

             Kxx   What do you return?
   ☐   Kxx   Dummy
             xxx
             Qxxx   Answer: Return a **D**. "When the dummy's on the right lead the...? *Weakest thing in sight.*
   You   Keep par with the dummy. Your A of Hs should catch the K of Hs, and your
   xxx   A of Cs should catch the Q of Cs. If you get lucky, your J of C may win too.
   AQxx
   xxx   If you play the A Hs *now*, you set up the K in dummy for a sluff, and/or your A
   AJx   may be ruffed by the declarer. Make the **switch** and let partner lead another H.

2. You discard on oppo's S trumps. How would you signal for a C?   Standard: high=like: 7C, 8C, 9C, or 10C
                                                                      Upside/Down: low=like: 2C, 3C, 4C (or 5C)

3. How would you signal you don't want a H?   Standard: low=no!: 2H, 3H, 4H, maybe 5H
                                                                      Upside/Down: high=hate: 7H, 8H, 9H, 10H

4. How would you show a doubleton while on <u>lead</u> in partner's suit?   Play high/low.

5. Do you need to signal your trump holding?   No.

6. What is the Rule of 11?   If partner leads 4th, subtract that # from 11
                                                                      to know how many higher cards are in the
                                                                      other three hands. Play accordingly.

7. Second hand usually plays____ and 3rd hand usually plays____?   Low/ high (as necessary)

8. If the dummy is to your LEFT, lead **to** the ____.   HEFT - Strength (that has gaps)

9. Win with the ____ ____ ____.   Lowest card possible

10. If partner leads a K...   Expect the Q

11. If partner leads a Q...   Expect the J10 or J9

12. If partner leads an 9 or 8...   He is not asking for a return **unless** it is
                                                                      a singleton. Check your holding and the
                                                                      dummy's holding to try to figure out
                                                                      partner's intent. If you are defending a NT
                                                                      contract, you may want to continue the suit,
                                                                      if the suit is a M, per partnership agreement.

13. If partner leads a 2...   It's 4th from *his* longest, or he's leading
                                                                      from 3-4 in *your* suit, showing an honor.
                                                                      Return the suit.

14. If partner leads a J...   He's led from an interior sequence. May
                                                                      also be a lead from J1098(x), or a short
                                                                      suit (J or Jx) if it's *your* suit.

15. Never lead an A from...   Space, as in Axxx. The A should catch
                                                                      an honor.

Tip: Did it ever occur to you that, once all the trumps are gone, *every hand becomes a NT hand?* Hmmm...

Building Bridges © 2022 Jeanne R. Wamack May not be reproduced in any form.   49

Lesson XIII BIG Hands

Among challenges for players are describing opening, overcalling, or responding hands that are greater than the minimum range.

THE OPENING HAND

AN OPENER WITH 16+ HCP

With 16 (to 18) HCP, the opener will JUMP IN HIS OWN SUIT to show his HCP with 6+ of a major or 6+ of a minor, or he'll JUMP IN PARTNER'S SUIT to show 16+ HCP. *The jump is strong.* He may also BID HIGHER, in a suit or NT.

Ex: (no interference) 1H - 1S - **3H** (instead of 2H). The pair may have game or slam. The responder should bid 4H with two+ in the H suit and 8+ HCP or perhaps 3NT, depending on his hand. *Did you notice the opener's jump bid?*

Ex: (no interference) 1H - 1S - **3S** or 1C - 1H - **3H.** Game invitational jump in partner's suit showing 4 card support. The responder needs 8-9 HCP for game, but he may have more points: his bid is unlimited and he may want to investigate slam. *He could have 5 of his M and knows his team has a **9 card trump suit.***

Ex: (no interference) 1D **-** 1H **-** 3D shows **6**+ diamonds, < 4 Hs or 4 Ss, and 16-18 HCP. The pair will need 28-29 HCP for game in a minor, *but who wants to be there anyway?* The responder might bid **3NT** with 8-9 HCP and the right holding. The length and strength in Ds should help the pair make the 3NT contract. *If not 3NT, 5Ds?*

For Future Study:

Ex: (no inter.) 1H/1S - 2D - **3C** shows 16+ HCP because of the **3 level rebid.** With fewer HCP, the opener must bid 2NT or rebid his 5 card M. *Though required to bid again, **raising the auction a level** indicates med+ HCP.*

Ex: (the opponents interfere) **1C** - [**1H**] - **X** - [**P**] - **2S** (instead of 1S) shows 16-17 HCP and a fit in Ss. Game invitational. *The responder could easily miss partner's jump bid, so the responder must be vigilant.*

Ex: (the opponents interfere) **1H** - [P] - **1S** - [2C/2D] - **2NT**. The opener, rebidding 2NT, **must have 16+ HCP.** If the *OPPONENTS* make the opener bid 2NT, **he must have extra values because he does not know exactly what partner holds.** The responder shows 6+ HCP but may have ONLY 6 HCP - barely enough to respond. *Yikes!* For success in 2NT or a 3 level contract, the opener must have a medium+ hand. The good news? A responder with only **9** HCP now knows that his side has game.

AN OPENER WITH 17+ HCP

A **17 HCP** opening hand needs only **8-9 HCP from the responder** for game. In what category are responder's 8-9 HCP? They're in the minimum category. How will the opener invite game over a weak response? He will invite by BIDDING THE SUIT AGAIN if the pair has the Golden Fit. *He asks partner if he is at the **top of his bid***.

Ex: (no interference) 1H - 2H - **3H.** This sequence asks the responder if game is possible. With 6-7 HCP, he would UNLESS he has a singleton or void that allows ruffing. With 8-9 HCP, the responder bids game. *There is no other reason to bid higher in an uncontested auction EXCEPT that the opener has a medium or medium+ hand.*

Same strength: 1H - 2H - **3D.** Game invitational. Opener wants to know if **partner has help in Ds** (A, K, sing, void).
Here's another: 1H - [1S] - P - [P] - **X**. Opener has a big hand and hopes resp has 3-5 HCP. *Bid **something**, partner!*
And it even works over a NT response: 1C - 1NT - **2NT**. The opener has **17-18 HCP**, game invitational.

• *The 17 (or 18) point hand may make the same bids as a 16 point hand - all the bids in the section above.* •

Note: Responder's "stop" bid doesn't mean he may NEVER bid again. The notion that a weak response is a stop bid is to emphasize to a beginning player that he should put the brakes on with a minimal hand. Many beginners are reluctant to pass if partner opens and overbid hands - with poor results. Conversely, some beginning players are afraid to bid with nice hands and pass, missing game.

AN OPENER WITH 18+ HCP

The opener may show **18-19 HCP** by a JUMP TO 2NT after a 1/1 bid (including 1NT) and no interference. Ex: 1H - 1S - **2NT.** If the auction goes 1S - 2D - 2NT it is part of the conversation, not a jump bid, so the opener **does not** show extra values.

AN OPENER WITH 19+ HCP

An opener shows **19+ HCP** with a *jump-shift* (J-S) bid. He'll bid a suit at the one level, then **jump** in a **second suit** to show game values if partner responds. Watch for jump rebids. **Without a J-S, opener's range is 12-18 HCP.**

Ex: (no interference) **1H** - 1S - **3D,** instead of 2D. *Go team!* Ex: 1D - 1H - **3C.** These are **game-forcing bids. (GF)**

AN OPENER WITH 20+ HCP

If an opener holds **20 HCP** (or 19) and a long M suit, he may bid 1M, then if he gets a *pulse* from his partner, HE WILL BID GAME SOMEWHERE. He has half the HCP! He may invite game with a long minor suit because he needs 28-29 HCP for game, or he'll get wild and bid game: 3NT or 5m if his hand is extremely distributional.

Ex: 1H (anxiously holding his breath since he does NOT want a pass) - 2H - **4H**, or 1H - 1S - **4H** with 6+ strong Hs. He could also bid **4S with a fit, or 3NT**. He found his game contract! Over a minor: 1C - 1D - **4D** is a strong game invitation. **The opener skipped 3NT,** so he thinks game or slam in Ds in the best contract. A jump to 3NT is strong too: 1C - 1D - 3NT. The responder should think about what the opener is telling him - he bid game with the promise of only 6 HCP in the responder's hand. *If the responder has a big hand too...is slam possible?*

RESPONDERS: Keep your wits about you. **THINK** what partner tells you when he invites or bids game with little apparent help from you. **Add your points together** and determine the approximate final contract.

If the opener has a 20 point hand and gets passed out, it will take every point he has to make his contract.

Tip: If you open 1 of a suit with a 16-20 HCP hand but your dependable partner NEVER responds, you'll want to **avoid jump rebids** because your partner won't magically grow HCP. You may continue vying for the contract by yourself with a long (6+) suit, or you may bid two different suits asking partner's preference. If there's a reason he couldn't bid but has HCP (4-9), the fact that you are continuing to bid by yourself **shows your strength**. Partner could enter the auction later. A second, perhaps dangerous option, is to **X** to make your reluctant partner bid.

THE NO TRUMP FAMILY

One level opening bid of a suit - 1 level response - 1NT rebid	= **12-14** HCP	(1D-1S-1NT) *Rarely 15 HCP*
A 1NT opening bid	= **15-17** HCP	
One level opening bid of a suit - 1 level response - 2NT jump rebid	= **18-19** HCP	(1D-1S-2NT)
A 2NT opening bid	= **20-21** HCP	*(see the following chapter)*
A 2C opening bid with a rebid of 2NT	= **22-23** HCP	*(see the following chapter)*
A 2C opening bid with a rebid of 3NT	= **24+** HCP	*(see the following chapter)*

THE OVERCALLING HAND

A one level overcall shows 8+ HCP and a two level overcall or TOX shows 12+ HCP, but what if the overcaller is even stronger, with perhaps 16+ HCP? How can he show his strong hand when RHO opens the auction?

AN OVERCALLER WITH 16+ HCP

The overcaller could bid his own long suit, then jump later with a strong hand, similar to the opener. If he overcalls and the advancer bids a new suit, he could **cuebid** to show game interest, or raise partner's suit. With 16-17 HCP and no long suit, the overcaller will first TOX, then **raise partner's suit one level** because he would PASS if he's minimal (12-15 HCP). The overcaller could also bid a TOX over a preempt. All of these bids are clues to allow the advancer to figure out the overcaller's strong HCP. The overcaller's and advancer's bids below are **bold**.

Ex: The opponent opens: [1D] - **X** - [P] - **1S** - [P] - **2S**. The TOXer has 16-17 HCP, shown by a low 2S raise over a non-jump advancer's bid, *as the advancer would jump with 10+ HCP.* He could X **again** if responder bids and partner passes: [1D] - **X** - [1H] - P - [2H] - **X**. *The overcaller is strong enough to demand a bid for the second time.*

Ex: The opponent preempts [2D/2H/2S] - **X** (the overcaller). *The overcaller should have 16+ HCP to TOX.*

AN OVERCALLER WITH 18+ HCP

As an overcaller, a takeout double followed by a suit, NT, or double-raise of advancer's suit **shows 18+ HCP**. A second seat player with a big hand, wondering how best to show his HCP, will TOX, then see what his partner bids. Ex: [1C] - **X** - [P] - **1H** - [P] - **1S** = 18+ HCP. If partner bids the TOXer's **best** suit, the TOXer will jump 2 levels, cuebid, or bid game (if he feels lucky, has a superb fit, or is distributional). If he bids the TOXer's **weakest** suit, then the TOXer may bid his **own** LONG suit, OR if the TOX bidder has the *opener's suit,* he may bid **NT** at his second bid. This bid reveals a lot of information to the advancer - the pair will find their game. The advancer may bid game with **only 7 HCP.** The direct seat 1NT overcall shows **15-17** HCP, while a TOX followed a NT bid shows **18+** HCP.

ADVANCERS: Know that a TOX may not be your partner's entire story. *Always watch his rebids and hope for more.*

THE RESPONDING HAND

When responding hands are medium to maximum+, the bidder needs to know what to do to keep the auction open. Thankfully, you're already familiar with many of these bids.

SUIT RESPONSES

A RESPONDER WITH 10+ HCP

A medium (invitational) or greater hand is initially shown by the responder bidding a NEW SUIT over the opening bid. A 2/1 bid is clearly invitational, but a 1/1 bid is an unknown quantity except that the responder must have 6 HCP, therefore it is not invitational or game forcing *yet*. A CUEBID over interference shows a 10+ HCP hand with 3+ card support: **1H - [1S] - 2S.** The responder might bid 2NT (10+ - 12 HCP), which is invitational, but is NF.

A RESPONDER WITH 11+ HCP

The responder may JUMP IN HIS OWN SUIT to show **11+** HCP and **6+** cards in his suit. This bid invites game, but the opener may **pass** since it's a NF rebid. If responder holds *more* than 11 HCP, he should bid game directly with a long, strong suit, OR he must bid a <u>new</u> suit to keep the auction open, then rebid his long suit later. He may not even need a great fit for game because he has several honors in his suit, so he may chance that partner has 1-3 cards in his suit and bid game, hoping for a reasonable fit and/or a favorable trump split. The opener should **strongly consider game** after the jump, knowing that responder has a long suit and medium HCP.

Ex: (no interference) 1C - 1H - 1S - **3H (shows 6+ H and 11+ HCP).** The responder hopes for a heart fit for a M game, or perhaps 3NT. With a strong suit, he can bid 4H himself. Remember, his first bid promises only **4** Hs.

A RESPONDER WITH 13+ HCP

The responder may JUMP SHIFT* or REVERSE *(explanation in chapter 17)* to show 13+ HCP and a **game force+** hand. *Remember, the responder could have significantly more than 13 HCP.*

Ex: (no interference) 1C - **1S** - 2C - **3H** - A jump shift: shows 5 Ss & 4-5 Hs. *The bid of 2H would be forcing as well.*
1C - **1H** - 2C - **2S** - A reverse: shows 5 Hs & 4 Ss, *not 4/4 since the* **opener denies 4 Ss.**

*Note: Some experts require that the responder's jump shift shows much more than 13 HCP, perhaps as high as 19 HCP, the same as the opener. Since a new suit bid by the responder is forcing in many auctions, **a jump shift may not be necessary to keep the auction open.**

A RESPONDER WITH 16+ HCP

If the responder has a maximum+ hand with **possible slam values**, he will first make a FORCING BID (1/1, 2/1), then the responder can further describe his hand without fear of a pass. Ex: (no interference) 1C - 1D, or 1S - 2C - the opener **must** rebid. You will NOT bid 3NT over partner's opening bid since it shows inclusively **13-15 HCP:** 1S - 3NT. *You state with your 3NT bid that, from your point of view, there is no higher score possible than game - it's a **closeout**. Oops!* Note that many game level bids are stop bids - "I'm not interested in slam."

If your points add up to a small (33+ HCP) or grand slam (37+ HCP), **no worthless doubleton,** *JUST BID IT!*

Remember: If the responder keeps bidding new suits or jumps in a previously bid suit, he is promising a nice hand - *at least high minimum and/or unusual distribution that increases it's value.* Keep step until the end - a definitive sign-off bid, a game contract, or a slam contract.

NO TRUMP RESPONSES

Medium, invitational	1 of any suit - **2NT** shows **11-12 HCP**	*Do **NOT** bid NT if you want to keep the*
"Game force"	1 of any suit - **3NT** shows **13-15 HCP**	*auction open. NT bids are non-forcing.*

See page 14 for a complete review of no trump responses and 10 HCP hands relative to NT responses.

Tip: *When a player with a powerful hand has to make a rebid, he may have to bid a strong short (3 card) suit showing stoppers to keep the bidding as low as possible on the way to a slam. If he rebids partner's suit because they have a fit (which is NF), he could miss showing stoppers that are in a **lower** suit, so he may show the stoppers instead as* **the new suit is forcing.** *He can show the fit with partner <u>later in the auction.</u> You'll know this hand when you see it.*

AN IMPORTANT ADJUSTMENT: FINE TUNING WITH DISTRIBUTION POINTS

Back in chapter two, you were encouraged to bid higher with **EXTRA PIZZAZZ** in your hand because it made your hand more valuable. Extra pizzazz means you have a very long trump suit, additional points, a two-suited hand, or a hand with a singleton or void. Obviously having more trumps and/or points is of significance. The advantage of *length*, whether LONG OR SHORT, is officially called **DISTRIBUTIONAL VALUE,** the final piece of the puzzle used to determine the true potential of your hand.

LENGTH POINTS are traditionally added to the **opener's count** because of a 5+ card suit(s). This line of reasoning goes with bidding systems that require 13 HCP to open the auction, so one length point added for a five card suit allows a 12 HCP hand to open, which is what we already do. How can length points benefit our system? If you have a good 5 card suit, you may add an extra point to your total. For a 6 card suit add 2 points, and for a 7 card suit add 3 points. Tally these points during your **initial hand evaluation.** You may decline to add length points right away for a poor 5 card suit unless partner raises you, then you'll have a reasonable expectation the suit can win tricks. Compare AJ532 to KQ1097 - which holding is better? Both suits have **5** HCP, but the second suit is superior because it has mid-range cards that will force honors, establishing the long suit. You have experience with length points: the Rule of 20+2 opening bid. *Length is why this bid works well: it's secretly an opening hand.*

Length points can help you bid a game or slam contract that you might normally miss. Carefully evaluate your hand, maximizing your length, once you have an idea where the contract is headed. If you're two-suited, remember the adage *"Six, five, COME ALIVE,"* and don't give up the auction too easily. You may consider adding in shortness points (see chart) **AFTER** you know you will be in a SUIT contract if you have extreme distribution, since your short suits and voids are DANGEROUS and/or USELESS in a NO TRUMP contract, but shortness points ARE CONSIDERED OPTIONAL for the opener in many circles.

SHORTNESS POINTS are added to the **future dummy hand** AFTER YOU HAVE FOUND THE GOLDEN FIT AND **ONLY AFTER** THE GOLDEN FIT IS FOUND. These points will help you zero in on your final contract. As far as shortness is concerned, you've noted the winning edge provided by a singleton or void in the dummy, allowing losers to be ruffed when you're in a **suit** contract. The unexpected tricks may make you exceed your contract such that you find you didn't bid high enough, so **do not delay** adding in the extra points. With NO fit, there is NO advantage to shortness, so do not add in ANY shortness points. *In a 6/2 trump fit, NEVER add points for the trump shortness!*

Can the responder add in length points? Traditionally, he would calculate only shortness points, but if he has a long running suit and access to it through a mutually held suit, or through As and KQs, he should add points for his long suit too. In a NT contract, as previously stated, any shortness is NOT beneficial, but the auction may reveal that the opener has the responder's weak suit(s) covered. **If the responder's long, strong suit is accessible, it is worth a great deal in ANY contract - use your card sense.** If the strong suit is accessible, and both hands show promise, the partnership may have a slam without the requisite points.

SHORTNESS OR DISTRIBUTIONAL POINTS		FURTHER ADJUSTMENTS:
Added **ONLY AFTER** the "GOLDEN FIT" is found, and BOTH charts apply. Do not forget the "further adjustments."		**-1 HCP** for a flat, totally balanced hand (4333). **-1 HCP** for zero aces in your hand.
Open. or resp. w/ 3 trumps	**Resp. w/ 4+ Trumps**	**Devalue your hand** with all your strength in SHORT SUITS (very bad), and/or in Qs and Js.
1 Doubleton	1	**Devalue** singleton or unprotected Ks, Qs, & Js.
2 Singleton	3	**Do not keep bidding competitively** if you have
3 Void	5*	no mid-range cards: 10s, 9s, (and sometimes 8s).

~ OR ~

**Add one point for each extra trump beyond three,
if your hand is semi-balanced** (5422, 4522).

Due to shortness, in the following auction you may bid a 5 HCP hand. Partner opens 1H and you have the following: x Kxxx Qxxxx xxx. You hold 5 HCP, a S singleton (+3), and an extra trump (+1), but no As (-1) = 8. Your hand is now valued at **8** points. *Bid 2H.* Your S singleton and your extra heart will help you make your contract.

* **Tip:** In standard bridge, a responder with extra trumps may **add 5 points if void in a suit.** This may or may not be too high a number when estimating true hand value. Why? 1. If the responder has top honors the opener will need to pull trumps, the responder may have few trumps left for ruffing. 2. The number may be affected if partner bids your void/singleton (a mismatch), or 3. There is a bad trump split. Adjust the number from 3-5 as you see fit, depending on the rest of your hand.

Doubletons can be overvalued and risky: two swift losers. Be wary when stretching for a M game permitting only 3 losers.

MORE DISCUSSION OF UNPROTECTED HONORS...

Sometimes you have a singleton K, Qx, or Jx(x) - **_unprotected honors._** You CANNOT count BOTH the honor points AND the shortness points in a suit contract. If your partner bid the suit, you might help him set up his suit or perhaps provide transportation one time. In that case, count only the **honor points.** If an opponent bid the suit, count only the **shortness points** as shown in the opener's count or which ever point count between the honor count and shortness count that is the SMALLER number. For example, you hold a singleton K of Hs. If partner bids Hs, count the K as **3** - the honor count. If the opponents bid Hs, count the K as **2** - the HCP value of a singleton in the opener's hand. You may even choose to count your singleton K of their suit as **0 HCP,** not an unreasonable assumption of it's true value to you. The K will likely be useful as a singleton, *but only after being lost to their A,* **costing one trick and three of your points.** Therefore...

DEVALUE ANY UNPROTECTED HONOR IN A SUIT BID BY THE OPPONENTS

If you and your partner each hold big hands, add in all the distribution points you can and try for the big score. Now is not the time to be hesitant - he who hesitates is lost! DON'T MISS THAT SLAM!

EXTRA TRUMPS

You hold: x J1098 KQ86 10986, NV. You evaluate 6 HCP initially, then add 3 HCP for the spade singleton AFTER partner opens with Hs: 6+3=9 HCP. Subtract a point because you have no aces and add 1 HCP for the extra H, a total of **9** HCP. All players bid: **1H** (part.) - [1S] - **2H** (you) - [2S] - **P** - [P] - **you?**

Each side has about the same number of direct high card points (not including distribution), but your hand has some extras. Can you bid again? You have a fourth trump, a S singleton, and you're at the top of your range. **Bid 3 Hs.** You can safely ruff partner's losing spades at least twice. *The extra trump and the opportunity to use trumps on the opponent's Ss tip the balance in your favor.* If you get set one or two tricks, it should still be a better score for you than passing. Can you get a read on what partner has? Probably 5 Hs, 4 Ss and either 2/2 or 3/1 in the minors. If the opponents have a 9 card S fit, your partner will have another card in a minor, which could mean a double fit in Hs and a m. Don't pass at the two level - they'll likely make their bid. Your clue? Partner passed at his second opportunity to bid, showing a minimal hand. It's up to you to bid again. If they bid 3S, *does a bad split await them since you have only one S?*

MORE FINE TUNING...

A positive feature you may have in your hand are **9s and 10s**. They are high level, non-honor cards that can force or trap *their* honors. Put with your own honors in a long suit, they become powerful. If you are wavering, look at the non-point strength of your hand. Do you have small cards, perhaps aces with spaces such as the A532, or do you have honors and mid-range cards such as the KQ1094? If you are heavy in the middle, GOOD! Your hand improves. This is the only time being "heavy in the middle" will make you happy. Enjoy it while you can.

Do you have a balanced (flat) hand headed into a suit contract? Will the declarer have to wait a while (lose a while) before he can ruff in your hand? Will that hurt the team? Weak three card suits are often calamitous in a game contract, especially if your partner holds three poor cards in the same suit - you'll feel like a sitting duck. Balanced hands play best in **NT**. Slightly devalue your hand if the two sides are battling for a suit contract.

EVALUATING YOUR HAND and CONCLUSION

Hand valuation is not finished when you count your HCP: you recalculate throughout the auction. Do you have the Golden Fit with your partner? **Add in those distribution points.** You may have a long two honor suit of your own, then the opponent **ahead of you** bids your suit. Your hand goes **UP** in estimation because you are positioned to take some of his winners. What if you support your partner's M and you can't wait for him to see your KJ10x holding in diamonds, hoping he has some Ds. Then the player **following you** bids diamonds. Uh oh! He's positioned to **take *your* winners.** Your hand goes **DOWN** in value. Don't keep bidding if the person behind you has your suit, unless you have the AKQ. If partner chooses to continue bidding in the auction he has a reason (a singleton or void in Ds?), but *you* don't!

What does all this mean? You may be battling the opponents for a partscore or a game, and whether or not you can bid higher depends on what happens in the auction, how well you fit with your partner, and your distribution: are you totally balanced OR 2-3 suited? Any voids or singletons? Extra trumps? Mid-range cards? All these questions have an impact on your contract. So...

Continually reevaluate your hand to determine the best contract.

Practice & Application Lesson XIII: <u>BIG</u> Hands *BIG hand and Distributional Values charts p. 94*

Only you and your partner are bidding. What do these bids mean? You are the responder.

1. 1H - 2H - 3H? Partner has 17+ HCP (or 16 HCP with distributional values). He asks if you are at the top of your point range. Bid game with 8-9 HCP. There is only one reason for him to bid again. If he has minimum opening values, he just made his contract more difficult for no reason.

2. 1H - 1S - 3C? Partner shows 19+ HCP, 5 H and 4+ Cs. Since you dared bid, you promise at least 6 HCP, game values. Do not stop below game.

3. 1H - 1S - 3H? Partner jumped in his suit, which promises 16+ HCP and 6+ Hs. If you have 8+ HCP, check to see if your distribution is favorable for game. Bid game with 9+ HCP. Partner could have *more* than 16 HCP, up to 18 HCP.

What does the bidding mean? The opponent's bids are in [ ].

1. 1H - [1S] - 2H - [2S] - 3H? Does this bid invite game? No. The opener is competing based on extra values in his hand, or if your pair is NV, he thinks your score will be better if you get set than if they make 2S. Pass. Everyone seems to have some points, so no game for you.

2. [1C] - X - [P] - 1H - [P] - 2H? Does this invite game? Yes. The overcaller has 16-17 HCP and asks if you are at the top of your bid, as you would have jumped with 10+ HCP. Bid game if you have 8-9 HCP.

3. [2H] - X? - P - Partner has a good hand - 16+ HCP. Jump in your long suit with 9+ HCP as game is likely. With fewer than 9 HCP, bid your suit at the lowest level. If you have good stoppers in the opener's suit, bid NT.

4. 1H - [P] - 1S - [P] - 2NT? Opener shows 18-19 HCP. Though 2NT is not a forcing bid, you should strongly consider game, as you only need 7 HCP or a good/distributional 6 HCP (with a fit) to make game.

5. 1S - [P] - 2NT - [P] - ? Game invitational. Responder shows 11-12 HCP and fewer than 3 S. With 12 HCP and only 5 poor Ss, pass. With more Ss or 13-15 HCP, rebid Ss or bid 3NT.

6. 1C - [P] - 1H - [P] - 1S - [P] - 3H? Responder shows 11+ HCP, 6+ Hs and searches for a fit. Game is possible, but 3H is NF.

7. 1C - [P] - 1H - [P] - 1NT - [P] - 2H? This is a **"<u>drop dead</u>"** bid. Responder has 5+ Hs and fears a bad outcome in NT. Pass. A rebid at the lowest level is a sign-off. The fact that the opener bid NT **implies SOME Hs** (2-3) because he didn't rebid 1S or 2C, effectively denying Hs.

8. [1C] - X - [P] - 1S - [P] - 2H? Partner shows 18+ HCP and a very nice heart suit. Bid game in a M or NT if you have 7+ HCP.

Tip: Distribution points help define your strength, but at times may encourage you to go overboard in your bidding. If this happens, do not become discouraged and stop adding in distribution points, but instead see how you might have played the hand differently for success.

Lesson XIV   HUGE HANDS

2NT and 2C

You've crossed over into another dimension..."The Twilight Zone."
It's strange, but disregard everything you thought you knew about the responder's HCP.

You've spent so much time learning the SA bidding system that you probably feel as if you have a complete encyclopedia inside your head. But in the wonderful world of bridge, as you already know, things are not always what they seem. Right when you think you've got it, you'll find there is *even more* information to process. However, you will really like these final two opening bids and their distinctive set of responses because they mean your team's **got it all!** You may pull out a 3-5 point hand and feel as if the future is hopeless, but DON'T GIVE UP YET!

THE 2NT OPENING BID

If partner opens 2NT, he is showing a balanced hand with **20-21 HCP.** How many points does your team need to bid game? **Only 4 or 5 HCP!** If you have 4 HCP (perhaps with a long suit) or 5 HCP, DO NOT LET THE CONTRACT STOP BELOW GAME. It is usually up to the responder to make sure the contract is in the right place. Normally you would not bid with fewer than 6 HCP, but the usual requirements for a minimum bid DO NOT APPLY.

How would you bid over a 2NT opener? **Just as you would bid over a 1NT opener, only one step higher.** You may use Stayman and Jacoby Transfers to describe your hand, OR bid 3NT if you don't have the configuration to bid conventions. If you have 10-11 HCP and a **long suit** with distributional values, consider a small slam. If you have 12+ HCP, a slam contract is coming your way. If both the opener and the responder have **balanced hands**, a slam would require the recommended combined point count - 33 for a small slam, and 37 for a grand slam. With fewer than 4 HCP and no long M to transfer, you may pass. *A 2NT opening bid is not forcing.*

Opener: **Responder and Meaning:**

2NT   **3C** =   Stayman (seeking a 4 card M) *Remember, you only need 4 or 5 HCP for game, so the usual requirement of **8 HCP for Stayman is OFF**.*

Opener makes the typical responses at the three level:

3D = no 4 c M   3H = 4Hs, maybe 4 Ss   3S = 4S, no 4 c H suit.

*The **responder** will place the final contract.*

or

3D =   Jacoby Transfer (I have **5** hearts). After the transfer (opener says "HEARTS"), the responder will pass, bid 3NT, or seek a higher contract.

or

3H =   Jacoby Transfer (I have **5** spades). After the transfer (opener says "SPADES"), the responder will pass, bid 3NT, or seek a higher contract.

or

3NT =   I have 5-9 HCP and don't think we have slam. I have no 4 or 5 card M or a long, trick-taking minor, and you, the opener, are expected to be balanced too.

or

4C =   **Gerber.** I have 11+ HCP. *See the following chapter.*

*As over a 1NT opener, the RESPONDER now becomes the **Captain** over 2NT or 2C. He is responsible for getting to the right contract since he is privy to the full count of the team's HCPs.*

HUGE HANDS

THE 2C OPENING BID

Two Clubs is the "crown jewel" of opening bids: it is **artificial** and **forcing.** It is the **ONLY** forcing opening bid, showing **22+ HCP,** no limit, and could be **any shape**. The opener might have a long suit, but shows his strength **first** to prevent a pass from a weak partner. **The responder must bid.** The responder needs only **3 HCP** for game. There are many response systems to use over a 2C opener. The response system we will employ follows.

The RESPONDER'S answers to the 2C opening bid:

2D: Waiting (+) — The responder wants the opener to tell more about his hand, **acknowledging game values** with his 2D bid. He has at least 3 HCP (an A, K, 2 Qs, or even 3 Js). The opener will bid his long suit, or if the opener is balanced, he'll rebid NT**.** Systems will be "on" for Stayman and Jacoby Transfers. If asked, it is "Positive Waiting." **See further explanations below.**

2H: WEAK (-) — A poor (negative) hand with 0-2 HCP. **_ALERT_** this bid since it doesn't show Hs. The opener will place the contract: 2S, 3H, 4S, 4H, a minor suit, 2NT, or 3NT. *He will infrequently pass.*

2S: Strong S suit — The responder has 5+ good spades (2+ top honors), **8+** HCP, & game values, possibly more. He must meet **BOTH** requirements in honors and HCP to bid Ss. Opener must rebid since the responder indicates a game+ contract. He'll support Ss with at least 3 spades (3S or 4S).

2NT: HEART SUIT — Responder has 5+ good **HEARTS** (2+ top honors) and **8+** HCP. As with 2Ss, **BOTH** requirements must be met for responder to bid 2NT. The 2H bid is for a "**_bust hand_**," so responder must have a way show a heart suit. Pair has game+ values. The opener must **ALERT** 2NT, & then rebid. If the opener has support for partner's Hs, he will play the contract, unlike Ss.

The opener rebids 2NT or 3NT after a 2D response:

2NT: If the opener rebids **2NT** after the responder's 2D "waiting" bid**,** he shows a balanced hand that is **limited to** **22-23** HCP. Stayman and Transfers may be used by the responder to show 4 or 5 c Ms, **OR** the responder can bid **3NT** with at least 3 HCP and no 4 or 5 c M. The responses are the same as if the opener opened 2NT - one step higher than over a 1NT opening bid. If responder does not bid a 5 c M directly over the 2C bid, but *chooses to make a transfer later,* after opener's 2NT rebid, he has a 5 c M with fewer than 2 top honors and/or a hand with fewer than 8 HCP. He may yet show his long M - he needn't despair! **Game** is still "on."

3NT: The opener can rebid **3NT**, **a jump bid,** with **24+ HCP**. Responder can try for a slam contract with 6-8 HCP and a **long, good** suit, and slam is "on" with **9+** HCP. If the opener has even greater HCP, he may want to assume control of the hand.

The opener rebids a SUIT after a 2D response:

If the opener rebids a suit, it shows **5+** cards in his suit and both players will continue the bidding until a **game contract** is decided. The responder's 2D "waiting" bid means he has **at least 3 HCP**. If the opener's suit is a M, the priority would be to play in the M, so a bid of another suit by the responder would show **no M fit** and either a long suit or stoppers for NT. If the opener rebids a m, the responder can bid a M showing 5, but fewer than 8 HCP and/or 2 honors. He may also bid NT, but **he would try to get the 2C opener with the big hand to be the declarer in NT**. Remain calm and think about what partner is trying to tell you. Attempts getting to the right contract after opening 2C can be somewhat stressful as you concentrate on how to respond.

The opener's rebid after the 2H weak ("Bust") response:

After partner's 2H bid, the opener will place the contract where it needs to be according to *his* hand. Rarely would the responder bid again, as he has told his story, but if he does, he is showing a lot of **length** (5-6+) *but no strength* in his suit/hand. The opener can pass, raise the suit if he has some honors, bid another suit, bid game or bid NT. Transfers are "on" if the responder rebids after a 2NT response by the opener and there is no interference.

The opener's rebid after 2S (showing spades as usual) or 2NT (showing hearts):

The opener will raise Ss to show a fit and to invite game or better; he may bid **3S** to show 22-23 HCP, or he may bid **4S** to show *more* HCP (PA). Over 2NT he will bid **3/4Hs** to put the contract in the correct **_strain_** (suit) if he has Hs, or the opener will bid his own suit and wait for a response. If no fit in a suit, the pair will likely bid a NT game.

Practice & Application Lesson XIV: HUGE, GIGANTIC, ENORMOUS HANDS *Chart p. 94*

What do these bids mean? No one else bids.

1.	2C, as an opening bid?	A 2C bid is the **only** forcing bid by the opener: 22+ HCP and could be ANY shape. The responder MUST bid no matter what his hand looks like.
2.	2NT, as an opening bid?	Shows 20-21 HCP and a balanced hand. With an unbalanced hand, bid a long suit and hope you get to jump-shift or big game. If your hand is extremely unbalanced (6511, for example, with a long solid suit), open 2C having so many points. You don't want partner to pass.
3.	2NT - 3C?	Stayman - do you have a 4 card M?
4.	2NT - 3H?	Jacoby Transfer - I have 5 S.
5.	2NT - 3D?	Jacoby Transfer - I have 5 Hs.
6.	2NT - 3C - 3D?	Opener does not have a 4 card M. Responder bids 3NT+.
7.	2NT - 3NT?	Responder has enough HCP for game and no 4 or 5 card M.
8.	2C - 2D?	Resp's waiting to see if the opener have a long suit or a balanced hand. Resp. has at least one A, one K, or two Qs. but does NOT have a superb M suit with two honors and 8+ HCP. However, he could have a 5 card M that is not strong.
9.	2C - 2H?	Resp. has fewer than 3 HCP. Opener sets the contract with his next bid, or passes if he prefers Hs. If he raises the Hs, it is an invitation to game showing extra strength. Resp. will bid game with **anything** positive in his hand - an extra long suit or 1-2 HCP. The opener must **alert** the 2H bid.
10.	2C - 2S?	Resp. has 5+ Ss, 2+ honors, and 8+ HCP. Opener can raise to 3 Ss if he has 3 or more Ss & 22-23 HCP. He may bid game if stronger. Responder will not stop below game and slam could be possible. Opener can bid any other suit or NT without a S fit.
11.	2C - 2NT?	Resp. has 5+ **Hs,** 2+ honors, and 8+ HCP. Natural bidding follows and the pair will bid game or a higher contract. Opener **alerts** the 2NT bid. The opener can "super accept" and jump to game to show extra HCP with H support, or make another bid.
12.	2C - 2H - 3D - 3S?	2H = a bust hand (< 3 HCP), BUT responder also has 5-6+ Ss. The opener could bid game with S support **and** distributional value.
13.	2C - 2D - 2NT?	2C opener is **limited to 22-23 HCP** and has a balanced hand.
14.	2C - 2D - 3NT?	2C opener has **24+ HCP** and is balanced. Slam is possible if the responder has at least 8 HCP, especially if responder has a long suit.
15.	2C - 2D - 2NT - 3C?	The responder asks the opener for a 4 card M: Stayman.
16.	2C - 2D - 2NT - 2H?	The responder transfers Ss.
17.	2C - 2D - 2NT - 3D - 3H - 3NT - ?	The responder makes a transfer to Hs, then bids 3NT to let the opener select the final contract. Note that the 2D waiting bid and the 3D transfer bid are unrelated. **In each of the last three auctions, it's as if the 2NT bid "resets" the system.** Hmmm...

Lesson XV   Blackwood & Gerber

You and your partner both have strong hands. Perhaps one of you jumped in the auction to show extra values and surprised the other who planned to do the same. The final contract appears as if it should be a slam. Do you *really* have it all? Investigate further by using one of these two special conventions.

BLACKWOOD

Blackwood is a convention used with **SUIT** contracts. In this convention, 4NT asks partner how many aces he has, and **if the team has them all**, he MIGHT ask for kings (5NT).* First, *agree on a suit*. If unable to clarify the suit for fear of a pass, start Blackwood over the last suit bid and place the final contract in the correct suit. **Do not use Blackwood with a worthless unbid doubleton.** If the bidding goes 1H - 1S - 3H... partner has 16+ HCP. If you have at least 15+ HCP too, BID 4NT! You are this close to slam AND partner has 6 Hs!

4NT is the "Ace ask."	**If you have all the aces, 5NT is the "King ask."**
5C = **Zero or four** Aces	6C = **Zero or four** Kings
5D = One Ace	6D = One King
5H = Two Aces	6H = Two Kings
5S = Three Aces	6S = Three Kings

To stop: bid your trump suit, **not** 5NT.

*__Be careful.__ You may be **committed** to the six level if your suit is a <u>minor</u> and you initiate Blackwood. Your partner's answer could **pass** 5C/5D, exactly where you'd want to stop. Make your decision **NOW**, before the ask.

If your suit is Hearts and you ask for Ks, should partner answer that he has 3 Ks (6S), you are committed to the seven level in Hs: ***6NT anyone?*** You may bid 6NT missing an A or K, or 7NT if you have all the As and Ks and a long suit either shared between the two hands, or a long suit that easily accessible in either hand.

Tip: Examine your hand and **count all the points for the outstanding As and Ks.** Is it possible that partner could have most or all of the missing As and Ks? For example, if your partner opens a minor, **not 1NT**, does he have a big hand or a minimal opening hand? Probably a minimal range opener, **unless** he jumps in his minor to show a big hand. He couldn't open NT because *he doesn't have a balanced hand.* Does he jump shift in a new suit? Does he rebid his original suit or bid a new suit at the **lowest possible level?** If the outstanding points add up to a bid your partner **doesn't make**, forget the slam bid. You are probably close, but not close enough. **If you have a void,** *that may change everything*. Think about which A(s) he could have and see how his A(s) might impact your hand. Can you toss a loser? Maintain control? Distributional hands are in a league of their own and are powerful. **Fine tune your hand with distributional points and decide game or slam based on the results.**

GERBER

Gerber is similar to Blackwood, but is used over the **first or last NT**. With Gerber, the auction doesn't get as high as quickly as it does with Blackwood, so you may end the auction at a lower level. Again, do not bid higher *without all four aces,* unless you have all the Ks. Ex (no oppo. bids): 1D - 1H - 1NT - 4C = Gerber.

4C is the "Ace ask."	**If you have all the aces, 5C is the "King ask."**
4D = **Zero or four** Aces	5D = **Zero or four** Kings
4H = One Ace	5H = One King
4S = Two Aces	5S = Two Kings
4NT = Three Aces	5NT = Three Kings

To stop: pass a 4NT response or bid the desired NT level.

For Future Study: _____

THE QUANTITATIVE RAISE

Partner opens 1NT, 15-17 HCP. You also have a balanced hand with **15-17 HCP**, so a small slam is possible. **Bid 4NT,** a Quantitative Raise, asking partner if he is at the top of his bid, and if he is, he'll bid **6NT**.

If you want to find a suit fit first, make a transfer to show your 5 card M, then bid 4NT to invite slam, or 5NT telling partner to "pick your slam." Must be a PA for both of you. Don't worry, these hands are rare.

Lesson XV: Blackwood & Gerber Baby!

Chart p. 93

What do these bids mean? The opponents are silent.

1. 1S - 4NT? — The responder is asking for As, Blackwood. Ss is the agreed upon trump suit.
2. 1S - 4NT - 5D? — The opener has one A.
3. 1S - 4NT - 5S? — The opener has three As.
4. 2C - 2D - 2S - 4NT - 5C? — Ss agreed suit. The opener has zero or four As. The auction and your hand should tell you - he has all four As *or* he has almost every K, Q, and J to be able to open 2C.
5. 1S - 2H - 2S - 4NT - 5C? — Ss agreed suit. The opener has zero or four As. He didn't open the auction showing a hand with a lot of points or jump when he rebid, so assume zero As. The responder knows what the opener holds. If Blackwood continues, *the responder has all the As!*
6. 2NT - 3D - 3H - 3NT? — Not Blackwood, simply a regular game contract. The opener can correct to Hs if he has enough (3-4). The responder is the captain.
7. 1S - 2H - 3NT - 4C? — Gerber, the A ask. Opener has **at least 15 HCP** since he bid game after partner showed 10+ HCP. Hmmm...
8. 1NT - 4C - 4NT? — Gerber - the response of 4NT shows three As.
9. 1NT - 4C - 4D? — Zero or four As. The responder will immediately know which count you have.

Answer your partner.

1. 4NT by partner and you want to show two As. — Bid 5Hs.
2. 4NT by partner and you want to show three As. — Bid 5Ss.
3. 4C by partner and you want to show four As. — Bid 4Ds.
4. 4C by partner and you want to show one A. — Bid 4Hs.

The following is continuously bid by both partners *after* initial bidding:

4NT by partner and you want to show zero As. — Bid 5 Cs...

...Then partner then bids 5NT. — Partner has all the As and asks for Ks...

...You want to show one K... — Bid 6 Ds. Partner will place the final contract.

    You may not have to use BW or Gerber if you know you have the combined points for slam. Partner opens 1NT, 2NT, or 2C illustrating his points well, and you have several points. The bidding may go 1C-1H-2NT, a jump bid showing 18-19 HCP. Again, the opener's hand is well defined. Trust the points and bid your slam.

    If the bidding goes 1H-1S-3H, partner is showing 16-18 HCP. Does he have 16 or 18 HCP? It may make a difference to you if you have 13-15 HCP with a certain shape of hand, so you may choose to use Blackwood to decide if a slam is possible. The check for As and Ks should confirm what you suspect, not be a hunt for what you desperately hope partner holds. If you bow out of slam, your points should be enough for a 5 level bid.

    Do not use BW with a worthless doubleton in a suit that neither of you bid, and be careful not to pass your best contract by asking for Ks when the answer may pass 6 of your suit. If you have a void and come up short an A after the A ask, **test your hand** to see if **any A** partner holds would benefit you. You may still be able to make slam with a void or singleton, IF you are in a suit contract.

Lesson XVI Scoring and *more* Offense/Defense

Bridge is a great competitive game. The more you know about all facets of the game, including scoring, the easier it will be for you to get to the right contract, pass when you should, and not overbid so that you make a **ZERO** - *horrors!* - *the worst score!* - if you continue in the auction.

You've been told to "check and respect" your vulnerability when you sort your hand, and by now you've probably noticed when you get set vulnerable, it **gives several points to the opponents.** But have you ever noticed your LOSING score was HIGHER than their partscore would have been? Higher than *ANY* partscore they could have bid? We'll get to the **real deal;** to understand vulnerability and its effect on scoring. The following is about duplicate bridge scoring and strategy. Social? Keep it positive.

First of all, know basic scoring.............

When successful below game, pairs receive the sum of tricks won **+ a 50 point bonus.** Vulnerability doesn't affect partscores. Big NV/V bonuses are added only to winning **game/slam** contracts.

Partscores - NV OR V

Making	1	2	3	4	+1
minors	70	90	110	130	**150**
Majors	80	110	140		**170**
NT	90	120			**150**

+1 = an extra trick: the team **underbid** - they should have bid a **game contract**.

The teams that made an **extra trick** not only missed a game, but the **bonus points** for making a game contract.

ALL of the above scores, *even the missed games,* are lower than **200**: the "Terrible 200" the equivalent of **getting set 2 tricks V.** Down 3 NV (-150) is a poor score as well. Moral of the story: DO NOT take chances, when competing for a partscore when you are **vulnerable.** *If you are NV, well...maybe.*

One isn't the "loneliest number," it's **170:** Your score if you make 10 tricks & DON'T bid a M game. A M game is **420 NV** and **620 V,** *a costly error in competition.* A missed NT/m game is **150** vs. **400/600**...also a costly error.

And know the basic penalties...............

Your pair's NEGATIVE SCORE becomes the opponent's POSITIVE SCORE.

# of tricks set	NV	V	NVX	VX
-1	- 50	-100	-100	- 200
-2	-100	**-200**	**-300**	- 500
-3	**-150**	**-300**	**-500**	- 800
-4	**-200**	**-400**	<u>**-800**</u>	<u>**-1100**</u>
-5	**-250**	**-500**	<u>**-1100**</u>	<u>**-1400**</u>

• The non-bold-print penalty scores are usually safe & competitive vs. their two level M contract. Most contracts, but not all, will be at the two level or higher.
• The **bold-print** penalties are dangerous *EXCEPT* when competing **NV** vs. their **V** GAME, and can be **appalling** if doubled.
• The **bold-underlined** scores may cause your dismayed partner to ask, *"Are you out of your mind?! We gave away too much - why did you keep going?"*

What do you see when you compare the two charts? That you can get set up to **TWO TRICKS** non-vulnerable, but only **ONE TRICK** vulnerable or non-vulnerable doubled to keep from giving the opponents a higher score than had you *PASSED* their partscore contract, in most cases. Ouch! So if you are bidding vulnerable, you must be careful not to bid **too high.** You can't "fall in love with your hand," or continue the auction hoping for *something* from your weak or non-bidding partner. If you want to compete more, but have bid as high as you feel is safe with your number of HCP, let PARTNER decide the final contract. He may be at the top of his point range or has extra trumps. *Then it will be HIS fault if things go awry.*

So what do you need to to know? Always bid your games and **NEVER, EVER** get set 150 - 200 points (or more) when competing for a partscore contract. *If you're that weak, don't push them into their* **unbid game.**

• *Beginners may skip to page 66 for more defensive tactics* • *Read 62-65 with game experience.*

Know when to hold 'em... What if they seem headed to a **V** game with a potential score of **600 or 620?** Suppose your pair is **NV** with a long combined suit, AND you are distributional with none or only one of their suit. Can you do anything to disrupt their game? Compare the penalty chart with this game chart.

Game Score	NV	V
5 minor	**400**	**<u>600</u>**
4 Major	**420**	**<u>620</u>**
3NT	**400**	**<u>600</u>**

Balanced: 4333, 4432,
Semi-bal: 5332, 5422

*Unbalanced: 5521, 5530, 6421, 6430, 6511, etc.

You can get set *more* tricks if they are in game, especially a **vulnerable game.** The bold-print penalty scores are much safer now. They'll make **600** or **620,** but you may **GET SET** as as much as **500** points (-3 tricks NVX) and still come out ahead. Will they double? They may if they know you are stealing their contract. Bid anyway, IF your hand is right - they're **V**, you're **NV and unbalanced*** with a nice long trump suit AND a second suit. *You may make your bid* - but that doesn't happen every time. If your hand is balanced or semi-balanced, forget it...you'll lose too many tricks to their strong holding in your weak suits - after all, they bid game and have the majority of the points. Finally, don't fall victim to the ghastly **<u>bold underlined</u>** penalty scores. You'll dejectedly say, "This one's on me. I am a complete idiot."

It takes a special hand to safely wreck their game. Don't blindly run over the cliff, smash yourself and your score into a million pieces on the rocks below and...never mind. You get the idea.

How the scoring is calculated in a game of duplicate bridge:
- *Pairs get 1 point for every team they <u>beat</u>, and .5 for every team they <u>tie</u>.*
- *The highest score (the top board) will be one fewer than the actual number of competing teams because <u>zero</u> is a possible score.*

Starting with a simple auction, let's see the scoring in action as it affects each bidder on a **<u>traveller</u>** (score sheet):

Traveller 1:
Neither side vulnerable. Best contract 2S by N/S for 110. Avg: 2 Dealer: W

N/S Pr.#	E/W Pr.#	Contract	By	Made	Down	N/S	E/W	Match Points N/S	Match Points E/W
1	4	2S	N	2		110		2	2
2	3	2S	N	2		110		2	2
3	5	2S	N	2		110		2	2
4	2	2S	N	2		110		2	2
5	1	2S	N	2		110		2	2

Analysis:

As I like to say, "No bridge player was harmed in the making of this contract." Not harmed yes, *but not helped either*. **Every** team gets a **50%** board because the scores are all the same. No one stands out. **It's un-American!** Nobody wants to be average!

Let's see what happens when **someone takes a chance,** since the teams appear evenly matched according to the auction: 1H - [1S] - 2H - [2S] - P - [P] - P. *How does that "someone" know they're evenly matched?* West opens 1H & there is a 1S overcall. The responder makes a minimum raise & advancer has opening count with S support. He trusts his partner to have **8+** HCP as a level one overcaller, which adds to 20 - half the HCP. *Never lie to your partner!*

SCORING AND MORE OFFENSE/DEFENSE

Traveller 2:
   The same board as before, but with that one daring soul who will not be average.

N/S Pr.#	E/W Pr.#	Contract	By	Made	Down	N/S	E/W	Match Points N/S	Match Points E/W
1	4	2S	N	2		110		2.5	1.5
2	3	2S	N	2		110		2.5	1.5
3	5	**3H**	E		1	**50**		**0**	**4**
4	2	2S	N	2		110		2.5	1.5
5	1	2S	N	2		110		2.5	1.5

Analysis:

One E/W team (5) understands the scoring. They know each side has around 20 HCP so they can safely make a NV sacrifice bid. If they make their bid, great. Top score! If they get set **one** trick it is only **50** points. That means they GIVE UP THE *FEWEST* POINTS. If they get set **two** tricks undoubled or 1 trick doubled NV, **their score would *still* be lower at 100** than the opponent's **110**. Also notice how the **one** sacrifice bid affects **all** the scores. The scoring indicates that EVERY E/W pair should have made the sacrifice. Those that didn't are penalized by a deduction in their points from the previous traveller. Now their scores are **below average.**

Traveller 3:
   The same board, but one N/S fought back...

N/S Pr.#	E/W Pr.#	Contract	By	Made	Down	N/S	E/W	Match Points N/S	Match Points E/W
1	4	2S	N	2		110		3	1
2	3	2S	N	2		110		3	1
3	5	3H	E		1	50		1	3
4	2	3S	N		1		50	0	4
5	1	2S	N	2		110		3	1

Analysis:

The game's afoot. Three N/S pairs play their optimum contract & end up in a three-way tie for top on their side. E/W pair 5 bids the 3H sacrifice that would have allowed them give up the fewest amount of points for a top score, *EXCEPT FOR 4 N/S*. They don't know silence is golden, so they bid again for a disastrous result. A bottom board: **ZERO!** Their negative score becomes the opponent's positive score, & no other N/S gives up any points to E/W but them. **Top score for 2 E/W**. N/S 4 would have been better off to **double the E/W sacrifice bid** for the second highest score on their side (+100). Oops!

Building Bridges © 2022 Jeanne R. Wamack May not be reproduced in any form.

Let's see what could happen to the scores in a bigger game with competitive players...

Neither side vulnerable. Best contract 3H by E/W. Avg. 3 (a 50% board) Dlr: W

N/S Pr.#	EW Pr.#	Contract	By	Made	Down	N/S	E/W	Match Points N/S	Match Points E/W
1	6	2S	N	2		110		6	0
2	1	2H	E	3			140	0.5	5.5
3	3	3H	E	3			140	0.5	5.5
4	5	3SX	N		1		100	3	3
5	7	2S	N		1		50	5	1
6	2	2H	E	2			110	2	4
7	4	2D	W	2			90	4	2

Analysis:

N/S 1 - N made a sacrifice bid of 2S which E/W didn't challenge or set. E/W has the lowest score because they gave up the most HCP on their side.

N/S 2 - E/W passed out in 2H and made 3H, one of the top two scores.

N/S 3 - N made a sacrifice bid that E/W bid over and made, so E/W is tied for top score.

N/S 4 - Again, N tried to push the score higher, but didn't stop at 2S and bid 3S over 3H. The way the rest of the game went, they ended up with an average board. The E/W pair didn't bid 4H, but did double the contract. They received an average board too. Had they not doubled, they would have been tied for second lowest on their side. Neither side was harmed nor benefitted by this board. *Had N/S been vulnerable, they would have given up **200 points**, top score for E/W.*

N/S 5 - N/S tried to sacrifice, but went down 1 trick. E/W didn't bid higher, nor did they double. N/S got a good score - second from the top, while E/W was second from the bottom. E/W would have had a better score had they bid 3H or doubled. N/S's sacrifice, even getting set, was **BETTER THAN E/W's potential 140**.

N/S 6 - N/S didn't try a sacrifice bid, but E/W got lucky because E should have made another trick. There is no penalty for not making the best possible score and they receive the second highest score on their side.

N/S 7 - **W preempted a minor** and got passed out. They ended with a below-average score because they missed their M fit, *even though they made their bid.*

We see sacrifice bidding here, good defense that worked, and we see pairs that bid well & didn't let their contract get stolen. We get score variation now - clear winners & losers.

Let's look at interference in a vulnerable game in which the opponents are not vulnerable:

Your goal is to bid your games (and slams). If you are battling for a partscore, you *may* have to sacrifice - you PLAN to get set one or two tricks NV to prevent the opponents from making a high score. In order to do this properly, you need to memorize the part-scores of all contracts to compare those points with the penalty you will receive for getting set.

The non-doubled penalty scores are easy to remember as they are in multiples of 50 NV or 100 V. Think "1, 3, 5" for NVX (100, 300, etc), and "2, 5, 8" for VX (200, 500, etc). You will continue bidding **only** if it is to your benefit. You will rarely, IF EVER, sacrifice vulnerable. **Compare the risk to the benefit.** Learning how to sacrifice takes time and practice. Be patient.

N/S Vulnerable. Best Contract 4S by N/S. Average score is 3 (50% board). Dlr S.

N/S Pr.#	E/W Pr.#	Contract	By	Made	Down	N/S	E/W	Match Points N/S	Match Points E/W
1	6	4S	N	4		620		4	2
2	1	4S	N	4		620		4	2
3	3	5C	E		3	150		1	5
4	5	4S	N	4		620		4	2
5	7	5CX	E		3	500		2	4
6	2	5S	N		1		100	0	6
7	4	5CX	E		4	800		6	0

Analysis:

N/S 1 Bid and made their contract for a good score - tied for 2nd N/S. (three-way tie)

N/S 2 Bid and made their contract for a good score - tied for 2nd N/S.

N/S 3 Poor N/S 3 - they were challenged by an E/W pair that found their C fit, but N/S didn't X for penalty. Bad board for them, great board for **E/W.**

N/S 4 Bid and made their contract for a good score - tied for 2nd.

N/S 5 Poor N/S 5 - they were challenged and not allowed to make their 4S bid, BUT at least they doubled the opponents and got a slightly below-average board for their side. The board is above-average for E/W.

N/S 6 Poor N/S 6 - they let themselves be pushed to the **5 level** and got set for the worst N/S board. That wicked E/W pair! They got the top board on their side!

N/S 7 The E/W pair had the right idea to challenge N/S, but either lacked the skills to pull off the theft, or the N/S pair defended exceptionally well. The attempt cost E/W dearly - **a deadly zero** for them and a top for N/S - which is exactly what E/W was trying to *PREVENT.*

Special Note: Every bottom board (0%) that you get has to be offset by a top board (100%) to have two 50% boards, scores that that neither hurt, NOR HELP YOU.

Don't aim to be **THE HERO** on every board because you will likely be **THE ZERO.**

Bid your hand, tell the truth, evaluate challenges, and follow up accordingly. A pass is not the end of the world. **Aim to be in the center of the pack**, not the **top dog,** especially on dangerous boards. Ruff, ruff!

SCORING AND MORE OFFENSE/DEFENSE

In summary, the auction is often a delicate daring duel between rival teams, neither of whom want their score to become a casualty. Be *aware* of the scoring and how if affects the outcome of each board, but don't let *fear* of the scoring stop you from proper bidding OR sacrificing, particularly in partscores. Most players will not double for penalty at the two level, so do not pass and let the opponents make an easy contract. Go ahead and compete in the auction, carefully analyzing each bid relative to your hand, and weigh your options. Do not necessarily be afraid of getting doubled either. I have been doubled MANY times and MADE my contract, even doubled at 5C by a professional player when I was a "bridge baby." I was tense, but I settled down, concentrated, and made my contract. When successful after a penalty double, I have the hardest time not laughing at the table (in relief), and I cannot control that little grin that comes on my face. *Instant top board!*

THE 3 AND 5 LEVEL BELONG TO THE OPPONENTS, SO THEY SAY...

How do you compete? *Watch the auction for clues as to the distribution of the HCP.* At the partscore level, one opponent opens and his responder bids 1NT or makes a simple raise, stopping at the one or two level. He doesn't have a big hand, which indicates that the points may be evenly divided between the teams. Fourth seat, you have a long, strong suit, opening count, and you are **NV**. Bid your suit. If you don't win the contract, at least you've given partner information or a lead. If your partner has no points, the opener has more and will probably advance. Suppose they open 1S and your partner overcalls 2H, indicating opening count, and you have three Hs and 9 HCP in your hand. It appears your side has half the points or better - compete! Suppose there are two passes before the auction opens, and the opener is willing to settle for a low contract, indicating the opponents are in a misfit or have few points. Will their contract succeed? If you think *any* of their two level contracts will succeed, don't let them stop in their **comfort zone.** Make a bid that comes flying out of nowhere like a winged monkey to seize the ruby slippers! Push their bidding to the next level, the **danger zone**, *but be prepared to play should they pass.* Have the right distribution and **vulnerability** so if they leave you there or worse, double your contract, you haven't gone on a suicide mission. FYI: Their three level contract might be difficult to make if the HCP are evenly divided, ***perhaps an ideal time to lead trumps,*** reducing ruffs on the short side of trumps.

What if your hand is extremely unbalanced? The good news is that your hand doesn't have to be quite as strong as a semi-balanced hand to compete. The bad news is that if you are two-suited, so are they, and the odds of them succeeding at the three level increase. Then it is easier and safer to interfere if your suit is the **higher ranked suit.**

Suppose you dare the opponents and they bid higher. If they can make their bid at the three level, you haven't lost anything. If they don't make their contract, hopefully the score will be good for your side because you give up fewer points.

As always, there is a caveat: *NEVER PUSH THEM INTO A MAJOR GAME THEY DID NOT BID.* Disrupt at the two level if it is SAFE for you to do so, but DON'T KEEP PUSHING at the three level. They may continue the auction and make game...along with all those bonus points they would have missed. Oh no!

If they bid a **vulnerable game** and **you are not vulnerable**, push them out of their 4M contract. *No easy 620 at this table!* If they make their five level contract, they would have made the extra trick anyway. If you get set bidding over them, you will have made a good score because you are **not vulnerable,** even if you are doubled, because you have the **right distribution** and go down very little. At game level, you SHOULD have extreme distribution. If you don't have the right distribution, vulnerability and a little support from partner (if needed), **let it go.** Sometimes you get a surprise - *on the same board, either team's contract can succeed.*

In your effort to compete vs. a partscore OR game, don't make ***phantom sacrifices***, which means you bid over the contract *they weren't going to make anyway* and GIVE them a score instead of RECEIVING a score. 'Tis NOT more blessed to give than to receive at the bridge table. Determining whether or not to continue can be a **cliffhanger.** Consider what "the rest of the field" is going to bid. How aggressive are the other players sitting in your direction? Will they take risks? Look at your trump holding - is it possible that your partner has a trump stack because you have only one? Sometimes you should sacrifice and sometimes you should let it go for a 50% board for everyone, if persisting is too hazardous. You have to understand you can't interfere **every** time. You'll end up with a convention card that has so many zeroes on it that looks like it was hanging in a pistol range, shot to bits.

If you ARE vulnerable, keep bidding only with a very strong distributional hand and you're near 100% certain you won't get set in a partscore. Otherwise, if you take chances, you'll have egg on your face. A rotten egg, AND an egg-shaped score. So basically, forget it, as nothing is guaranteed in this game. *If you take chances vulnerable, you might as well wrap up all those contracts and put them under their Christmas tree.*

SCORING AND MORE OFFENSE/DEFENSE

Don't forget to preempt M suits as often as possible, m suits too (though they are not quite as menacing to the opponents), to disrupt their bidding and/or to keep them out of a makable NT or slam contract.

Finally, you must realize PASS is NOT a dirty 4 letter word. It may describe your hand p-e-r-f-e-c-t-l-y. Let partner keep bidding if he can, then support him at the 11th hour with the right holding: a weak hand, maybe (partner shows a strong hand because he continues bidding alone), but one with extra trumps and EITHER a void/singleton in their suit, OR several cards in their suit. *One of you will ruff their winners*. If they continue to bid, the bad split in their trump suit could be troublesome.

Always tell your partner **the truth** about your hand so he can make the best decisions for your side.

THE PENALTY DOUBLE

We have learned about the takeout double, the negative double, and briefly mentioned the penalty double, but what is it for and when does one do it? A penalty double (the same card) is for **punishment.** Near the end of the auction, your opponents put the red X card on the table because they do not think you are going to make your contract, and they want to make your penalty **worse** since it will be a **better score** for them. If you make your contract, *they* will be punished, and your score will be much higher than "the field." Vice versa, you might double your opponents for the same reason, but you hope that *your* team isn't the one punished. Penalty Xs are most often imposed by beginners after the auction passes 3S - the start of game level bids.

That is why distribution is so important when you are competing against the other team with the threat of a double, especially at game level. *They* may have THE POINTS, but *you* have THE SHAPE. If you have a balanced hand, you will have more losers, probably too many, than you will have if you are unbalanced, should your rivals have the majority of the HCP.

Suppose you've decided you want to X your opponent's suit contract. What do you need? First, if you make a penalty X, you'd better be certain of your prowess on defense. You and your partner MUST be leading clearly and reading signals at **every** opportunity. Second, in a suit contract, you should have a **solid trump stack.** You must have solid trumps because your X just told LHO where all the missing trumps are located and he, the declarer, will make a plan to get your trumps - perhaps coming from dummy through you to get them ALL, if you are his RHO. Yikes! Finally, you must have HCP (As and KQs) in their **secondary suit** and/or in the unbid suits. **Forget the AK in your own suit.** They are not going to have much, if anything , in your suit *which is why they bid higher.*

Defending a NT contract, you should have a long suit and access back into your hand, something like Ax Axx QJ10xx xxx, *or better* as defender. Lead Ds every time you can, starting with the Q lead, then the J, then the 10 as you get back in with your As. You hope the declarer doesn't have 4 Ds, specifically the AK9x! **If you lead your As**, you will **NEVER** get all your tricks in Ds. *Use those As as reentries* into your hand.

DURING THE AUCTION

BALANCING

If your LHO opens at the one level or preempts 2D followed by two passes, consider your hand. If you have HCP and a long suit, bid it especially if it is a **major** suit. If you have a good hand but have flat distribution, **X** to get partner to bid, or bid NT with Ds. Remember in 4th seat, 1NT shows 12+ HCP and **implies stoppers,** but does not necessarily **promise** the best of stoppers since you're balancing as a defensive move. In particular, don't let them get by with a one or two level *minor* contract. If they don't have the Ms, your team probably does.

If LHO opens and is followed by two passes, think about where the points are. If your 4th seat hand is poor you might pass: the opener could have a big hand because your partner didn't overcall or TOX. Hmmm... What is going on if no one else bid? Either the opener has the majority of the HCP (and your bid will enable him to rebid or X) or *partner has the opener's suit and the missing points*. If you make a TOX because you have a nice hand, and partner DOES have the opener's suit, he will have to decide whether to bid NT or leave the X "in." If he leaves the X in, he should have **points, high cards and length** in the opener's suit, AND the opener should be **vulnerable.** Top board if the opener gets set *ONE trick*, **unless your side has a vulnerable game or slam.**

What if there are three passes to you and you have 10-11 HCP? If you don't have a long M suit, *especially Ss*, **pass.** Don't open the auction and let them find *their* M suit fit and contract. Dare I mention **Cansino Count,** aka **Pearson Points?** To give you a clue if you should open 4th seat after 3 passes, add your HCP together with your number of Ss. If the sum is 15, open the auction. *This is also known as the Rule of 15*. I use it regularly. It has saved me from disaster many times - at least a 65-70% success rate. **No M = no bid.**

Now for something easy, fun, and helpful...

DOUBLING AN ARTIFICIAL BID

Think of Stayman and Jacoby Transfers (or Blackwood and Gerber), the most common artificial (conventional) bids. As you know, **they do not necessarily mean the bidder has the suit he shows**. If you have winners in those suits, partner would love to have a clue as to what he should lead since it is obviously their auction. **If you double the artificial bid**, it tells partner to LEAD THAT SUIT. You should have high honors - AK, KQ, KQJ, but NOT the QJxx, Qxxx or Jxxx. Show your **winners** and gain control. *Take every chance during the auction to give partner information.*

Ex: [LHO opens 1NT] - P - [2C - Stayman by the responder] - **X** (you): You're asking for a **CLUB LEAD**.

If you **DON'T** double a conventional bid made by the opponents, your partner should **lead a different suit** if he is trying to locate your strong holding.

Ex: [RHO opens 1NT] - P (you) - [2H - opener says "Spades"] - **X** (partner). What did your partner do?
He asked for a H lead. You'll happily oblige because you weren't sure what to lead anyway.

PLAY OF THE HAND: THE DEFENDERS

SIGNALING

By now you should be using signals. Get into the habit of signaling on discards **immediately** - do not wait if you haven't started. You will find great pleasure in signaling as your winners stack up.

ATTITUDE

Signaling also applies to **partner's leads**. If partner leads an A, in standard signaling you will play a **high** card to tell your partner you **like** his suit. In Upside-down, you'll play a **low** card to show you **like** his suit. You've shown him where the K and/or Q is located, most likely the Q since he should have the K when leading the A. If you signal him you do not like his lead, he should stop playing his suit to **avoid setting up the declarer's winners.** If partner leads a low card in a new suit, you will not be able to signal since *third hand plays high.* Does his lead of a low card mean something? **Any lead of a low card in a NEW suit should be promising.** If partner doesn't want the suit returned, *he should lead a high card.*

PLAYING HIGH/LOW TO SHOW A DOUBLETON

Once you start attitude signals, playing high/low to show a doubleton on **partner's opening lead** of an A or K will CHANGE and be covered by ATTITUDE (like/hate) instead. A high or low card, depending on whether you use standard or U/D attitude signals, could mean "I like your suit, keep playing it! You don't know it yet, but I'll ruff *their* third round winner so that we stay in control!" Do you completely give up playing high/low? No. You will still play a doubleton high/low when **you're leading partner's suit**, and you might play high/low to show a doubleton on the **opponent's** lead of an A or K, per PA. Hmmm...

COVER AN HONOR WITH AN HONOR

Wait a minute! Aren't honors valuable as winners? Yes they are, but sometimes they can be used to **promote** a card you or your partner hold. This will either make a loser a winner, or prevent a long suit from getting established by the opponents.

Ex: The declarer, South, leads the **JACK.**

<pre>
Suit contract   Dummy: AQx
                     You: K10xx □ 9xx
                                      J
</pre>

If you do not cover the J with the K, **you will get NO TRICKS IN THE SUIT.** The declarer will let the J "ride", then finesse the same way again. If you cover the J with the K, you'll have **promoted your 10**, and cost the declarer two honors to pull one. If you don't have the 10 and don't see it, you may want to cover with an honor to promote *partner's* possible 10.

If the honors are in the **dummy,** and you follow the dummy, cover the **last honor** if you see a sequence of honors, if covering will benefit your side. If not, wait it out, especially vs a NT contract.

PLAY OF THE HAND: THE DECLARER
REMEMBER THE AUCTION

Did either competitor bid? If so, you know something about the bidder's hand. If he opened a M, you know he has **at least** 5 of the M and **at least** 12 HCP. If you are wondering where missing honors are in that M, you have a good clue where to find most or all of them. You know something else too - any 5 card suit means a short suit somewhere else. The bidder has at best a doubleton or could have a singleton or void in addition to the long suit. His most balanced holding would be 5332. Hmmm...*watch out!*

Did he open a minor? He might have a balanced hand with at least 12 HCP. Did he bid his m again at the lowest level possible? Then he has 5+ of his minor (he should have 6 for a rebid, but as you know sometimes openers rebid a 5 card suit for various reasons) and fewer than 16 HCP because he didn't jump when he rebid.

Did his partner bid a new suit, or did he support the original bid with a simple raise or a limit raise? Did anyone bid two suits? If an opponent opened a M, then bid a second suit, he has shown 9 or 10 of the cards in his hand. That means he only has three or four cards divided between the other two suits. Did anyone make a negative X? Did anyone overcall? At what level was the overcall?

Suppose the auction proceeds [RHO: 1H] - 1S (you) - [2H] - 2S - P - P - P. Which opponent has the most HCP? RHO opened. Which opponent is weak? LHO has shown 6-9 HCP.

LEADS

What did the opponent lead? A promising low card? A discouraging high card? A high card in partner's suit? An honor from a sequence? The opponent's lead tells what he has in his hand just like your leads give information to your partner. Pay attention **from the very first card led to your contract.**

FOR EVERYONE
COUNTING CARDS IN A SUIT

Bridge players know to pull trumps early, with some important exceptions, and to be sure they have all of the outstanding trumps they count to 13. This is a good skill to develop for **all the suits**. Start by counting your trump suit, then add a second suit, perhaps your next longest combined suit. Gradually add a third suit. Think of the *division* of the 13 cards. If a suit has gone around twice, with 8 cards falling, what is the split of the remaining five cards? Are you in danger of being ruffed, or if all the competitor's trumps have been pulled, are your remaining cards winners? Counting is what the best bridge players do. Many new players struggle with counting. I prefer to count the *outstanding cards.* For example, my partner and I have the Golden Fit and win the contract. To start with, there are 5 outstanding trumps. I count to **5** instead of 13 as the trumps are played.

COUNTING OPPONENT'S POINTS

Another tip from the experts: **count everyone's points.** As declarer, start with your hand and your dummy's hand. Count all of your HCP and subtract your total from 40 to see how many points are held in the opponents hands. Who bid? You can actually determine where the missing points are and learn who is out of winning cards as each player throws point cards.

TAKE A DECK OF CARDS AND...

deal them out face up at home. Study the hands to see the relationships among the cards and suits in all the hands. You'll notice how the bidding works, why 5 card suits are bid once, how finesses work, why we lead as we do, why the three level is risky if you are vulnerable, and more. Set up hands you played poorly and study them to see how the contract should have been played. Turn the cards face down in each hand after play to see how the remaining cards relate to each other. *You will have an enlightening experience.*

AND REMEMBER THE AUCTION! REMEMBER THE AUCTION!

Several of these concepts are difficult right now. When you are ready, the information to help you grow as a player will be right here, patiently waiting for you...

...and then you'll be ready for Book 2: **Continuing Construction.**

SCORING AND MORE OFFENSE/DEFENSE

Practice & Application Lesson XVI: Scoring & a sprinkle of potpourri *Complete Scoring chart p. 95*

1. What are the highest partscore (under game) bids in Ms and ms? — 3H, 3S, 4C and 4D
2. What is the <u>score</u> if these are bid and made? — 140, 140, 130, and 130
3. How many tricks can you get set NV for a better score? — Two: -100
4. How many tricks can you get set V for a better score? — One: -100
5. What is the score for down 3 NV? — 150: NEVER give 150 points in a partscore!!!
6. What is the score for down 2 V? — 200: NEVER give 200 points in a partscore!!!
7. When you see a 4NT bid on the table, what does it often mean? — Blackwood initiation - Ace ask.
8. How would you show two As? — 5Hs
9. Only you & your partner bid: 1H - 1S - 1NT - 4C. What is 4C? — Gerber initiation - Ace ask.
10. What should you have if you are cheeky enough to X the enemy? — Good trumps, good cards in their second suit, good cards in the unbid suits & good defense.

The opponents bid Stayman and Jacoby Transfers over a 1NT opening bid.
You know this because they told you when they sat down, or you have checked their convention card.

1. What does this X mean?
   o1NT
   X ☐ P
   2C
   The X asks for a C lead

2. What does this X mean?
   o1NT
   X ☐ P
   2D
   The X asks for a D lead.

3. What do the following bids mean in the pass out seat?

   o1C
   X or 1NT ☐ P
   P

   • The X shows opening count or so and 0-2 of the opener's suit; asks for partner's best suit. Partner may leave the X "in" for penalty.
   • The 1NT bid shows 12+ HCP and implies stoppers in Cs. Continue as usual over 1NT, per partnership agreement. Some partners do not choose to use conventions in this auction, but make "natural" bids: a suit bid is "to play," showing a 5+ card suit.

<u>How would you play this hand?   Make a plan.</u>

	♠	♥	♦	♣	
					What is your best bet to win? *It depends on what the opponents*
Lead: a low H	x	Q	A	x	*lead after taking 2 H tricks with the K & A, AND the S & D splits.*
Contract:	x	x	K	x	• **If they lead a 3rd H,** disregarding your J, you are likely
An optimistic 4S	x	x	x	x	home free. Toss a C, even if RHO ruffs, then get control, pull
				x	trumps, and play a low D to the A and run the rest of the Ds.
		☐			If the Ds split unfavorably, concede one, ruff the next lead,
					then play the rest of the Ds to win.
	A	J	Q	x	• **If they lead a D,** win with the A, pull trumps, & later toss a C on
	K	x	x		the Q of Hs, hoping for a favorable D split. The Ds might not split
	Q		x		well; that is why the opponent led into the AK. Lose one round
	x		x		of Ds, ruff the next lead, and finish playing the rest of the Ds.
	x		x		• **If they lead a C,** that is the worst scenario. Now you are forced

to take risks. After two H losses and one C loss, pull two rounds of trumps and hope for a 3/2 split. After playing two rounds of trumps that go favorably, the only way to make your contract is if the Ds also split favorably. Play two rounds of Ds. If both opponents play Ds, draw their last trump and finish the D suit. If Ds do not split well, plan to ruff the 4th D round in the dummy, and hope that the player with the last trump also has the 4th D.
• **If they lead a trump,** pull trumps, play a D to the A, toss a C on the QH, & run the rest of the Ds, perhaps conceding one trick if you have an unfavorable D split. *Success in this contract **depends** on favorable splits. Good luck!*

Lesson XVII BONUS CHAPTER: Rebids and Review
Prerequisite: BIG Hands
NON-FORCING BIDS: A REVIEW

- **Some bids are "stop" bids on the responder's part** - a simple raise of the opener's suit or a response of 1NT. These bids do not demand another bid of the opener. If the opener bids again, he has a good reason for doing so.

All bid:
1. <u>He is competing in the auction:</u> 1H - [P] - 2H - [2S] - **3H**. **He has extra points, extra trumps,** distributional value, **OR** he thinks he will get set only one or two tricks, NV. *He believes the 2S bid will be successful, so he chooses to intervene. Lesson 16 explains why.*

2. He is **two-suited** (unsuited for NT) and asks responder for his **preference**: the BEST, not necessarily PERFECT fit: 1S - [P] - 1NT - [P] - 2H - [P] - ? The responder could opt for a spade contract **with TWO Ss**. *If the responder seems to have a choice between putting partner in a **5/2** or **4/3** fit, he should opt for the **5/2** fit.* The opener could have up to **18 HCP**. *With 19+ HCP, he'd jump-shift.*

3. He has a **big hand** (17-18 HCP) and invites **game**: 1H - [P] - 2H - [P] - **3H**, or 1H - [P] - 2H - [P]- **3C**. The responder bids game if he is at the **top of his bid** with **8-9** HCP, & in the second auction he'll bid game with 8-9 HCP AND C support (A, K, singleton or void), *as the opener asks for help in the C suit.*

4. He has **19+ HCP** and knows the pair has game values: 1H - [P] - 2H - [P] - **4H.**

- **Preemptive bids**, made by either partner, **do not require** further bidding - the preempt says it ALL in one bid: it is not a forcing bid. After partner's opening preempt, a weak responder with a great fit may continue bidding to interfere with the opponent's possible game or slam, or he could bid a higher level to override interference (over a TOX, for example), OR a **strong** partner could bid **game** for his team (see the Rule of 17, page 18).

<u>Opening Preempts:</u>	<u>Preempts by an overcaller OR responder with an intervening pass:</u>		
• 6 in suit: 2D, 2H, 2S	1C	2D, 2H, or 2S	Hands too weak (< 6 HCP) to make further bids,
• 7 in suit: 3C*, 3D, 3H, 3S, etc.	1D	2H, 2S, or 3C	showing *length and strength* in one bid. Their
5-10 HCP, disciplined if VUL	1H	2S, 3C, or 3D	value is not only in the length of the preempt suit,
*A 3C preempt shows **6 OR 7** Cs	1S	3C, 3D, or 3H	but in obstruction.

- **A bid made by a previously passed partner is non-forcing.** All bid: P-[P]-1S-[P]-2H. The 2H bid is not forcing.
- <u>2NT rebids/responses aren't forcing:</u> (Oppo. don't bid) 1S - 2NT or 1S - 1NT - 2NT. Here 2NT invites, but is NF.
- **A non-jump, minimal rebid after a 1/1 auction is NF:** (Oppo don't bid) 1D - 1H - 2C, or 1H - 1S - 2D. Though new suits are bid, the two level bids are NF; after all the opener HAD to rebid over **the responder's new suit.** The responder could have **only** 6 HCP. *In either auction a jump in a new suit (a jump-shift) would force game.*

For more information on forcing bids, see Appendix B.

1/1 AND 2/1 BIDS: THE BIRTH OF REBIDS

As openers, we often have to bid again based on what our partner does - a bid he makes that is not from one of the categories above. He makes a different bid - a forcing bid. A bid of 1C - 1S by you and your partner alone (responder has **never** passed) **requires a rebid** on the opener's part - he cannot pass. Any 1/1 or 2/1 bid cannot be passed **UNLESS there is an intervening bid which holds the auction open,** even if the opener's hand has been completely described in one bid. Does the example of 1C - 1S show the responder's holding of 6 Ss and 13 HCP? No. **The opener has to allow the responder to finish telling about his hand,** and the opener's rebid will be very informative for the responder. *Tip: Many openers already have a rebid planned when they begin an auction.*

The six 1/1 Bids			The six 2/1 bids		
1C - 1D	1C - 1H	1C - 1S	1D - 2C	1H - 2C	1H - 2D
1D - 1H	1D - 1S	1H - 1S	1S - 2C	1S - 2D	1S - 2H

These are all unlimited bids: *none* of them may be passed if it is the responder's first bid, no previous pass. As you know, the difference between stop bids and forcing bids is that the responder bids a NEW SUIT. New suits bid late in the auction by the responder show extra strength. Ex: (Opponents do not bid) 1C - 1S - 2S - **3H.** The responder shows a big hand. The auction will continue.

Let's start with some general 1/1 and 2/1 bids. What should the opener rebid & why? The opponents are silent.

1C - 1D - ?   **Since the responder DOESN'T have a 4 c M**, his first choice to respond, the opener should rebid...
- **1NT** if minimal and balanced. Expect **12-14 HCP** because he didn't open 1NT.
- **2NT** with **18-19** HCP and a balanced hand.
- **3NT** makes no sense here because with 20-21 HCP, the opening bid should be 2NT, as the opener would have to have that many HCP to bid 3NT. However, the opener could have a long, strong **C** suit, stoppers in the Ms, and 1-2 poor Ds with no stoppers. He expects the responder to have the Ds stopped, so he now bids 3NT instead of perhaps 5Cs.
- **If NT is impossible** due to a void, singleton, or very weak M suit, he'll rebid Cs with 6 (5 if desperate) OR support partner's Ds, **jumping with 16-18 HCP.** *The responder can bid NT.*
- **If the opener rebids 1M**, he shows a stopper in the M. *Does resp. have the other M stopped?*
- **If the opener jumps in a M,** his jump-shift shows **19+** HCP.
- **The team's last resort** would be a minor contract.

1C - 1H - ?   **#1 Priority: The opener should support the Hs with 4 Hs of his own.**
  <u>With H support and distributional values added:</u>
  - If the opener is minimum (12-15), he'll bid **2H**, the lowest response.
  - If the opener is medium (16-18), he'll bid **3H**, a **jump which invites game.**
  - If the opener is maximum (19+), he'll bid **4H**, game. Otherwise he'll...
- **Bid 1S** with 4 Ss and < 4 Hs. Opener has **12-18 HCP** w/out a jump-shift & resp could have 4 Ss.
- **Bid 1NT** with 12-14 HCP. <u>***Bidding NT implies a balanced hand with 2-3 Hs.****</u>
  If he is void or singleton in Hs, a better description of his hand may be to rebid Cs, even with only 5 Cs, if he doesn't have 4 Ss. *He has to rebid with no intervening bid.*
- **With 16-18 HCP,** he'll jump in Cs with 6+ clubs, or **bid 2D**, a reverse, showing 16+ HCP (per PA). *The reverse bid is described on pages 74-75.*
- **With 18-19 HCP** and a balanced hand, he'll bid 2NT. **His last choice** would be to rebid Cs.

*If the opener bids 1C/1D/1H and partner responds 1M (1S over 1H), a 1NT rebid **implies a balanced hand with 2-3 of the M & 12-14 HCP**. If opener is unbalanced with only one of the M, he'll rebid his first suit with 6+ (or 5 if trapped for a rebid), or he'll bid his second suit if of a lower rank than his first suit. If opener rebids NT, this is one time the responder can **rebid a 5 c M if he's minimal**. He's more afraid of a **terrible NT contract** than a **poor M contract**. With 0-1 of partner's suit, you <u>must</u> have more of your first suit, or you have a second suit. If your hand is 1444 with only one S, open **1D** and rebid **Cs** with no interference: 1D - 1S - 2C. You cannot rebid 1NT because you are too unbalanced - **it would encourage partner to bid 2Ss with only 5 Ss**.*

Except for this situation and a few others, <u>the rebid of any suit without support, M OR m, should show SIX.</u>

1C - 1S - ?   **#1: The opener will support the Ss with 4**,** jumping or bidding game with HCP as above, or
- **Bid NT** based on his HCP, **1NT** implying 2-3 Ss, bal. & minimal HCP, no fit, **2NT=18-19** HCP, or
- **Rebid Cs** with 6+ good Cs (12-15 HCP), or only 5 Cs if minimal and stuck for a rebid, or
- **Jump to 3C** with **16+** HCP and 6+ Cs, or
- **Bid 2D or 2H** with **16+** HCP (PA), a reverse, OR if he'd rather, he'll
- **Jump-shift with 19+ HCP** (if he doesn't reverse), and bid **3D** or **3H.**
  Remember: If the opener has a 1444 hand, he'll open 1D to plan for a possible rebid of 2C.

1D - 1H - ?   **#1: The opener will support the Hs with 4**,** jumping in Hs with **16** HCP, etc. or he'll
- **Bid 1S** with 4 Ss, < 4 Hs, HCP range between 12 and 18 (no jump-shift); **2S** with **19+** HCP, or
- **Bid NT**, implying 2-3 Hs, bal, no 4/4 fit, any jumps based on his HCP (**2NT** rebid=**18-19** HCP), or
- **Bid 2D** if minimal with 5-6+ Ds, **3D** with **16-18** HCP (6D), or **2C** if 2-suited and minimum-medium, or
- **Bid 3C** with good Cs and **19+** HCP, a jump-shift bid.

1D - 1S - ?   **#1: The opener will support the Ss with 4**,** the level of his rebid showing his HCP, or he'll
- **Bid NT,** the level of his NT bid telling his HCP & implying 2-3 Ss no fit, or
- **Bid 2H** showing **16+** HCP (PA), 5Ds and 4 Hs, a reverse, or
- **Bid 2C** if two-suited and minimal-medium, or **3C**, a jump-shift showing **19+**, or
- **Rebid Ds** with 5-6+ Ds and no better option, the level of his forced rebid showing his HCP.

** *The expert player might raise with three extremely strong cards in support: You may see this in bridge literature.*

Building Bridges © 2022 Jeanne R. Wamack   May not be reproduced in any form.

REBIDS AND REVIEW

1D - 2C - ?   **The opener may bid 2NT** (12-14 HCP) **or 3NT** (15+ HCP) *unless* his D suit is very long and he has no protected HCP in the Ms that would make NT possible. Partner does not guarantee M strength (< 4 in either M). In that case, the team may have to be in a m contract. Part. shows 5+ Cs, 10+ HCP, and **no** 4+ c M. A rebid of **2H** or **2S** would be a reverse - shows **16+** HCP & 4 c M.

1H - 1S - ?
- **The opener will rebid 2Hs** with 6+ Hs and a minimal hand, **12-15** HCP, or he'll
- **Rebid 3Hs** with 6+ strong Hs and a medium hand, **16-18** HCP, or he'll
- **Rebid 4Hs** with 6+ very strong Hs and a maximum hand, **19+** HCP, OR he'll
- **Support the Ss with 4,** jumping to show his category of strength (including dist points), or he'll
- **Bid NT** with 2-3 Ss, only 5 Hs, semi-bal, the level of NT showing his HCP, or
- **Bid his long minor,** jumping with **19+** HCP. Without a jump, the m bid is NF.

1H - 2C - ?
- **The opener will rebid Hs with 6+,** how high based on his HCP, or he'll
- **Support the Cs with 3+;** he'll bid 3C if min, 4C with **16+** HCP, invitational: *Is it ok to pass 3NT?*
- **Bid 2S,** a reverse showing **16+** HCP (per PA) and at least 5 Hs and 4 Ss, or he'll
- **Bid 2D** if it's his 2nd suit, showing 4-5+ & min/med; he'll **jump to 3D** with **19+** HCP, or he'll
- **Bid 2NT** - a minimal balanced hand (< 15 HCP), no 2nd long suit, no fit in Cs, or
- **Bid 3NT** with **15+** HCP, no fit, since resp. shows 10+ HCP. Responder may continue with more HCP.

1H - 2D - ?
- **The opener will rebid Hs with 6+**, jumping in Hs with extra strength; or he'll
- **Supp. Ds w/ 3+;** jumping with **16+**. He'll pass 3NT; *Is slam possible, or is 3NT the best contract?*
- **Bid 2S,** a reverse showing 5+ Hs, 4Ss and **16+** HCP (PA). The resp has < 4 Ss but may have 3+ Hs;
- **Bid 3C** with 4+ Cs & 16+ HCP (the 3 level bid shows game interest), or **bid 4C** with **19+** HCP. He'll pass 3NT, but he may be strong enough to bid slam with a superb H suit, OR he'll bid **2NT**.

1S - 2C/2D - ?
- **Same as above - rebid Ss with 6+,** jumping to show **16+** HCP, etc. or
- **Support the m with 3+,** or bid the *other* minor to show a second suit (3C over 2D=extra HCP), or
- **Bid 2Hs to show 4+ Hs** (not a reverse) with 12-18 HCP to show his second suit, or
- **Jump in a new suit** with **19+** HCP, or
- **Bid 2-3NT,** showing an otherwise balanced hand and his points. The 3NT bid shows **15+** HCP.

1S - 2H - ?
- **The H bid shows 5 Hs** and 10+ HCP. The opener may support Hs with 3, jumping to game to show extra strength (**15+** HCP), or he'll
- **Rebid Ss** to show 6+, jumping with extra HCP, or he'll
- **Bid 3C/3D** to show a second suit and extra values (without extra values, bid something else), or he'll
- **Bid 2NT** to show an otherwise balanced hand, with < 3 Hs, or he'll
- **Bid 3NT** with **15+** HCP and m stoppers.

If at any time one side bids a game contract, from that point-of-view, there is no slam: 1S-2H-4H, or 1H-1S-2C-3NT. The partner may continue the auction.

NO TRUMP BIDS, AGAIN

1 of any suit - 2NT - ?   Shows 11-12 HCP & bal; no M fit. If resp. is a previously passed hand, 10-11 HCP. Opener may pass. **Not a 2/1 bid.**

1 of any suit - 3NT - ?   Responder has 13-15 HCP, balanced, no M fit. *If opener has 17+ HCP, slam may be possible, especially with a long strong m, which prevented a 1NT opening.*

If resp has 16+ HCP, he'll start with a forcing bid, **not 3NT**, to allow the opener to show a big hand if he has one. For the responder, 3NT is a bid limited to 13-15 HCP. *This is an occasion when an auction may start 1C-1D.*

1C - 1S - 2NT, 1D - 1H - 2NT   The opener shows **18-19 HCP**, invitational, no M fit; **too strong** to open 1NT, **too weak** to open 2NT.

1C - 1S - 3NT, 1D - 1H - 3NT   The opener shows **19-21 HCP**, game values, no fit; too strong to open 1NT, too distributional to open 2NT. *Partner must have filled in the missing suit.*

1H/S - 2D/2C - 3NT.   The opener has at least **15 HCP (up to 18 HCP,** no jump-shift or temporizing bid) because he bid <u>game</u>. He doesn't want to bypass 3NT by jumping in the m, and he can't rebid his M because he only has 5. The responder can bid 4M with support, or try for slam.

Building Bridges © 2022 Jeanne R. Wamack May not be reproduced in any form.

REBIDS AND REVIEW

Sometimes the opener MUST rebid but has meager selections

He doesn't have 6+ in his first suit, and he too unbalanced to rebid NT. His second suit is four cards long, but they are "without honor" (or even mid-range cards). If the *intervening* opponent bids, the opener may **pass** since the opponent's bid will **hold the auction open for partner.** If the opponent doesn't bid, the opener must bid again. If his first suit is *extremely strong* - AKQ10x - he can rebid it *with no better choice,* an exception to the rebid rule. Otherwise, he will have to bid the poor four card suit, *provided that he doesn't bid at the three level with a minimal hand.* He will see what the responder rebids, then pass or bid the safest contract. Perhaps the opponents won't lead his weak suit.

RESPONDER'S REBIDS

After the opener's rebid, the responder will have an idea of how high the partnership should climb. If the opener rebids a suit at a low level, jumps in his own suit or responder's suit, jump-shifts, bids game, **or** if he opened 1NT, 2NT or 2C, the responder will **add his points** to what the opener holds and shouldn't be afraid to stop in a partscore, bid game or investigate slam. If the pair has no fit, or has a minor suit fit, he might bid NT (if he shares a suit, often a minor, with partner), or he'll get out of the auction ASAP in the safest contract. He may even bail with game values. Why? Because the TRANSPORTATION will be an issue. Singletons or voids in partner's suit are NOT helpful in NT. If this is the case, **place the contract in the longest known fit and stop bidding.**

If the responder has a big hand, he should BY NO MEANS make a **weak** or **stop** bid, but should make forcing or jump rebids so the opener keeps the auction open until the right contract is reached, even if he has to make a ***temporizing bid*** (usually the bid of a strong **short** minor suit) to hold the auction open. *If you HAVE to exaggerate your length, try to do it in a minor, NOT a Major.* How can the responder remember what to do? In SA, FIRST bids are made to start the search for a fit, perhaps showing a long suit, and LATER bids reveal points, summarized with a handy bridge saying:

First bids show length, second bids show strength.

There are well over 600 trillion hand combinations, and at times describing hands may be difficult. Since the language of bridge is limited by a small 38 card vocabulary, partners should do their best and glean a tip from that which does not go well.

WITH INTERFERENCE

You usually have options to tell your partner your HCP, some more creative than others. If your pair initiates the auction, assume the opener shows an above average hand. If you are in the direct seat after an opening bid, you will overcall or make a TOX showing strength. If you are the responder you may negative double, cuebid, or enter the auction by bidding higher than the overcaller, which shows your points, or you may pass initially and bid later, showing partner weakness with support OR a long suit with few HCP: either are discouraging bids. As responder OR advancer you may bid a long weak suit preemptively, a bid which will either gain the contract for your side or interfere with the opponents. The advancer may cuebid to show strength and support. Talk to your partner to ascertain what you are promising with each of these bids, and **do not pass when you have a bid**. *The earlier you get into the auction, the better.*

REVERSES

We've learned how to bid "big" hands, and there is one more "big bid" to learn - ***the reverse.*** I hate to write about it in a beginning program, but you need to be aware of it, even if you (sort of) choose not to bid it yet, as it is part of the system by which we show strong hands. You don't want to reverse without at least **16** HCP because the order you bid your suits may make partner bid too high in a desperate attempt to find a fit. *What is a reverse?*

A reverse bid shows an unusual, two-suited hand: a **long, low-ranking** suit (5+) that is bid first, with a **shorter, higher-ranking** suit that follows in the auction. Expect a distribution of 5/4, 6/4, 7/4, 6/5, etc. AND the hand has 16 to 21 HCP - with 22 HCP, you would open 2C. The lowest HCP requirement is a partnership agreement: some partners reverse with **16 HCP,** while others reverse with **17 or 18 HCP.** Should your team decide to require more HCP for a reverse, make a note of that in the rebid information of this chapter.

In a reverse, the distribution and bidding order are the OPPOSITE of the norm: the higher ranked suit is usually bid first, then the lower-ranked suit. The TYPICAL auction (opponents pass): 1H-1S-2C. Opener has 5 Hs & 4+ Cs. The REVERSE auction: 1C-1S-2H. The opener has **5+**Cs and 4 Hs. If he had a 5 card M, he'd open 1M as usual, though some experts would open a longer m suit. With two 5 c suits, he'd bid the higher ranked suit first. Why are so many HCP required for a reverse? Showing the second suit is risky because the responder **DENIES** having enough of that suit to bid it. So why would the opener take the risk? *To show his two-suited shape and his points.*

REBIDS AND REVIEW

Without at least 16 HCP, the opener **CAN'T** show his second suit. He'll have to make another bid - perhaps rebid his first suit or NT. Why? Because the pair could rise to the three level, requiring **22-24 HCP** for success and the responder may have only **6** HCP. Remember, the first suit is **longer** than the second suit when a player reverses - it gives an "out." Weak responses to opener's reverse: a low rebid of the responder's M (showing at least 5), 2NT, or 3 of the opener's first suit. Any other response shows strength, and the responder could jump to game. *Some experts say 2NT or 3 of the opener's first suit is a **strong** bid - it's a partnership agreement*

For some partners, reverses are used to show big hands when the bidder's **second suit is higher ranked** than his first suit, and jump-shifts are used when the bidder's **second suit is lower ranked** than his first suit. That is why they prefer the higher range of HCP when reversing.

If opener's reverse suits are a M and a m, should the responder bid the opener's M on his first bid, (what would have been the opener's second bid) the opener will **jump bid** in responder's suit (16-18 HCP) or bid game (19+): an ordinary auction. Ex: 1D - 1H - 3H/4H. Had the responder bid 1S instead, the opener would rebid 2H.

HOW TO RECOGNIZE A REVERSE (No one else bids)

1. **The opener's first bid suit is of a lower rank than his second bid suit.** Ex: **1D** - 1S - **2H**.
   As you know, Ds is a minor, a lower ranked suit than Hs.
2. **The responder skips over the opener's 2nd suit in his initial bid.**
   A S bid is higher on the bidding ladder than a H bid. The responder **could have bid Hs,** but bypassed Hs to bid Ss, **technically denying 4 Hs**.
   *Then the opener rebids a suit in the **SPACE** between the two suits on the table.*
3. **The bid of the opener's 2nd suit is higher than a rebid of his 1st suit.** Ex: 1D - 1S - **2H**.
   The opener's rebid of 2H is **higher** than a bid of **2D**, the rebid of his first suit. If the responder has a hand with 5 Ss and 4 Hs, he may now support the Hs. Without 4 Hs, he can rebid Ss with 5, bid NT, or he can bid Ds. Responders will need an "out" should they have few HCP. Remember, the opener's distribution is at least 5 Ds, with only 4 Hs.
4. **If the responder wants to bid the opener's first suit, he must go to the three level.** Ex: 1D-1S-2H-**3D**.
5. **A reverse can never be made over a 1S opening bid.**
   You would have to jump, jump-shift or keep bidding new suits, etc. to show a big hand.

If the first two requirements are met, it's a reverse, and the rest of the requirements confirm it. If you "don't play reverses," these hands are difficult to bid: they can lead to the **"death spiral"** of overbidding, so in reality, *EVERYONE* plays reverses to avoid disastrous auctions. *No rebids in skipped suits if the opener is minimal.*

A reverse FORCES for 1 round, and it is game forcing if bid by the responder. Yes, the responder can reverse too. He can do almost everything the opener can do.

The **ten reverses** made by an opener: (no opponent bids in any example)	1C-1H-2D, 1C-1S-2D, 1C-1S-2H, 1C-1NT-2D, 1C-1NT-2H, 1C-1NT-2S, 1D-1S-2H, 1D-1NT-2H, 1D-1NT-2S, 1H-1NT-2S. (Can be bid over 1NT)
Example of a reverse by a responder:	1C - 1D - 2C - 2S Shows 5 Ds and 4 Ss, a game forcing bid. Opener denies 4 Ss. Responder may jump-shift with a very big hand, per PA.
These are NOT reverses: (not all requirements met)	1D-1H-2S (A jump-shift bid by opener: the H bid did not bypass Ss)
	1C-1H-1S (H bid did not pass Ss and 1S is not higher than 2C)

Special note about reverses with the **minors**...

The example 1C - 1H - 2D shows at least **5 C, 4+** Ds and 16+ HCP. **With a minimum hand, bid the Ds then the Cs**. *This is why the order by which we open minors is so important!* Plan for a rebid from the start.

GOT IT?

With all these rebids and all this information exchanged, NOW DO YOU SEE WHY THE BIGGER THE HAND YOU HAVE, THE SLOWER/LOWER YOU BID? The jumps should come *after* basic bidding groundwork is established to show extra strength. Give your team room to find that 2-6 M fit. Why the rush with a frenzied jump bid? Your side has ALL the HCP. TAKE YOUR TIME! Let the early jump bids (preempts) do their dirty job - take bidding space away from the **opponents.** And the reverse eliminates the need for a jump while showing strength.

Questions about rebids...

I showed my partner a stop bid, and he bid again. What do I do?

Did partner rebid after suit agreement (no interference), jump in his suit, your suit, reverse, or jump-shift? If so, he is showing a big hand and doesn't want to miss game. Did he bid a new suit at the lowest level over your 1NT? Then he is minimum to medium with two long suits and wants you to pick the suit you prefer. Pick one **even without a great fit** because he could have unknown extra length. Give preference to the **Ms.** Ex: 1H - 1NT - 2D. Opener should have 5 Hs, 4-5+ Ds and up to 18 HCP. Bid Hs if that is the best fit, **even holding just two**, or pass if you prefer Ds, holding 4+ Ds. Any auction similar to this is known as a **preference auction.**

My partner rebid his M at the lowest level and we still don't have a perfect fit since I have only one. I am minimal. What do I do?

You'll pass. He has a long suit (6+) so be glad of that, even without a perfect fit. Maybe your luck will hold and you will have a favorable split in trumps. You don't have to "rescue" him. His bid is not forcing.

My partner bid two suits and I don't like either one. We have game values.

Bid the lowest available NT and hope for the best if transportation is an issue, or take a chance on 3NT, assuming you have strength in the other two suits and at least a doubleton in one of partner's suits. If your own suit is extra long, you may rebid it to see if partner fits with your suit after your rebid, or to see if your long suit improves his hand or transportation. Your other option is to choose one of his suits and stop bidding since you appear to be in a misfit. Depending on the auction, he may asking your preference. Settle on a M or NT contract whenever possible.

The bidding went 1H (partner) - [P] - 2H (me) - [2S] - 3H (partner). What is this?

Partner is competing in the auction, not inviting you to bid game.

We bid this sequence, having no interference: 1H - 1NT - 2NT. Does that show my partner has 18+ HCP?

He shows 17-18 HCP and 5 Hs with an otherwise balanced hand (5332 shape). He would bid game (3NT) with 19+ HCP, since you've shown 6-10- HCP. Instead, he invites you to game if you're at the **top of your range.** Somewhat similar is the 1/1 bid with a jump rebid of 2NT showing 18+ HCP, though the 1/1 bids are each **suit** bids. If you think about the points partner must have to invite game in such auctions, *you can figure it out his HCP.*

My partner passed my forcing bid. We have game values.

Your **score** will remind him to bid properly. Sometimes it takes a bad result for a partner to understand rebids.

My partner, who opened, liked my M suit. I have a good hand with 11 HCP. How do I invite game?

Rebid your suit to invite the opener to game. **You have found your fit.** Ex: (no oppo. bids) 1C -1H - 2H - **?** The opener shows 12-15 HCP & 4 Hs. If you bid 3H, you are asking him to bid game if he is at the **top of his bid, including distribution points**. You have extra values, but not enough to go by yourself. With his 14-15 HCP plus the 11 HCP in your hand, you have game. If he has 12-13, you have values for 3H. This is similar to the opener's game invitational bid: 1S - 2S - 3S - ? The opener has 17-18 HCP, an invitation. He asks the responder to bid game if he is at the top of his minimum bid. If you are distributional or have **5+** of your M, *bid game yourself.*

I opened 1D and my partner bid 1S. I have 13 points, 4 Hs, bal. Can I bid my hearts?

A heart rebid would show a bigger hand than you have, since partner denies 4 Hs. You could rebid the LOWER suit, Cs, but rebidding a higher suit than your first suit says you have more Ds than Hs and a big hand - a reverse. If you're otherwise balanced, bid 1NT and see what happens. If partner bids Hs now, he shows **5 Ss and 4-5 Hs.** *Pick your poison!* You have a double fit if you have 3 Ss. Partner's not showing a big hand - your 1NT rebid **gave him the opportunity to see if you had support for EITHER M.** With a big hand (13+), the responder can **jump** in Hs, per PA as a new suit is forcing anyway. Another ex: 1C - 1S - 1NT - 2H...shows 5 Ss and 4-5 Hs in responder's hand.

Having 10 HCP, I passed. Partner opened 1H. The intervening opponent bid 1S. How do I show my 10 HCP and 3 Hs?

You will CUEBID the opponent's suit by bidding **2S**, showing support and 10-11 HCP. Do not bid 2H as this DOES NOT describe your hand. You are too strong to bid 2H.

1C/D - 1S - 1NT - 2H: An important bidding sequence; shows **5** Ss & **4-5** Hs in resp's hand. You may yet find that *elusive* 4/4 H fit, or you may uncover a S fit. He'd bid Hs first with **4/4** in the Ms. Responder's upper limit is 10- HCP.

REBIDS AND REVIEW

Practice & Application Lesson XVII: Rebids: Here we go again!

Chart: F & NF bids p. 94. Also see BIG hands chart p. 94.

What do these rebids reveal to you? Only the opener and the responder bid.

1. 1H - 1NT - 2H? The opener has minimal points and 6 Hs (possibly just 5).
   Both opener and responder have made "stop" bids.

2. 1S - 1NT - 2D? The opener is min/med, and is 2-suited. **Preference auction:** responder chooses suit.

3. 1C - 1S - 3S? The opener has 16-18 HCP, 4 Ss and invites game, but it is not a forcing bid.

4. 1S - 2H - 4H? The opener has 3-4 Hs and 15+ HCP. Responder can ask for As or pass if minimal.

5. 1H - 2D - 3D? The opener is minimal to medium with 5 Hs and 3+ Ds. Is a H or NT contract possible?

6. 1C - 1S - 2D? The opener bids a reverse showing a big hand with 16+ HCP (or 18+ HCP per PA). He has at least 5 Cs and 4 Ds, and < 4 Ss or 4 Hs. The responder can rebid Ss with 5+, bid 2NT, 3NT, bid 3Cs with 3+ clubs and a minimal hand, or make another bid.

7. 1S - 2S - 4S? The opener has 19+ HCP and the responder is minimal.

8. 1C - 1H - 4H? The opener has 19+ HCP. The responder knows whether slam is possible. His bid is unlimited.

9. 1C - 1H - 1S - 3H? The opener has a min-med hand, but the responder is at least game invitational with 6+ good Hs and 11+ HCP. The opener will pass if minimal with no support, as in he opened a weak hand (10-11 HCP) in a weak moment or Rule of 20, but the team should *usually* bid game because the *low* end of responder's points is 11; he could have more. The opener needs only 2Hs for a fit. The 3H bid is not forcing.

10. 1C - 1H - 1S - 2D? The responder bid a new suit, asking the opener to tell more about his hand. The responder has a good hand or he would have bid 1NT instead of 2D. This is not a reverse by either side.

11. 1C - 1H - 2NT? The opener is showing 18-19 HCP, game values. He does not have 4 Hs or 4 Ss.

12. 1S - 1NT - 3H? The opener made a jump-shift showing 19+ HCP, game values. He has 5+ Ss and 4-5 Hs. He could have more Ss but cannot rebid them *because it would not be forcing.*

13. 1C - 1S - 2H? This is a reverse showing 16+ HCP, or 18+ HCP depending on partnership agreement. The opener has at least 5 Cs and only 4 Hs. Without a strong hand, the opener can't bid 2H because the responder has in effect **denied** four Hs by bidding Ss. The opener will have to bid 2Cs or 1NT as **either 2H or 2D are reverses.**

In this series, the second bid is an **overcall.** No hand has previously passed.

1. 1C - [1S] - 2H? The responder has 5+ Hs and 10+ HCP. The opener will bid again.

2. 1H - [1S] - 2S? The responder makes a **cuebid** showing 3+ H support and 10+ HCP. The opener must bid again.

3. 1S - [2D] - X? The responder shows either 4H/4C and 8+ HCP, OR 5+ Hs, some Cs and < 10 HCP.

4. 1H - [1S] - 2H? Responder is minimal with support. He is able to make the normal responses, even with interference.

Lesson XVIII   More Bridge Etiquette, Tournaments, and Final Thoughts

You have learned how to do many things expected of players in duplicate bridge outside of bid and play: how to use your bid box, how to say, "Any questions, partner" with a face down opening lead, and how to respond to partner's discards, "No ____, partner"? You know to announce transfers and to state the point range of 1NT opening bids. You know to keep a poker face during the auction, and to make NO comments that would be considered information, **even if partner's explanation of your bid is <u>wrong</u>.** You are on your way to the winner's circle! All these courtesies are known as **bridge etiquette,** and there is more etiquette.

You should have a prepared convention card with you at all times. A convention card is a public record of what you play on the outside, and a private record of how you played on the inside (your score). The card shows the agreements and conventions you and your partner adhere to, and you and your partner's convention cards should MATCH. Every player should have a card filled out and should abide by the agreements set forth. As you fill out your card, you normally start in the upper right hand section with your name, then you progress down the right side of the card, checking boxes or making notes about your bids and what you expect with M, m, and NT openings, responses, conventions, etc. The left side lists overcalls, doubles, defense, signals, etc. Every section doesn't have to be marked; only mark the sections that apply: what you know and play. Information and sample cards are found in Appendix A. Other etiquette - greet opponents, keep your table neat, take your trash with you, clean up spills, be prompt, etc. is the same as you should act anywhere you visit.

If there is irregularity in the bidding, say "Director, please," and get help to solve the problem. In fact, CALL THE DIRECTOR WHEN THERE IS **ANY** BIDDING IRREGULARITY, including simple mistakes. The rules are there to protect **everyone**. One or two times, as a new player, I was "nice" to **save time** and the opponents were **not nice** and took advantage of the unauthorized information revealed by their partner to benefit themselves and harm our score. You are not being **rude or mean** to call the director. Many times the options for correcting a problem are so complicated that you should never attempt to set the record straight yourself. There are players who will try to intimidate you. Don't let them. **You are entitled to a fair game.**

Now that you are fully prepared, you should play in <u>tournaments</u>. Tournaments are a lot of fun, and tournament directors want to encourage new players by having low stratified games (***strats***) for new players to play with other new players in a stress-free environment (more or less). Occasionally there are 0-5 games for free. You will make friends from all over the United States and many foreign countries. All levels of players compete in tournaments, not just high level players.

Let's prepare for tournament play. And don't worry - **it's bridge as usual.**

PAIR GAMES

Arrive at the tournament a little early and find your partner. Know the amount of your ***masterpoints*** (points won at bridge), if any, pool your entry fees, and one of you will go to the sign in table. You will fill out a form (both players on one entry) with your name, address, blah, blah, blah, and **your ACBL number.** Be sure to bring your number with you. If you forget to bring it, a director can get it for you.

Tip: Many players have address labels preprinted with their name, address and ACBL number.

If you aren't a member and don't have a number, you'll have to pay a little more to participate. When you start accumulating points, you'll want them registered with the ACBL. They track all the points won in duplicate bridge played at clubs, through tournaments, and on cruise ships, so join if you haven't yet. You've worked hard for those points and want to keep them. You may join online.

Go with your partner to the table listed on your entry form and soon your opponents will arrive, if they are not already there. Each pair will put the entry slips on the table beside North, and a caddy or director will retrieve them. Greet the opponents pleasantly, as you will all of your opponents, then play the boards as soon as they arrive. The boards are usually "play ready." If not, you will prepare the boards as shown on printouts from the director.

If you must prepare the boards pass the trays to the players, then each player will divide his deck into suits. Put the suits face up into the slots and stack the boards in order in the center of the table. The easiest and fastest way to prepare the cards is for each player to take a suit and hand it out according to the diagram given to the table by the director. Make sure the diagram corresponds correctly with the board directions - NSEW. If the directions are correct, North will pass out his cards looking at an **upside down diagram.** Therefore, **North**

should pass out spades, the easiest suit to see since it will be at the top of the list. Each direction should check his hand for accuracy before putting it back face down into the slot. Listen for further directions on how to move this set of boards. You'll not play them. The director or a caddy will pick up the diagrams. Place them by North.

North is in charge as usual. Sometimes the playing area gets crowded, or the next table to move the boards to is located far away, so changing boards is like running an obstacle course. North should be anticipating where the opponents will be coming from, because someone is always lost, and he should find out where the table is located for board delivery.

On to the round: play each board as usual, then enter the scores immediately after each board is played if the electronics are ready. Keep your table from getting behind. You or your opponents will then move as usual. Tournaments are timed events with three games a day, so talk after the card play is over. If a morning game runs late, players may miss lunch - so keep pace. After the event is over, scores will be displayed somewhere nearby. Look for the crowds if you can't find the posted sheets.

PARTNERSHIP DESK

If you don't already have someone to play with, you may pick up a partner at the tournament, (or online before you go). There is always a partnership desk. Some players love bridge so much that they will attend tournaments by themselves. Other players may have travelled with their bridge club to the tournament. Their usual partner becomes ill, but he/she still wants to play and needs a partner. A couple may love to play bridge but they can't play together for marital harmony, so they each find someone at the tournament (to play bridge with). Meet ahead of time and discuss M and m opening and NT expectations, as well as any conventions you play with your new partner. Allow at least **15 minutes** for discussion. Later, if your new partner makes an unusual bid that you do not understand, try to keep the bidding open at least one round for clarification.

TEAM GAMES

Many of the notes above apply to team games too. You should greet the opponents courteously and always have a prepared convention card. The most common team games are Knock-Outs (KOs), compact KOs, or Swiss Teams. Board-A-Match (BAM) is another type of team game, but it is not as common.

As in pairs, arrive early and find your partners, but this time add together all individual masterpoints (the current ACBL summary), pool fees, and one player signs up the team at the entry table while the others wait at a designated location. There is always a big crowd around the table, waiting on assignments. Have the total number of team points with you because KO game stratifications are usually based the cumulative points of the team. If not based on the team points, the stratification will be based on the points held by the highest-ranked member of the team. All members of the team will put their names and ACBL numbers (or labels) on the single entry form. Regular KOs can have up to 6 team members, while compacts are limited to four members. The captain, the person whose name is at the top of the entry, will go get the section letter and playing table number from the pocketed schematic hanging up by the entry table and will inform team members where to go. **Remember your team number.** There may even be an overhead projector with all the match-up information, which is much easier to see.

In the card pocket above your team number, or beside your number on the projected information, will be a **section**, shown by a letter of the alphabet, and a **number**. **North/South will always go to the section and table shown in the pocket**, and E/W will go to the corresponding section and table. The letters are in pairs: A-B, C-D, E-F, G-H, etc. If the pocket shows "**A1**," N/S will go to section **A**, table **1**, and E/W will go to section **B**, table **1**. If the pocket shows "**E 12**", N/S will go to section E, table 12 and E/W will go to section F, table 12. Sometimes the letters are reversed. If the pocket holds "**B1**," N/S will go to section **B**, table **1** and E/W will go to section **A**, table **1**. At large tournaments, the letters will be on a stand, high in the air to be seen easily. At a smaller tournament, look at the table cards as you walk by to see if you are headed in the right direction. Each letter has it's own uniquely colored table card, so once you get to the letter, you can find your table by following the numbers. If you get lost, ask a director to point.

In team games, your N/S will play the opponent's E/W, and vice versa. The boards are not predealt, but are shuffled by the players. In *rare* cases, for beginners, there may be predealt boards. In a regular KO, head to head, you will play the half the boards, and when done, you will call a caddy to switch boards with the rest of your team. At the end of the play of all the boards, you will compare scores to see if you are ahead or behind, then you will reshuffle and play all the boards AGAIN to determine the winners. In a **round robin**,

things get complicated. If you are N/S, you sit and play. If you are E/W, you will play a team, take the boards to your home table (**no talking** - drop the boards and flee), then go to the third team's table to play, compare scores and do it all over again. Ask the director for help in your first round robin. If you are in a round robin, you may have an extra chance to win because you usually have to beat only one team. There is no score comparison in the compact KOs; it's all or nothing unless there is a tie, and the director determines the tie-breaker. You may be in a round robin in a compact too. N/S stays at one table and E/W plays, drops boards, goes to the third table, plays the rest of the boards, compares, and that round is over. Compacts play fewer boards for fewer points, but they're just as much fun and are briefer in duration.

Example of a Round Robin. *Tables 1, 2, and 3 are in a RR:* **All N/Ss stay put.** *Pair 1E/W goes to table 2 first round, Pair 2E/W goes to table 3 first round, and Pair 3E/W goes to table 1 first round. After all the boards have been played, they are taken to the N/S home team and dropped off. Then Pair 1E/W goes to table **3** for the second round, Pair 2E/W goes to table **1** for the second round, and Pair 3E/W goes to table **2**. Each E/W pair goes to a **new** table for the second round - not their home table nor the table where they just finished. The E/W pair do not play their own N/S, and the teams are never head-to-head with the same teams playing each other. Think of it as a circle, hence the name. It's easy once you get used to it.*

In both types of KOs, the winning team moves ahead to the next session's match whenever it is scheduled, and the losers are finished with the event. They can enter another game according to the tournament schedule or rest, eat lunch, run an errand, etc. In compact games, the losers may play in a consolation round for an opportunity to get some points for a win.

In Swiss Teams, no one is knocked out, but all teams continue to play the entire session (or in both sessions). There will be a chart with team captain's names or numbers listed and the points accumulated by each team. Whether you win or lose, you can look on your scorecard (a different one from the usual type of convention card) and you can find out how many points you will get for the round, based on the 20 or 30 VIP (victory point) scale. The director chooses the scale. If you win, you get a portion of the allotted points, and your opponents will get some points too, unless the round was extremely lopsided.

After the first round of Swiss teams is over, losers play other losers and winners play other winners in a "King of the Mountain" type scenario. Bridge lore says that losing in the first round is best because it is the easiest loss from which to recover.

Your VIP points are added together each round. Lower level winners can jump to a higher level and attain a higher score than in their own level if they win continuously, and they will ultimately get more masterpoints than their level because of their fine play. If you lose a round at Swiss, you can still come back and win. Forget any poor playing and jump back into the game! You'll get points for each win.

The word "tournament" sounds much more intimidating than is the actual event. As you can see from the information in this chapter, the play is the same as duplicate play in pair games, and the team games are a different, head to head, exciting type of game, played at each table as **regular old bridge.** Good luck at your first tournament!

THE END and the BEGINNING

This is the end of *Building Bridges*. I hope you find this manual helpful to you as you progress in your knowledge of this great game. Use it as a resource now and in the future. There is no greater frustration for a new player than being unable to find a solution to his bidding problem. Hopefully this book, with it's charts and explanations, will be of assistance. I started writing it **BEFORE I forgot what it was like to be a struggling beginner,** maintaining that perspective so that YOU can identify with the information herein. It has taken several years to complete, but it's been worth every minute as my students develop and grow as players, taking pleasure in this pastime. As stated in the introduction, there is a lot of information that we simply cannot cover in class, so invest the time to learn the nuances of each concept. Don't forget much of the material is condensed into study guides, allowing for an expeditious review. You will find that you understand the concepts to a greater degree as you play more bridge, and the more bridge you play, the better will be your ability to interpret hands and to bid or defend properly.

As noted earlier, this book was designed to get you ready for bridge in sixteen weeks. Most players do not want to devote endless months to class after class after class, but want to play as soon as possible. *Building Bridges* prepares you for play as rapidly and as thoroughly as is reasonable. Each topic was carefully chosen

based in it's relevance to the game, and if you genuinely familiarize yourself with this book, you will be a formidable beginner to intermediate player.

If you want to enhance your play further, you must become a student of the game. You may choose to read other books or search the internet. If so, find sources that state they represent the Modern Standard American style of bidding, or the Five Card Major style of bidding. Both of these bridge methods are generally the same as what you've learned. Ask other players what to read, or refer to the Baron Barclay Bridge Supply website as they list books by levels. **Frank Stewart's** column appears daily on this site for those who are interested in pursing the finer points of advanced bridge concepts. **By the way - a heartfelt thanks to you, Frank, not only for your bridge wit and wisdom enjoyed the world over, but also for your suggestions and encouragement.** Join a bridge club because you will have the privilege of using their library, if they have one. There are many easy-to-read books with good explanations for the beginner. I have found it helpful to read a book (or part of it), take a break, and either reread the information, or continue to a new section. Then I read it all AGAIN. Baron Barclay gives a discount to ACBL members. And don't forget to read the *Bridge Bulletin* that comes monthly to ACBL members.

Ask more experienced players for guidance. They will not offer an opinion unless asked by someone who wants to learn. **Gracefully and gratefully accept criticism of your game.** No one wants to hurt your feelings - they want to help you. You are a beginner. No one thinks poorly of you because you are new to the game. Trust me - they are excited and delighted to have you! Perhaps you will be fortunate enough to find a special mentor like I did - the late Doug Hoadley. Doug initiated our Mentor-Mentee program and coached almost everyone at our club, which is how I met him. He gave his time at several regional tournaments to help Barbara, my partner, and me become Life Masters.

Discuss your bidding system with your partner(s). Review boards that scored poorly. The partners I have the most "heated" discussions with are my best partners. Through "review", ahem, we learn to understand each other. Don't lose your friendship - *focus on the game.* Different beginner bridge materials may present slightly different instruction methods, and point requirements for minimum - maximum levels may be slightly higher or lower. Work through and resolve your differences if your partner took a different beginner course.

Try new conventions and **be prepared to make mistakes at first**. It's okay to "mess up" and you will learn from the experience. I can't tell you how many times I forgot I had to have 8 HCP to use Stayman. My poor partner! (She must have forgiven me - she still plays with me). Practice does make perfect - or gets you closer inch-by-inch.

You now have a basic foundation in Standard American style bridge. Take any classes or attend any seminars offered on conventions in this book to sharpen your skills - Stayman, Jacoby Transfers, Blackwood, Gerber, TOXes, negative Xs, cuebids, or signaling. There may be other conventions or styles of play you choose to learn in the future, but do not rush to learn them now - resist the pressure. UNDERSTAND THE BASICS WELL before you add to the mix. My partners and I didn't learn a convention just to feel like we were 'real' bridge players: we waited until we noticed the same perplexing issue over and over, then we sought a means to fix the problem. You will figure out what to do as you gain experience.

Some of the bids in this series will eventually change to conventional bids or will become bids with new meanings in the future, and this is a sign you are MATURING as a player. **Do not become frustrated when the bids with which you are comfortable change!** Think how helpful Stayman and Transfers are over partner's 1NT opening bid instead of bidding your suit directly. If you bid your five card suit, then what do you do? Does partner like it? How would you show a four card suit? In bridge, the learning never ends - it is lifelong.

Other worthwhile conventions not in this book: Cappelletti or DONT (defenses over a 1NT opening), Michaels Cuebid, and the Unusual 2NT. The follow-up book of this series, *Continuing Construction*, describes these conventions. Even if you decide not to play these conventions yet, it WILL help you to understand what the OPPONENTS are doing. Your defense may get a boost!

Good luck to you in all your bridge endeavors!

Royally and loyally yours,

"Queen Jeanne"

APPENDIX A

Bridge definitions, tips, charts, convention card instructions, and summaries are located here. The material is presented in several forms to accommodate different learning styles and **may not be reproduced.**

Bridge definitions	83
Lead table	87
Major Bidding Study Guide	88
Minor Bidding Study Guide	88
Rule of 20 • Preempts • Basic Overcalls	88
The 1NT - Stayman and Jacoby Transfer Study Guide	89
Approximate HCP Needed for Level 1-4 Bidding	89
Flow Charts	90
Negative Xs • Cuebids • Common Finesses	93
Play of the Hand • Defense	93
HUGE Hands	93
Blackwood and Gerber	93
BIG Hands • NT Family • Advanced Overcalls	94
Distribution Values Chart	94
Forcing/Non-forcing/Invitational/Game force bids	94
Complete Scoring	95
Gems of Wisdom: a compilation of adages and tips from *BB*	95
The Point Scale	97
The Breakdown of Points	98
Instructions for the convention card	99
A sample convention card	100
Questions to ask a new partner	102
Basic Bidding Study Guide	103
Stayman and Jacoby Transfers Study Guide 2	104

Bridge Definitions

The definitions are listed as they are found sequentially in the text of each lesson, so they are not in alphabetical order. Some definitions are explained as they apply to this introductory book. Many of the definitions are best understood in context, so be sure to **study each chapter.**

Lesson I

Duplicate boards	The four-slot playing card trays rotated from table-to-table in a duplicate bridge game so that players sitting in the same direction have the same hands with which to compete. It's important the boards remain in the center of the table at all times to avoid card replacement errors. Such errors would affect every player in the room and would be difficult for the director to remedy. (p. 3)
Bid box	The container that holds all the calls (suit, no trump, pass, and double) a player can make in bridge. Using the box means a silent auction so that the integrity of each board is protected. (p. 3)
Bid or Call	The suit, NT, pass, double, or redouble card pulled from the bid box and placed on the playing table. (p. 3)
Traveller	A score sheet that is folded and tucked into the north slot of a duplicate board. The paper is folded such that the scores are hidden inside the paper, but the board number shows. The traveller is not opened until **after** the board is played. (p. 3)
Spades	The higher major suit (or strain). Spades are black and look like a short upright shovel. Each S trick is worth 30 points in bridge. (p. 3)
Hearts	The lower major suit (or strain). Hearts are typically red. Each H trick is worth 30 points. (p. 3)
Diamonds	The higher minor suit (or strain). Diamonds are typically red. Each D trick is worth 20 points. (p. 3)
Clubs	The lower minor suit (or strain). Clubs look like a tree and are black. Each C trick is worth 20 points. (p. 3)
Honors	The top five cards of a suit: the ace, king, queen, jack and ten. The highest four cards of the honors are the only cards in the deck assigned a point value. The points help determine the strength of the hand. The ten is considered an honor, but it has no point value, so when players refer to the honors, especially regarding trick-taking ability, they often refer to the top four cards of a suit. (p. 3)
Director	The person who is in charge of the game, having authority via established contract bridge rules to settle disputes and restore equity after errors, ensuring fair play for all. (p. 4)
Auction	The successive bids made by the players in order to win the competition. The process ends after three subsequent passes, or if there are four passes in a row with no numbered bid. (p. 4)
Pass	A call made by a player. He places a green card from the bid box on the table to indicate that he does not choose to make a suit, no trump, double or redouble bid at his turn, so the opportunity to bid moves to the player on his left, unless his is the third pass. (p. 4)
Opener	The first person to make a <u>numbered bid</u> in an auction. He is said to have "opened the auction." Passes made by the dealer or subsequent bidder(s) do not open the auction. (p. 4)
Trump suit/Trump	The suit that is the dominant suit for the single board; the top suit; the triumphant suit of the auction. A card played from the top suit can only be beaten by a higher card of that suit. A trump can be used to capture cards in any other suit, provided the player is void in that suit and is not overruffed. (p. 5)
No Trump	A bridge board played with no "top suit." Since there is no top suit, the highest card in the suit first led wins the four cards contributed by each player. Each player must contribute a card in the originally led suit if he has one. If the card is not of the original suit, it cannot win the trick, even if it is of a higher number or honor than any card on the table. (p. 5)
Ruff	The play of a trump card on a non-trump card to take a trick. To many players, *ruff* is synonymous with *trump* for the act of prevailing over another player's winner. (p. 5)
Follow suit	A player must contribute a card in the suit first led if he has one. (p. 5)
Revoke/Renege	The failure to play a card in the suit that was first led when the player has a card in that suit. (p. 5) The director should be called to rectify the mistake. The revoke could penalize the revoking pair by costing them one to two tricks, because the revoke could affect the legitimate outcome of the board.
Open	The act of making the first numbered bid in an auction. (p. 6)
Contract	The final numbered bid made in an auction, determined by three subsequent pass cards. (p. 6)
Declarer	The person who named the winning suit or NT first on his side; he plays his and the dummy's cards and sets the strategy for play after observing both hands. (p. 6)
Trick	A group of four cards placed on the table in play. There is one winner of the set of cards. (p. 6)

DEFINITIONS

Book	The first six tricks taken by the declaring side. They may be taken in any order. (p. 6)
Set	The failure of the declarer to win the amount of tricks needed to fulfill his contract. (p. 6)
Dummy	The hand placed face-up directly on the table; the hand belonging to the declarer's partner. (p. 6)
Leader	The person to the left of the declarer who plays the first card of the contract. (p. 6)
Lead	The card that is played first in each set of four cards. The *opening lead* is the first card played in a new contract. The lead may give clues to promising suits in the leader's hand. (p. 6)
Defenders	The pair or team who did not win the contract. Their goal is to defeat the contract. (p. 6)
Round	The play of all the boards on the table, a timed event. International bridge rules allot 7.5 minutes per board as a reasonable amount of time for play. (p. 7)
Contract card	The card from the bid box that represents the final bid. All possible scores are listed on the back of the card. (p. 7)
Convention card	The pair information/pair agreement sheet required of each player, also used for recording scores. (p. 7)

Lesson II

Golden Fit	A total of eight or more cards held by a pair in a one suit. The suit can be in any combination of 8. (p. 9)
Responder	The title given to the opener's partner. (p. 9)
Rebid	The second call by a previous suit or NT bidder, not necessarily in the same suit as before. (p.10)
Limit raise	A medium range invitational response with the feature of at least one extra trump in a M (4). To show this type of support, the responder jump bids in his partner's suit. (p. 11)
Jump bid	A bid made higher than necessary in an auction. Depending on when the bid is made, it signals weakness OR strength. Also known as a "skip" bid. (p. 11)
Major game	A contract of 4H or 4S. Game contracts add a significant bonus to the total number of tricks won, much greater than the partscore bonus. (p. 11)
Partscore	A final contract that is below "game"; the most common contract. The score is the sum of the tricks won, plus a fifty point bonus for success in fulfilling the contract. (p. 11)

Lesson III

Up the hill	In standard bridge play, two four card majors are bid from low to high - hearts then spades. Also referred to as bidding "up the line." (p. 13)
Down the mountain	In standard bridge play, two five card majors are bid from high to low - spades then hearts. In fact, in any hand with two five card suits, the higher suit is bid first, then the lower suit, if circumstances allow (HCP, bidding level, partner's bid, etc). Also called "down the line." (p. 13)
One-over-one (1/1)	Bids between opener and responder that stay at the one level while introducing a new suit: 1C - 1D, 1C - 1H,1C - 1S, 1D - 1H, 1D - 1S, or 1H - 1S; no suit is repeated, nor is the lowest possible NT bid. There are six 1/1 bids. A one-over-one bid by an unpassed responder forces a second bid of the opener since a new suit has been shown. (p. 15)
Two-over-one (2/1)	Bids between opener and responder that introduce a new suit at the two level: 1D - 2C, 1H - 2C, 1H - 2D, 1S - 2C, 1S - 2D, or 1S - 2H. There are six 2/1 bids. These bids are invitational to a game contract, as the two level bid promises at least 10 HCP. It forces a rebid on the opener since a new suit has been shown, unless the responder has previously passed. (p. 15)

Lesson IV

Quick tricks	High honors that win early in play. Each A equals 1 quick trick, while a Kx(xxx) equals 1/2 quick trick. The K may NOT be a singleton. If the A and K are of the same suit, the combination equals 2 quick tricks. The KQ combination equals 1 quick trick, while the AQ combination equals 1 1/2 quick tricks. Many players will not open an auction without at least 1 1/2 or 2 quick tricks. (p. 17)
Preemptive bid	A high-level bid made by a player with a long good suit, but an overall weak hand, in order to win the contract quickly, or to interfere with the opponent's bidding by crowding the auction. (p. 17)

Lessons V & VI

Balanced hand	A player holds a low number of cards in each of the four suits in a single hand. There are no voids, no singletons, and rarely is there a 5 card suit. These hands are also referred to as "flat" hands. The typical suit configuration is 4333 or 4432. A 5332 or 5422 holding is often labeled semi-balanced. When opening a NT hand, indicating balanced distribution, ACBL rules allow for a singleton A, K, or Q, but the traditionally the shortest suit is a doubleton. (p. 20)

Building Bridges © 2022 Jeanne R. Wamack May not be reproduced in any form.

DEFINITIONS

Announce	The bidder's **partner** states information about his bid, if required. For example, he'll say aloud the point range of a 1NT opening bid. The bidder himself DOES NOT give information. It's unethical and illegal. If there is **ever** a question about a bid, **the question is addressed to the partner.** (p. 20)
Convention	The bid of a suit, following a specific auction, that does not mean length in the suit as usual. It is a specialty bid - an artificial bid. It legally gives extra information and/or creates an advantage in the auction. (p. 20)
Free finesse	A lead into a fourth hand holding which wins with a low card, lower than the A. This prevents the fourth hand player from having to create a winner in the suit on his own, a play that could cost him a trick. (p. 20)

Lesson VII

Overcaller	The first opponent who bids after the opener; may be be a second OR fourth seat bid. (p. 27)
Distributional value	A bridge hand that is unbalanced, having one or two long suits with outside shortness (a sing or void): provides an opportunity for extra tricks from ruffing in a suit contract, thus a potentially higher score. Also refers to the points added to hands with a Golden Fit for short suits to ruff. (p. 27)
Distribution	The number of cards held in each suit. May also be referred to as the "shape" of the hand. (p. 27)
Takeout Double (TOX)	A bid made by an overcaller that shows 12+ HCP, 0-2 cards in the opener's suit, and an otherwise balanced hand (no long suit and no doubleton other than in the opener's suit). The doubler shows he can support **any** of the three unbid suits. The bid is made using the red X card from the bid box. (p. 27)
Free Bid	A player makes a call when he is not required to bid. This type of bid is often made in response to a takeout double and is bid by the advancer over the intervening opponent's bid. (p. 28)
Systems on	The pair bids as usual when the overcall is 1NT, provided there is no interference from the responder. This means Stayman and Jacoby Transfers may be used to describe the advancer's hand. (p. 28)
Stoppers	High cards or promotable length in an opponent's long suit that ends their control of or the continuous run of their suit; gives protection, especially in a NT contract. (p. 28)

Lesson VIII

Negative double	A **response** to partner's opening bid made in conjunction with an intervening bid by the opponent. The play of the double card means the responder is expected to hold at least 4/4 in the unbid suits. If either of the unbid suits is a M, the bidder MUST have at least 4 in the M. If one of the suits is a m, the requirement is not as strict. If the m is extremely weak or short, the bidder should have another option: a "landing place," such as NT or rebidding partner's original suit, in the event of a misfit. (p. 31)
Tolerance	Applies to a minor suit when a negative double is bid, so that the pair will have protection in the minor suit should the team be in a misfit and bid a NT contract. It is a short suit with stoppers. (p. 31)
Cuebid	The bid of an opponent's suit. Commonly shows support for partner's suit and at least 10 HCP. (p. 32)

Lesson IX

Perfect sequence	Consecutive (touching) honors such as the AKQ, KQJ, or QJ10 (QJ9 is acceptable). Such cards are **equivalent in value** to the holder. Leading the top card shows the next highest card in the suit. Leading from such a holding is one of the best, most informative leads in bridge, and is s good lead vs either a NT or a suit contract. (p. 34)
Broken sequence	High honors in a suit missing one of the sequence - AKJ10x, AQJ10x. Also called a tenace. With high consecutive honors such as the AK, the suit is a good lead. Holding the AQ, the player should wait and not lead this suit to try to capture the K in case the declarer has it, if partner has not shown support for the suit. However, support in the auction does not guarantee partner has the missing honor(s). (p. 34)
Interior sequence	Honors and high cards further down a suit missing one of the sequence and at least one other, higher card - KJ10xx (here missing the AQ), Q1098x (here missing the AKJ). Leading from an interior sequence is a good lead against the opponent's NT contract, but may be a poorer lead against the opponent's suit contract, as the holder may be better positioned to *capture* cards. However, any time partner shows support in the auction should the suit have been bid, the suit may become a good lead. The lead should be the top card of the consecutive cards. If there are no consecutive cards, the holding is not an interior sequence, so the lead should be the fourth card down from the top of the suit: KJ954 (p. 34)
Unsupported	A lone honor card in a suit accompanied only by low cards. Examples: A642, K83, Q532. This holding has defensive value, but little trick-taking value. (p. 35) This differs from *unprotected honors:* K, Qx, Jxx.
Post-mortem	The dialogue/debate regarding the recent play. Any discussion should take place after ALL the boards at the table have been completed, and should be held in hushed tones so the other players will not overhear any result concerning their coming boards. (p. 35)
Trap	An honor card in a hand that is sandwiched between a low honor to it's right and a higher honor to it's

DEFINITIONS

	left. If played to defeat the lower honor, it will be captured by the higher honor in the following hand; the act of trying to force that card to be played to it's eventual loss. (p. 36)
Block	A high card that prevents a suit from being continually played for trick-taking purposes because the highest card of the suit is located outside the hand with the long holding of the suit. Sometimes <u>partners must throw high cards in the lead suit early</u>, even when it seems counter-productive at the moment, to allow partner's long holding to be "set-up." This is why leads are not often random - partner is describing his hand with his first card, asking for help in creating a running suit (p. 36)

Lesson X

Finesse	The attempt to make a non-ace honor card (or any non-honor card), likely a losing card, a winner by not leading it directly, but by leading <u>to</u> it from the opposite hand in order to gain tricks. The card will now be the third card played instead of being the first card played. (p. 38)
Promote	The rise in value of lower cards when high cards are played in a suit. When the A of a suit is played, the K becomes the highest card. If the A, K, Q, and J are played, the 10 becomes the highest card, etc. All players must pay attention to the cards that fall and <u>note which mid-range cards have risen in value</u>, as former losers will become winners. (p. 38)
Split honors	At least two honor cards that are not held in one opponent's hand, but are divided between the two opponents. Depending on what happens in a finessing situation, the declarer may be able to determine where missing card(s) are located. (p. 39)
Limited entries	Few cards (one or two) held in partner's long suit. This prevents the suit from being run or easily "set up" to play for extra tricks because of the opponent's length in the suit, unless the suit is extremely strong (AKQJx), or there is another entry into the hand (an outside A or KQ). (p. 40)
	Limited entries may also refer to any weak <u>hand</u> with few winning cards.

Lesson XI

Play for the drop	The continuous "run" of a suit from the highest honor to the lowest card in the suit, hoping that all the outstanding cards in that suit will fall and not take a trick, especially any honors. This is attempted only with long holdings, 8-9 cards or more, or by a shorter holding with all of the top honors. (p. 41)
Transportation	The ability to move back and forth between the hands of declarer and dummy. (p. 41)
Duck	When a player does not put down a winning card at the first (or later) opportunity, but allows another player to take the trick. (p. 41)
Establish	Making a suit capable of winning tricks by removing or capturing any outside honors or other high cards that prevent the continual play or "run" of the suit. (p. 42)
Clear a suit	A player gets rid of all holdings in a suit. (p. 42)
Cross-ruff	The ability to trump losers in either hand, continually back-and-forth, because each hand is void in a different suit and has an adequate number of trumps for ruffing. Also called cross-trump. (p. 42)

Lesson XII

Sluff	The act of dispensing a losing card. The card can be thrown on a winning card or another losing card (loser on loser play). The correct spelling is 'slough', but bridge players like for the spelling to match 'ruff'. See the next definition. (p. 46)
Ruff and Sluff	The opponents lead a suit that is a void suit for both the declarer and dummy. The declarer is able to trump the lead card while throwing away a losing card in yet another suit, creating an extra trick for his side. (p. 46)
Switch	A player, usually a defender, makes a decision to change suits while on lead instead of continuing the current suit (usually led by partner), because he sees an advantage for his side by playing the new suit, OR he is forced to make a change in suits because partner's card will be lost to the dummy, which usually has the A, other high cards, or a void in partner's suit. (p. 47)

Lesson XIII

Jump-shift	The opener bids one of a suit, then at his next turn, bids a new suit, and the second suit is bid higher than necessary, a skip bid. This shows a maximum strength hand for the opener and is game-forcing. The responder may also jump-shift, and it is a game-forcing bid, points **per PA.** (p. 50)
Unprotected honors	High cards without enough small cards to promote them safely: K, Qx, Jxx. These honors are often lost to higher honors of the opponents, so the value points they possess are nearly useless to the holder. (p. 54)

Building Bridges © 2022 Jeanne R. Wamack May not be reproduced in any form.

DEFINITIONS AND LEAD TABLE

Lesson XIV

Captain of the hand	When one partner makes a bid revealing his holding within a known range of points, the other partner decides the level of the contract since he more accurately knows the total points held by the pair. Such defining opening bids are 1NT, 2NT, or 2C followed by 2NT. The responder usually makes the decision of where the final contract should be placed. Less well-defined, but similar, would be the responder's limited bid: 1S-2S. Here the opener is responsible for the contract. (p. 56)
Alert	When a player makes a conventional bid that does not necessarily mean he has the suit he bid (or NT), the player's PARTNER must say "Alert" to notify the opponents that the bid is artificial. (p. 57)
Bust hand	Over a 2C opening bid, a responding hand with fewer than 3 HCP, shown by a bid of 2H. (p. 57)

Lesson XV

Phantom sacrifice	A high bid made to prevent the opponents from stopping in what appears to be a makable contract. However, the opponents were *not* going to succeed in their contract, so the declaring team gives the opponents a positive score, rather than a negative score, with *their* loss. (p. 66)

Lesson XVI

Temporizing bid	A rebid that shows stoppers or honors, but not the usual length of a suit. Such bids are typically made in minor suits, occasionally in M suits, and are usually a very strong three card holding. This type of bid is made to hold the auction open, to ask partner for more information, or to force game. (p. 73)
Reverse bid	A low ranked suit followed by a rebid of higher ranked suit showing HCP and suit lengths in one bid. (p. 74)

Lesson XVII

Strats	The stratifications or levels within a larger bridge game, so that peer groups ultimately compete against each other. (p. 78)
Masterpoints	Points won by a player in an ACBL sanctioned game: in a club, at a tournament, or on a cruise ship. (p. 78)

Chapter 9   LEAD TABLE: USE IF YOU HAVE NO BETTER CLUES FROM THE AUCTION   p. 34

Partner bid a suit & you're on lead	You bid/Have a suit/Part didn't bid	Leads vs. **Suit** contract	Leads vs. **NT** contract
• Lead his A first, if you have it: A, A7, A52, A643, AJ3	• Lead the **top of a sequence**: AKQx, KQ(J)x, QJ10xx, QJ9x	• Partner's suit	• Partner's suit: lead as usual*
• Lead a singleton in his suit.	**Vs suits:** Lead hi from seq. of **2+**	• Your suit:	• Your own long suit:
• Play a doubleton **high/low** K8, QJ, J6, 104, 73	**Vs NT:** Lead hi from seq. of **3+**	- Top of sequence: AK, KQ(J)	- You may lead away from A in NT **IF** you're setting up a long, decent suit: AJ976.
• With **2+** honors, play the highest honor, then the next honor, then small: KQ2, QJ7, KQJ	• Lead fourth down in a strong or long suit with **no sequence**: K1065 2, Q1083, KJ97, 97653	- Fourth down longest suit: KJ85, K9642, Q7532	- Lead seq: **top of 3** or lead 4th.
• With **1** honor, lead low from 3-4: K96, K642, Q63, Q753, J32 The low card is encouraging.	• Do not lead the A from space: A642 Maintain control of the suit.	- Top of nothing: no *better* lead	• Lead a M since they're in NT: *Stayman misfit, 1NT-2/3NT*
• With **0** honors, lead the middle then the higher card from **3** small: 1072, 753, 642, 987 The order of play denies a doubleton or honor. *Know your cards may be imperfect for completely accurate signaling.*	• Do not lead J753. The J could stop *their* long suit OR get promoted into a winner.	• Trump in a partscore - they need ruffs for success.	• Lead the unbid suit
	• If you have no good lead, lead the top of nothing: 9543, 8654, 9873 At least tell partner to return any other suit, but **NOT** this one.	• Singleton if warranted: See pg. 36.	• Do NOT lead your suit if they bid it: Make them come to you so you'll get tricks.
		• A doubleton is about the worst lead, unless it's the AK. Play it KA.	• Top of nothing.
		• Lead a X'd artificial bid.	• Lead a X'd artificial bid.
		• **Pay attention to the auction:** you may need to make a non-standard lead.	• If you are weak, part may be strong. Try to figure out what long suit (4+) he has, if any.

*Careful - do not block partner's suit in NT. You may agree to lead all honor(s) first (incl 10), saving a small card to return suit to partner.

Broken and interior sequences may be led more confidently if partner ever supported the suit. If not, you're making the best lead you can.

		vs Suits	vs NT
	Broken sequence lead:	AKJ76, AQJ76 (try to wait)	AKJ76, AQJ76
	Interior sequence lead:	KJ1076, Q10976 (use to capture)	KJ1076, Q10976
	Other leads:		J1094, J1082, in a **M**

You have **AKxxx** - a nice suit.
• How would you play this holding vs their **suit** contract?   You would play the A, then the K if it's safe, and maybe continue.
• How would you play this holding vs their **NT** contract?   You would lead fourth down - a small card. Why? You want to set up your long suit and may need help from partner. If he only has **two** cards in your suit, **let them take their winner,** and the next one of you to win can lead the suit **again** to get the maximum number of tricks in the suit. If you play the AK, partner can't lead that suit back to you. It's hard to lead a small card, but it is the correct way to play this holding vs NT.

Building Bridges © 2022 Jeanne R. Wamack   May not be reproduced in any form.

MAJOR OPENERS & RESPONSES • MINOR OPENERS & RESPONSES • RULE OF 20+2 • PREEMPTIVE BIDS • BASIC OVERCALLS

THE MAJORS p. 9

1S	RESPONSES	**1H**	RESPONSES		OUR GOALS
5+ Ss	MIN	5+ Hs	MIN		1. To find the GOLDEN FIT of **8** in a **M** suit.
12-21	2S = 3-4 Ss, 6-9 HCP, NF	12-21	2H = 3-4 Hs, 6-9 HCP, NF		2. To bid GAME with enough HCP. (25)
HCP	1NT = < 3 Ss, 6-9 HCP, NF	HCP	1NT = < 3 Hs, 6-9 HCP, NF		

1S = **4+** Ss & **6+** HCP, F
HCP UNKNOWN: *weak OR strong*

STRENGTH
Opener		Responder
12-15	MIN	6-9
16-18	MED	10+ -12
19+	MAX	13+

MED+
2C = 4+ Cs, 10+ HCP, F
2D = 4+ Ds, 10+ HCP, F

MED+
2C = 4+ Cs, 10+ HCP, F
2D = 4+ Ds, 10+ HCP, F

2H = **5+** Hs, 10+ HCP, F

3S = 4 Ss, 10-12 HCP, LR, NF

3H = 4 Hs, 10-12 HCP, LR, NF

2NT = < 3 Ss, 11-12 HCP, NF
3NT = < 3 Ss, 13+ HCP, NF: GAME

2NT = < 3 Hs, 11-12 HCP, NF
3NT = < 3 Hs, 13+ HCP, NF: GAME

NF = Non-forcing bid
F = Forcing bid
LR = Limit Raise (jump=med. hand)

1/1, 2/1 BIDS: No previous pass, **F** and unlimited.

OPENER'S REBIDS
1. He'll rebid a 6+ M suit.
2. He'll bid a 4+ card suit, his second longest, lower ranked suit.
3. He'll raise partner's **minor** suit w/ 3+
   He'll raise partner's H suit w/ 3-4 Hs
   He'll raise partner's S suit w/ **4** Ss.
   M suit raises show a GOLDEN FIT.
4. He'll bid NT with a balanced hand and no "better" choice.

THE MINORS p. 13

1C	FIRST PRIORITY RESPONSES	**1D**	FIRST PRIORITY RESPONSES
3+ Cs	1H = 4+ Hs, 6+ HCP, F	4+ Ds	1H = 4+ Hs, 6+ HCP, F
12-21 HCP	1S = 4+ Ss, 6+ HCP, F	12-21 HCP	1S = 4+ Ss, 6+ HCP, F

Another level one response:
1D = 4+ Ds, 6+ HCP, F
NO FOUR CARD MAJOR

UNLIMITED (UNKNOWN) HCP

UNLIMITED (UNKNOWN) HCP

OUR GOALS
1. To find the GOLDEN FIT in a **M** suit
2. To bid GAME* with enough HCP (?)

STRENGTH
Opener		Responder
12-15	MIN	6-9
16-18	MED	11-12
19+	MAX	13+

MIN, NF
2C = **NO 4 CARD M,** 5+ Cs, 6-9 HCP
1NT = **NO 4 CARD M,** < 5 Cs, 6-9 HCP

MIN, NF
2D = **NO 4 CARD M,** 5+ Ds, 6-9 HCP
1NT = **NO 4 CARD M,** < 5 Ds, 6-9 HCP

OPENER'S REBIDS
1. First choice: Raise resp's M w/ 4.
2. If R bids 1H, rebid 1S w/ 4 Ss & **< 4 Hs.**
3. If no M fit, strive for a NT contract.
4. O's NT rebid = a balanced hand.
5. Rebid a m w/ **6** (or 5 if no better rebid).

MED+, NF
3C = **NO 4 CARD M,** 5+ Cs, 11-12 HCP, LR

MED+, most NF*
3D = **NO 4 CARD M,** 5+ Ds, 11-12 HCP, LR

2C = **NO 4 CARD M,** 5+ Cs, 10+ HCP, F

2NT = **NO 4 CARD M,** 11-12 HCP
3NT = **NO 4 CARD M,** 13+ HCP, GAME

2NT = **NO 4 CARD M,** 11-12 HCP
3NT = **NO 4 CARD M,** 13+ HCP, GAME

RESPONDING IN THE MAJORS:
4/4: Bid Hs first, then Ss
"HIKE UP THE HILL"
5/5: Bid Ss first, then Hs.
"SKI DOWN THE MTN"

NOT ALL 10s ARE CREATED EQUAL

"A RICH 10"		"A POOR 10"	
A	K K	A K x	J
K	Q Q	x Q x	x
Q	x x	x	x x
J	x x		x
10			x

***GAME = 100 points**
M tricks = 30 points each
m tricks = 20 points each
NT = 40 1st trick, 30 after

4 tricks + book = 10/game
5 tricks + book = 11/game
3 tricks + book = 9/game

CORRESPONDING AKQJ POINTS
M game = 25-26 HCP
m game = 28-29 HCP
NT game = 25-26 HCP (preferred to m)

TWO MORE OPENING BIDS: p. 17

RULE of 20 (+2)
If the # in your 2 longest suits **+** the # of your HCP = 20 -AND-
You have 2 quick tricks...
A+A, AK, AQ + K, KQ + KQ
Open the auction at the 1 level
HCP *MUST* be in your long suits.

PREEMPTIVE BIDS
2 level: NV = **5-10 HCP** & a decent suit
V = 7-10 HCP: 2 of top 3/3 of top 5 honors
With a **6** card suit...**open at the 2 level**
With a **7** card suit...**open at the 3 level**
With a **8** card suit...**open at the 4 level**
Many initial jump bids are preemptive.

BASIC OVERCALLS p. 27
Level 1: 8+ HCP & **5** card suit w/ 2+ honors
Level 2: 12+ HCP & **5** card suit w/ 2+ honors:
w/ fewer than 12 HCP, a 6 card suit & a sing/void.
TOX: 12+ HCP & 0-2 cards in opener's suit -
promises at least Jxx in the other 3 suits.
1NT (direct seat) = 15-17 HCP & stoppers
1NT (balancing seat) = 12+ HCP, stoppers
Over Preempt: 14+ to bid suit, 16+ to TOX
If you don't fit any category, you must PASS.

Building Bridges © 2022 Jeanne R. Wamack May not be reproduced in any form.

THE 1NT OPENING BID • PIG • STAYMAN • THE JACOBY TRANSFER • APPROXIMATE HCP NEEDED FOR 1-4 LEVEL BIDS

Chapter 5   **1NT OPENING BIDS & CONVENTIONAL RESPONSES**   p. 20

Expectations of a 1NT opening bid: 15-17 HCP (announced) • Balanced hand, no 5 card M (per PA) • No voids or singletons lower than the Q (ACBL rules allow a singleton A, K, Q) • One weak doubleton permissible. Many responses are conventions - artificial bids. SUIT bids over 1NT may not mean the bidder has the suit he bids

THE PIG

A response you will use EVERY TIME partner opens 1NT.

Tells him how many HCP you have. He'll *usually* place the contract.

Open	Resp	HCP	Meaning	The
1NT	PASS	0-7	Poor hand	"P"
	2NT	8-9	Invitational	"I"
	3NT	10+	Game	"G"

If responder PASSES:
The opener will play 1NT unless the opponents intervene.

If responder bids 2NT, an opener:
With 15 HCP will PASS
With 16 HCP will CONSIDER game
With 17 HCP will BID GAME

If responder bids 3NT, the opener will PASS.

With interference, conventional bids are off and the responder will bid "naturally."

*A natural bid would mean a **5 card suit**. No jump in suit = no interest in game. A jump bid is game-forcing, whether opener bids game in the M suit or NT.*

The responder may also bid 2NT/3NT.

Responder will not be able to show a 4 card M.

STAYMAN

I have a FOUR card M, do you?

Responder's requirements:
1. The resp has 1 OR 2 four card Ms.
2. The resp has 8+ HCP.

Opener	Responder
1NT	2C = Stayman

Only 3 responses for the opener...

1. 2D: NO 4 card M
Bids the PIG:
2NT = 8-9 HCP
3NT = 10+ HCP
Places contract/passes.

2. 2H: 4 card H suit, unknown S count. Bid 4/4 Ms Hs first, then Ss.

With HEART fit:
3H = 8-9 HCP
4H = 10+ HCP
Shows a 4/4 H fit

With SPADE suit:
2NT = 8-9 HCP
3NT = 10+ HCP
Shows no H fit -
Resp's suit is **Ss**.

Places contract/passes.

If opener is 4/4 in the Ms, he may bid Ss over 2NT or 3NT because he KNOWS partner has Ss. Why else bid Stayman?

3. 2S: 4 card S suit, < 4 Hs

With HEART suit:
2NT = 8-9 HCP
3NT = 10+ HCP
Shows no S fit -
Resp's suit is **Hs**.

With SPADE fit:
3S = 8-9 HCP
4S = 10+ HCP
Shows a 4/4 S fit

Places contract/passes

Note: without a "hit" on his suit, responder bids NT. He will <u>never</u> bid the four card M.

THE JACOBY TRANSFER

I have a FIVE c M. _YOU_ bid it.

Responder requirement:
A 5 card M.
Transfers may be bid with 0 HCP.

Opener	Responder
1NT	2D = transfer to **Hs**

Says "HEARTS"
& bids **2H** - no
no matter what

Bids the PIG:
With 0-7 HCP - PASS
With 8-9 HCP - 2NT
With 10+ HCP - 3NT

Places contract -
in suit with a fit or
NT without a fit if
responder doesn't pass.

Opener	Responder
1NT	2H = transfer to **Ss**

Says "SPADES"
& bids **2S** - no
matter what.

Bids the PIG:
With 0-7 HCP - PASS
With 8-9 HCP - 2NT
With 10+ HCP - 3NT

Places contract -
in suit with a fit or
NT without a fit if
responder doesn't pass.

APPROXIMATE HCP NEEDED FOR LEVELS 1-4

*Generally, level one bids=**18-20** HCP • Level two bids=**20-22** HCP • Level three bids=**22-24** HCP • Level four bids=**25-27** HCP*
Slightly MORE HCP needed for NT contracts • Slightly FEWER HCP needed with extra trumps, extra length or a singleton/void

Building Bridges © 2022 Jeanne R. Wamack May not be reproduced in any form.

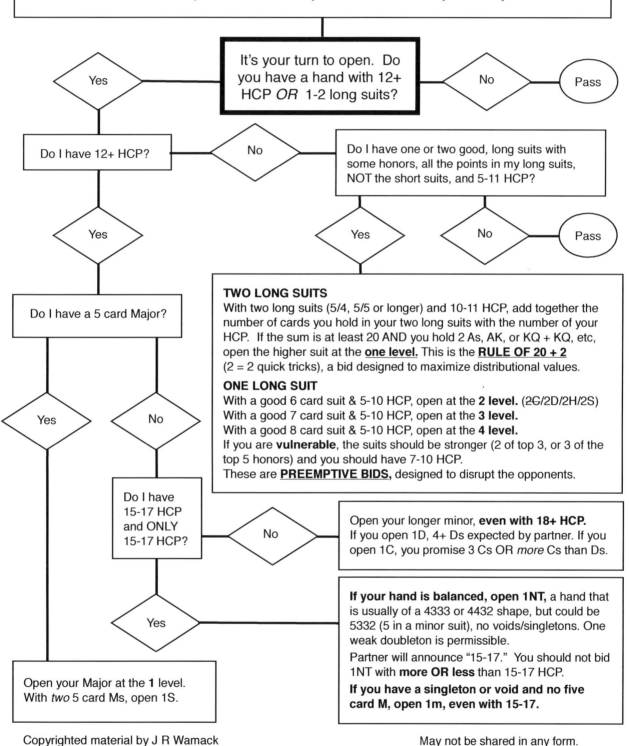

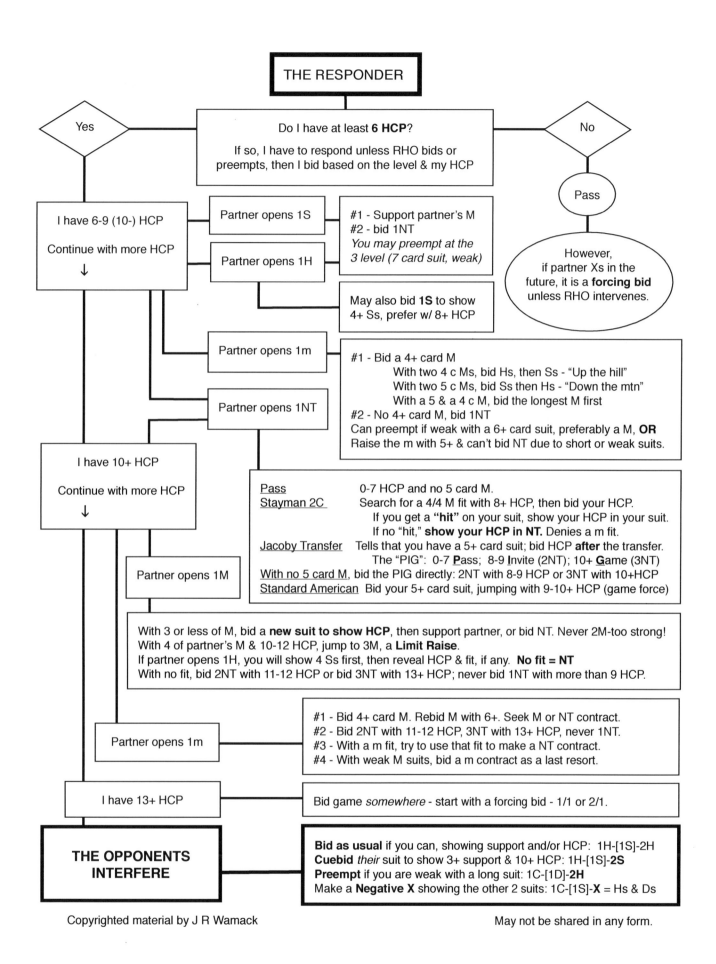

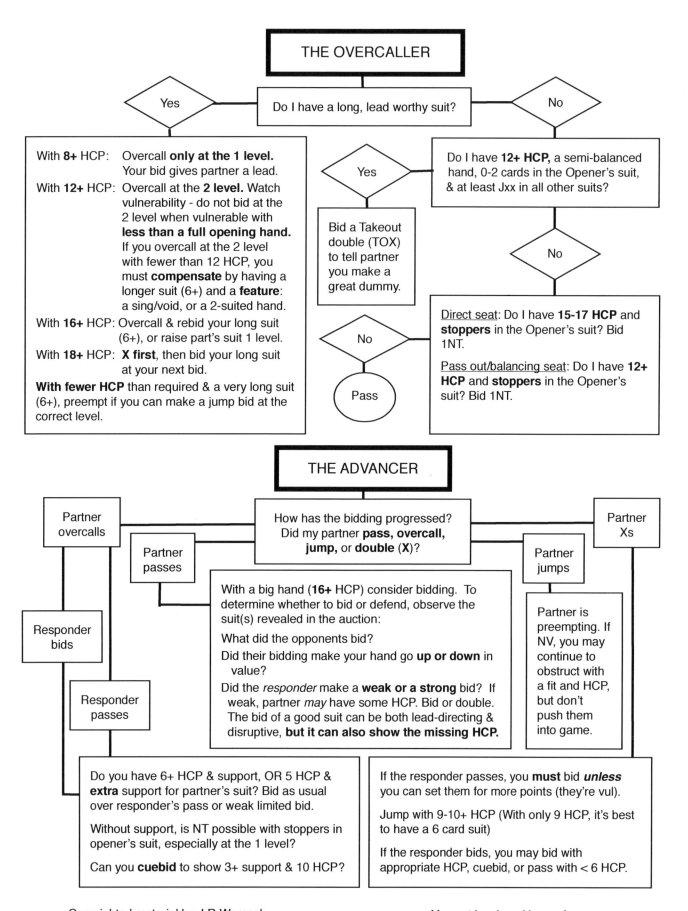

Chapter 8

NEGATIVE DOUBLE
Partner opens 1? & the following opponent overcalls another suit:
X = the two **UNBID** suits, guaranteeing 4 card M(s). ***Show your M.***
Xer may <u>not</u> have a 4 c minor suit; must have min QJx (a tolerance).
If weaker/shorter in the m, he must have a **LANDING PLACE**...
1. **NT** showing stoppers in oppo's suit & several HCP, OR
2. Length in partner's **original suit**.
After a H overcall: X shows **4 Ss** & direct bid of Ss shows **5+ Ss.**

CUEBID   p. 31
A bid of the **opponent's** suit showing **support and 10+ HCP.**
May be used after interference, after a previous pass,
  or if partner is an overcaller. **Forcing for one round.**
After interference, a cuebid shows a limit raise or better.
After an overcall, encourages further competition or game.
After a previous pass, a cuebid shows 10-11 HCP, a strong hand.

Chapter 10 — COMMON FINESSES (pp 38-40)

	1. N	2. N	3. N	4. N	5. N	6. N	7. N
	A	A	A	K	K	A	A
	Q	x	x	Q	x	Q	Q
	x	x	x	x	x	x	10
	x	x	x	x	x		x
	☐	☐	☐	☐	☐	☐	☐
	x	Q	Q	x	x	J	x
	x	x	J	x	x	x	x
	x	x	10	x		x	x
						x	
	S	S	S	S	S	S	S

1. Lead low to the Q from the S hand.
2. Lead low to the Q from the N hand.
3. Lead the Q from S. If the K shows, play the A.
   If the K doesn't show, let the Q "ride."
4. Lead low to the K or Q from S. If the finesse
   succeeds, repeat it. You may play either the
   K or Q as they are touching (equivalent) cards.
5. Avoid suit: lead low to K when you must play it.
6. Lead low to the Q from S. If the K shows,
   play the A. If the K doesn't show, let the
   Q ride. If she loses, cash the A later then lead
   low to the J.
7. Double finesse. Lead low from S to the Q or 10,
   most often the Q. If the K shows, play the A.
   If necessary, next time lead to the 10.

Chapter 11 — PLAY OF THE HAND

NT CONTRACT — COUNT WINNERS
If short of tricks, see where to get more:
  Usually in your 2 longest suits.
Develop winners in your long suits:
  Finesse/play for the drop.
Manage your suits properly:
 - Play high from the short side first.
 - Look to UNBLOCK suits.
 - Give up losers while you have stoppers.
 - Save short suit winners until the end.
HOLD UP the A in a short suit if they lead it.

SUIT CONTRACT — COUNT LOSERS   p. 41
Use your LENGTH & SHORTNESS to get rid of losers.
Set up long suits for tricks & tosses:
  As usual, finesse/play for the drop.
Ruff in the **short** holding of trumps for EXTRA TRICKS.
DO NOT ruff early in the LONG trump holding.
With a balanced dummy (no shortness for ruffing), draw
  trumps early and COUNT them.
TIP: If it won't break your train of thought, stop and
  reevaluate/recount tricks during a natural pause
  in the middle of the hand.

Chapter 12 — DEFENSE

THINGS YOU NEED TO REMEMBER WHILE ON DEFENSE   p. 46
The opening lead.
Usually return the opening lead <u>unless</u> partner's bid suit (or known long suit) will be overtaken or ruffed.
VS their NT contract - win (in partner's suit or another suit) and return the HIGHEST card you have in part's suit.
Dummy on the LEFT, lead to the HEFT - fill in a hole, get back in control.
Dummy on the RIGHT, lead the WEAKEST thing in sight.
Second hand usually plays low <u>unless</u> it's a short suit (doubleton) and you'll lose a winner.
3rd hand usually plays high: look at the cards already played & the dummy to decide how high a card you must play.
Keep par & win with the lowest card possible.
SIGNAL with your preferred method. Upside/down: high = HATE   low = LIKE   Standard: low = NO!

Chapter 14 — HUGE HANDS

2NT = 20-21 HCP, balanced
Responses:
3C = Stayman, seeking a 4 c M.
3D = Transfer to HEARTS
3H = Transfer to SPADES
3NT = no 4 or 5 c M, game HCP.
PASS = < 4 HCP, no 5+ M suit.

2C = 22+ HCP, any shape, F
Responses:
2D = Positive waiting, 3+ HCP, GF
2H = Negative*, < 3 HCP, game unk.
2S = S suit w/ 2+ honors, 8+ HCP
2NT = HEART suit*, 2 honors, 8+ HCP.
*Alert

2C Opener's rebid: p. 56
Any suit = 5+ cards in suit, natural
2NT = 22-23 HCP, bal, "Systems on"
  See 2NT responses to the left.
3NT = 24+ HCP. unlimited, bal.
  May support partner's M bid.
  May place contract over 2H neg bid.

Chapter 15 — BLACKWOOD AND GERBER   p. 59

BW Ace ask:	4NT	BW King ask:	5NT	Gerber Ace ask:	4C	Gerber King ask:	5C
0 or 4 Aces	5C	0 or 4 Ks	6C	0 or 4 Aces	4D	0 or 4 Ks	5D
1 Ace	5D	1 K	6D	1 Ace	4H	1 K	5H
2 Aces	5H	2 Ks	6H	2 Aces	4S	2 Ks	5S
3 Aces	5S	3 Ks	6S	3 Aces	4NT	3 Ks	5NT

Building Bridges © 2022 Jeanne R. Wamack May not be reproduced in any form.

Chapter 13 BIG HANDS
p. 50

OPENER w/ **16** HCP: jump in your suit or partner's suit.
OPENER w/ **17** HCP: rebid agreed suit (no int), bid new suit after agreement (no int), X to force resp, + all bids above
OPENER w/ **18** HCP: 1/1 bid, jump to 2NT, + all bids above.
OPENER w/ **19** HCP: jump-shift into a new suit, or rebid game in your suit, partner's suit, or NT.
RESPONDER w/ **10** HCP: bid at the 2 level (your first or second bid), cuebid if interference.
RESPONDER w/ **11** HCP: jump in own long suit (6+), bid 2NT.
RESPONDER w/ **13** HCP: bid a new suit at your first bid, cuebid to force partner to bid again, or bid M game/3NT.
RESPONDER w/ **16** HCP: bid a new suit or cuebid to keep the auction open. May consider slam: depends on auction.

NT FAMILY:
1/1 auction, 1 NT rebid:	**12-14** HCP
1NT opening bid:	**15-17** HCP
1/1 auction, jump to 2NT:	**18-19** HCP
2NT opening bid:	**20-21** HCP
2C, rebid 2NT	**22-23** HCP
2C, rebid 3NT	**24+** HCP

Some players will open 3NT w/ 25+ HCP

OVERCALLS AND THE REST OF THE TOX STORY
Level 1: 8+ HCP, good 5+ suit.   **Level 2:** 12+ HCP, good 5+ suit.
Level 2 with < 12 HCP: A good 6+ suit and a singleton or void
1NT direct seat: 15-17 HCP, **1NT** in 4th seat: 12+ HCP, stoppers
TOX: *(Partner will jump w/ 10+ HCP)*   **12-17** HCP
TOX vs 2 level preempt/3 level preempt   **16+** HCP/**18+** HCP
TOX, raise partner's suit 1 level: **16-17** HCP
TOX, raise partner's suit 2 levels: **18+** HCP
TOX, then bid own suit: **18+** HCP
TOX, rebid NT: **18+** HCP, stoppers

DISTRIBUTION POINTS/VALUES
see p. 53

Length points: Opener: +1 for good 5 card suit   +2 for 6 card suit   +3 for 7 card suit.
Opener typically adds length points during initial HCP evaluation.

Responder: +1 for a good 5 card suit   +2 for a 6 card suit   +3 for a 7 card suit   *(optional)*
Resp adds length points ONLY if partner supports his suit, or if it's accessible via outside As & Ks.

Shortness points: added **AFTER** finding the Golden Fit: **NEVER** added for underlined doubleton trump support or in a underlined NT contract.
*Shortness points are added to a hand in anticipation of **extra ruffs** due to the short suit.*
Shortness points are considered optional for the opener by some experts.

Opener & Responder with **3** Trumps		Responder with **4+** trumps	
Doubleton	**1 point**	**1 point**	*Add with careful consideration of actual hand strength:*
Singleton	**2 points**	**3 points**	*Whether or not you have an unbalanced hand, your holding*
Void	**3 points**	**5 points***	*in the trump honors (ruff or draw trumps), mid-range cards.*

~OR~ you may add one point for each trump beyond 3 if your hand is somewhat balanced.

Devaluations: **-1 HCP** if 4333 (flat),   **-1 HCP** for strength in short suits,   **-1 HCP** for too many Qs & Js, not enough As & Ks.
-1 HCP having 0 As,   **-1 HCP** for no 10s, 9s, & 8s   **-1 HCP** for unprotected honors (K, Qx, Jx or Jxx).

Chapter 16   Rebids and Review
p. 71

NON-FORCING BIDS
1C, 1D, 1H, 1S, 1NT opening bids
Simple suit raises:*
Simple 1NT or 2NT raises:*
    1NT-2NT, 1C-1S-1NT-2NT
Preemptive bids
Preference auctions:
    1H-1S-2S-4H (4S?),
    1H-1NT-2D (pass-prefers Ds)
Bid by previously passed partner
Low level bid of "old" suit:**
    1H-1S-1NT-2H
Non-jump rebids after 1/1:
    1C-1H-1S
    (up to 18 HCP, NF)
Penalty doubles
Game level bids
Limit raises

FORCING BIDS
1/1 auctions
2/1 auctions
New suit bids**
Cuebids
    1H-[1S]-2S
Takeout Xs (no interference)**
Neg Xs (no interference)
2C openers
Reverses
    1C-1S-2H
Conventions:
    Stayman
    Jacoby Transfers
    Blackwood
    Gerber

INVITATIONAL BIDS
1NT opening bid
Limit raises
2NT bid or raise by O/R
Jump in own suit
Jump in partner's suit
Rebid of suit after
    simple raise, no int:
    1H-2H-3H
Bid of new suit after suit
    agreement: 1H-2H-3D
Jump in "old" suit by O or
    R: 1H-1S-3H
Jump rebid by responder***
    1C-1H-1S-3H
1/1, then jump to 2NT by O

GAME FORCE BIDS
Opening 2C - 2D response
Opening 2C - 2S response
Opening 2C - 2NT response
Jump-shift by O or R (resp**)
3 level bid of new suit after
    1/1 or 2/1 auction

**List is incomplete as
every auction cannot
be represented.**

* simple = non-jump bid
** exceptions
***may be GF per PA

***See also BIG hands study
guide at the top of the page.***

Building Bridges © 2022 Jeanne R. Wamack   May not be reproduced in any form.
94

Chapter 16 **SCORING:** p.61 also p.19

Minors=20 points each; Majors=30 points each; NT: 1st trick= 40 points, rest=30 points each **GAME = 100 points**

Contracts:	Combined HCP Requirements:	Title:	Bonus:	Vul/NonVul:
Level one contract	**18-20** HCP *Add 1-2 HCP for a NT contract*	Partscore	+50	NV or V
Level two contract	**20-22** HCP *Add 1-2 HCP for a NT contract*	Partscore	+50	NV or V
Level three contract	**22-24** HCP *Add 1-2 HCP for NT,* **3NT=Game**	Partscore M/m	+50	NV or V
Level four contract	**25-27** HCP	**Game:** M or NT	+300 NV	+500 V
Level five+ contract	**28-30** HCP *Borderline for slam if unbalanced*	**Game** in a minor	+300 NV	+500 V
Level six contract	**30-34** HCP *33+ HCP if both hands are* **balanced**	Small slam	+500 NV	+750 V
Level seven contract	**35+** HCP *37+ HCP if both hands are* **balanced**	Grand slam	+1000 NV	+1500 V

Why are more points required for NT? The declarer cannot gain **extra** tricks from ruffing, and he's **balanced** - no long suits to run.
Why are 28-30 points borderline for slam? If one partner is unbalanced (a long, strong suit and a void), his hand is **extra** valuable.
As you can see from the bonuses - DO NOT MISS YOUR GAMES, ESPECIALLY YOUR VULNERABLE GAMES!

SET:	NV	V	NVX	VX	
-1	- 50	-100	- 100	- 200	Non-vulnerable set tricks are 50 points per trick.
-2	-100	-200	- 300	- 500	Vulnerable set tricks are 100 points per trick.
-3	-150	-300	- 500	- 800	Non-vulnerable doubled set tricks are 200 or 300 points more per trick. Think "1, 3, 5..."
-4	-200	-400	- 800	-1100	Vulnerable doubled set tricks are 200 or 300 points more per trick. Think "2, 5, 8..."
-5	-250	-500	-1100	-1400	Sacrifice when the opponents are vulnerable and you are not.

If you know scoring, you'll know WHEN to sacrifice and when NOT to sacrifice.
It **may** be to your benefit to get set 1 or 2 tricks NV, or 1 trick V, etc.

♛ GEMS OF WISDOM ♛

♛ **#1-Never lie to your partner.**

♛ **BIDDING** ♛

If your call doesn't fit it, you mustn't bid it... *make a BETTER bid to describe your hand.*
Bid 4 card majors "up the hill"... *even if the other one is prettier. "Hike up the hill..."*
Bid 5 card majors "down the mountain"... *and hope your partner figures it out. "Ski down the mountain..."*
He who knows - goes!... *Don't miss a game!*
Opening count + opening count... *equals game.*
The minors are... *the icing on the cake or the gravy on the rice - NOT the final contract.*
Roberta says, *"Diamonds are for your finga and clubs are for the golf course."*
Queen Jeanne says, *"Clubs are for cavemen and diamonds are for 'minors.' "*
First bids show length... *second bids show strength.*
Six, Five - COME ALIVE!... *the power of LENGTH.*
Check and respect... *know your vulnerability.*
PIG... *Pass, Invite, Game responses.*
Avoid the "Terrible 200"... *- 2 Vulnerable. You might throw a tantrum over your score.*
The 3 and 5 level... *belong to the opponents.*
Don't make "phantom sacrifices"... *and don't push them into an unbid game.*
Don't try Blackwood... *with a worthless unbid doubleton.*
Don't double for penalty... *without a stack of trumps AND with As & Ks in opponent's second suit or in UNBID suits.*
With LIMITED RANGE hands (1NT, 2NT, 2C followed by 2NT)... *your partner is the captain of the ship.*
Never lie to your partner... *and promise greater or fewer points than you have.*

♛ **LEADS** ♛

Lead partner's suit... *make your partner happy.*
Lead the A in partner's suit... *if you have it.*
Lead doubletons or singletons... *when they are in your partner's suit. Play the doubleton high/low.*
Lead the bottom of 3/4 with an honor in partner's suit... *unless you have two+ honors, then lead highest honor.*
Lead the lone (non Ace) honor in partner's suit... *only in a NT contract, if that is your partnership agreement.*
Lead the middle card from junk in partner's suit, then high... *so he won't think you have a doubleton or an honor.*
Return partner's opening lead... *help him win a trick or two or three.*
Lead the top of a perfect sequence... *to set up YOUR suit.*
Lead the top of touching honors of a broken or interior sequence... *to set up your suit vs their NT contract.*
Lead 4th from your longest and strongest... *not headed by the A or J.*
Lead a trump... *in a partscore.*
Lead the top of nothing... *when you have no better option.*

Don't lead an Ace from space... *because aces take faces.*
Aces take faces... *not worthless junk!*
Don't lead from Jxxx... *because it sets up a cheap trick.*
>*There is a famous Rock and Roll Hall of Fame band known as Cheap Trick. They must be bridge players.*

If they started in NT and/or end up in NT... *lead a M and keep leading it.*

♔ PLAY OF THE HAND ♔

When playing in a NT contract, count your WINNERS... *and see where you can make up for a shortfall.*
When playing in a suit contract, count your LOSERS... *and see where you can get rid of them using your length and shortness.*
In NT set up your long suits... *before you lose your stoppers in your* <u>short suits.</u>
HOLD UP your Ace... *to ROB the partner.*
Watch your transportation... *don't burn entries early.*
Play high from the short side first... *so you don't block yourself in your own long suit.*
Lead low to the card... *you want to win a trick.*
Finesse... *then hold your breath!*
If you lead an honor in a finesse... *you WANT it to be covered. f you don't want it covered, don't lead the honor.*
Get the kids off the street... *pull your trumps UNLESS you need to ruff in the dummy's short holding of trumps.*
When you ruff on the short side... *each one is an EXTRA TRICK.*
Throw a loser... *on a loser.*
Count your suits... *start with trumps, then add another suit...and another suit...and another suit.*
An EVEN number of outstanding cards... *tend to split oddly.*
An ODD number of outstanding cards... *tend to split evenly.*

♔ DEFENSE ♔

Never give them a "Ruff and a Sluff"... *lead something else.*
Lead to strength and through to weakness... *when the dummy's on the RIGHT, lead the weakest thing in sight.*
>*... when the dummy's on the LEFT, lead to the heft.*

Second hand low... *usually!*
Third hand high... *only as high as necessary.*
Cover an honor with an honor... *especially if you don't know where the 10 is, or if YOU have it.*
Signaling: *Think "low=NO!" if you play standard, or "low-like" if you play Upside-down.*
The player behind the dummy... *should cover what is in the dummy.*
The player behind the declarer... *should cover what the declarer plays.*
Win a trick... *as cheaply as possible.*

♔ FEW FUN TIPS ♔

The Rule of 7: When playing a NT contract and they lead your weakest suit in which you only have an A, you know you should "hold up" or "duck" but how many times should you do it? Add together the number of cards you and the dummy have and subtract that number from 7. This tells you how many times to duck before taking your A. *This tip is not found in the text - if you've read this far to study and learn bridge, you will become a great player!*

The Rule of 10: To double or not to double their suit contract? Add together the level of their bid + your # of trumps + the # of honors you have in their trump suit. If you count to 10, double the contract. (Sometimes 9 works too)

The Rule of 11: If the leader has led his 4th card from the top, subtract the number of his card from 11 and that number will tell you how many cards are in the other three hands that are higher than the lead.

The Rule of 15: When opening 3rd or 4th seat, add your points with the number of spades you hold - if you count 15 or more, open 1S. Known as *Cansino Count*; has morphed into *Casino Count*. It is a gamble at times.

The Rule of 17: When partner preempts at the **two** level, add your HCP + the number of trumps you hold. If you get 17 or higher, bid game.

The Rule of 20 + 2: Add the number of your two longest suits with your HCP. If your sum is 20+, open the auction if you have two quick tricks: AA, KQ-KQ, AQ-Kx(x...), etc.

The "Kiss of Death" ... *in a suit contract is 4333 distribution.*
Remember bridge etiquette and have your convention card ready.
And finally, don't lie to your partner... *or you will be searching for another partner.*

THE POINT SCALE: ADD YOUR POINTS TOGETHER - HOW HIGH CAN YOU BID?

CONTRACT		MIN HCP*		ADDITIONAL INFORMATION
Grand Slam	**7NT**	37+		**Declarer must take all 13 tricks**
	7S			Pair must have **all** of the aces
	7H			Missing **3** points *or fewer;* one K or equivalent - QJ, or JJJ.
	7D			The missing K *may* mean this contract depends on 1 finesse.
	7C		Clues:	Part opens 2C & you planned to open 1NT (or equiv HCP) & **vice versa.**
				Part opens 2C & you planned to open & jump in your suit (16+ HCP).
				Partner opens 2NT & you planned to reverse.
				Partner opens 2NT & you planned to open 1NT (17 HCP) & **vice versa**.
				Partner opens 2NT & you planned to open, then jump-shift w/ 19+ HCP.
				Partner opens 1NT & you planned to open, then jump-shift w/ 20+ HCP.
				Partner opens & jumps in his suit or jump shifts, which was your plan.
				*Contract can be made w/ **fewer HCP**: 2 Strong distrib. hands with long, superb suits and void(s) The long running suit(s) make the difference.
Small Slam	**6NT**	33+		**Declarer must take 12 tricks.**
	6S			Dangerous if missing 1 Ace; must have a void/all Ks to compensate.
	6H			Missing **7** points *or fewer;* 2 Ks & a J or equivalent.
	6D			Contract *may* be dependent on 2 finesses; depends on distrib.
	6C		Clues:	Partner opens 2C & you have 10+ HCP.
				Partner opens 2NT & you planned to open the bidding.
				Partner opens 1NT & you planned to open 1NT.
				Partner jump-shifts & you have opening values.
				*Cont. makes w/ **fewer HCP**: 2 Strong distrib. hands (long suits) w/ void(s)
	5NT	28+		Declarer must take **11** tricks.
	5S			
Game in a minor	5H		Clues:	Partner opens & you have more than opening count.
Game in a minor	5D			Partner shows extra HCP by jumps, jump-shifts, or reverses.
	5C			Partner opens 1NT & you have opening count (12+).
				NT & Ms @ 5 level often bid w/ interference by oppo. at game level.
	4NT	25+		Declarer must take **10** tricks
Game in a Major	4S			
Game in a Major	4H		Clues:	Partner opens & you have opening count.
	4D			Partner shows extra HCP by jumps, jump-shifts & reverses. You may be min.
	4C			Partner opens 1NT, you have 10+ HCP & end up in a M.
				Partner TOXs, then bids his own suit & you have 7+ HCP.
Game in NT	3NT	25+		Declarer must take **9** tricks.
				*NT contracts require slightly more HCP than suit contracts because
Partscores	3S	22+		a NT contract cannot add tricks thru ruffing.
	3H		Clues:	Partner opens & you have 8-11 HCP w/ a fit. Partner never shows extra HCP.
	3D			Partner overcalls; you have 15 HCP. Partner never bids again, so he's weak.
	3C			You have extra trumps.
	2NT	22+**		Declarer must take **8** tricks.
	2S	20+		Minimal + minimal
	2H			
	2D			
	2C			
	1NT	20-21+**		Declarer must take **7** tricks.
	1C/D/H/S	18+		Minimal + Minimal

*HIGHLY DISTRIBUTIONAL HANDS & VOIDS **ALTER** THE HCP RANGES, REQUIRING **FEWER** HCP. ADD IN LENGTH & SUPPORT POINTS TO GET THE TRUE PICTURE OF THE VALUE OF YOUR HAND IN A SUIT CONTRACT, ESPECIALLY IF YOU FIT UNUSUALLY WELL WITH PARTNER'S SUITS. THE HCP RANGES ABOVE ARE FOR SEMI-BALANCED HANDS WITH BALANCED TO SEMI-BALANCED SUPPORTING HANDS. BEWARE OF WEAK DOUBLETONS IN UNBID SUITS AS THEY ARE OFTEN THE LEAD. ******SLIGHTLY MORE HCP NEEDED TO MAKE THE LOW NT CONTRACTS SUCCESSFUL.

THE BREAKDOWN OF POINTS - WHAT CAN YOU DO WITH WHAT YOU HAVE?

*The chart can be read **across** to see what you should bid with your points, or it can be read from the bottom upwards to understand what to expect within the point ranges. It is the easiest to understand after attending Lesson 14.*

The Points		All NT Ranges	Opener's Suit Ranges	Responder's Ranges
S	40 Total HCP in deck	40	40	40 **Overcaller's Ranges**
	39	39	39	39 *18-19+ TOX & bid own suit or NT;*
L	38	38	38	38 *Bid game or try for slam if partner*
	37: GRAND slam ↑	37	37	37 *jumps w/ 10+ (may ask for As);*
A	36	36	36	36 *May invite/bid game w/ fit in part's suit*
	35	35	35	35 *& distributional values (void, sing).*
M	34	34	34	34 *If partner doesn't jump after TOX,*
	33: Small slam ↑	33	33	33 *raise his suit **2 levels** to invite.*
G	32	32	32	32
	31	31	31	31 *16-17 TOX & raise part's suit **1 level***
A	30	30	30 2C↑	30 *to invite game w/ support;*
	29	29	29 2C	29 *Bid game if part jumps after TOX.*
M	28: minor game ↑	28	28 2C	28
	27	27	27 2C	27 *15-17 Bid a long suit, 1NT or TOX.*
E	26	26	26 2C	26 *Invite after TOX w/ 16-17 HCP.*
	25: Major/NT game ↑	25 2C, rebid 3NT ↑	25 2C	25 *Game if partner jumps (10+).*
P				
A	24 ↓	24 2C, rebid 3NT	M 24 2C	24 *12-14 Bid good 5+ suit at the 2 level,*
R	23	23 2C, rebid 2NT	A 23 2C	23 *or **X** & pass. May invite game w/ 14*
T	22	22 2C, rebid 2NT	X+ 22 2C: Forcing bid, any shape↑	22 *& dist. value if part jumps over TOX.*
S	21	21 2NT Opening	M 21 2NT; *May* open 2C (so no pass)	21
C	20	20 2NT Opening	A 20 2NT; 1/Suit-jump to 3N/game	20 *8-17 Overcall at the 1 level w/*
O	19	19 1/1, rebid 2NT	X 19 Jump shift or bid game	19 ↑ *a lead-worthy suit (2+ honors)*
R	18 ↑	18 1/1, rebid 2NT	M 18 Jump to 2NT; Invite game	18 Ask for As with this strength,
E		*Resp. asks for As/bids 4NT*	E w/ support; Bid @ 3 level	especially with a long suit; slam
O	17	17 1NT Opening	D 17 Invite/jump in suit/reverse	17 Bid game or slam
P	16	16 1NT Opening	16 Jump: partner's/own suit	M 16 Jump shift
E	15	15 1NT Opening	M 15 Bid game if invited & at	A 15 Reverse (16+ per PA)
N	14	14 *Responder* bids	I 14 top of range (14-15)	X 14 New suit at the 3 level
I	13	13 *3NT; max (13-15)*	N 13 W/ 12-13, no 3 level bids:	13 Jump to game in own/part's suit
N	12	12 *Opener* rebids 1NT:	12 Minimum opening count	M 12 Jump w/ 6+ in suit; bid game
G		Bal. hand 12-14	O Open & rebid 6 c suit	E w/ 12 HCP and distrib. value.
	11	11 *Responder's* 2NT	T 11 Rule of 20+2	D 11 Jump w/ 6+ in suit; invite w/ 11
	10 AVERAGE HAND	10+ range: Med (10-12)	H 10 Rule of 20+2, or	10 Bid new suit @ 2 level.
		10- *Responder's* 1NT	E Preempt **V**, NV	M Raise partner 1 level with fit, or
B	9	9 range - a minimum	R 9 Preempt **V**, NV	I 9 bid 1NT w/ no fit. May bid a new
E	8	8 bid; no 4 c M over	O 8 Preempt **V**, NV	N 8 suit at level 1: 1S-2S, 1S-1NT,
L	7	7 minor opening, no	P 7 Preempt NV	7 1H-1NT, 1H-1S, 1C-1D/H/S, 1D-1H/S.
O	6	6 fit over M opening.	E 6 Preempt NV	6 *No 2 level bids unless preempt*
W	5	5	N 5 Preempt NV	5 Bid if forced by a X, or if partner
A	4	4	I 4	4 opens 1NT (may transfer), 2NT
V	3	3	N 3	3 or 2C. May bid if on the high
E	2	2	G 2	2 end w/ many trumps & partner
R	1	1	S 1	1 continues bidding over your
A	0	0	0	0 passes (add in distrib pts.)
G				
E		START HERE ↑	START HERE ↑	START HERE ↑

Partscore: Minimum & Minimum, Minimum- (12-13) & Medium- (10-11), Medium & Minimum- (6-7)
Game: Minimum & Medium+, Minimum & Maximum, Medium+ & Medium, Min- & Max, Med & Min+, Max & Min-
Small slam: Medium & Maximum+, Maximum+ & Medium, Maximum & Maximum
GRAND slam: Maximum+ & Maximum+

***ALL** contracts subject to distribution. Many 2-suited or unusual hands may be bid higher than their points indicate.*

HCP vs. Extreme distribution (one or two long suits & a void)**: The two are near equivalent in value.**

Instructions For Filling out a Convention Card

Black lines: typical SA (no alert), Blue lines: announcements, Red lines: alerts
Use this list when filling out your Convention Card. **Two sample cards follow - old and new style.**
You and your partner should fill these out together & **you should always have matching cards when you play.**

NAME: Find the space where you write your name, top right. Jot down your name and partner's name. DONE.

GENERAL APPROACH: You will write "Standard American" on the line for the bridge system you play; Check the box for 2C as a forcing bid. DONE. *American Standard, as some players write, is also correct.*

NO TRUMP OPENING BIDS: On the top blue line write 15-17. The blue line means you **announce** the point range as "15 to 17." Skip down to 2C and check Stayman; 2D transfer to Hs, check box; 2H transfer to Ss, check box, remember to announce transfers; 2NT write in 8-9 HCP; DONE.

2NT: Write in 20-21. You will open any bigger hands 2C, not 3NT (you'll need to explain to partner 2NT and 3NT rebids over 2C). Check the Jacoby box since you would transfer over 2NT. DONE.

MAJOR OPENING: You expect 5 of a M in any seat so check the 5 box twice; a double raise (which is a limit raise) is invitational per PA; Check weak in After Overcall section (a jump is now preemptive since we cuebid, which is a limit raise+), skip down to 2NT and check invitational and write in 11-12; at 3NT write in 13-15. DONE.

MINOR OPENING: You expect 4+ D if partner opens 1D (expectations are not always met), and 3+ Cs if partner opens 1C, so check the corresponding boxes (see the bottom of page 16 for clarification on opening minors); A double raise (which is a limit raise) is invitational - check box; After Overcall a double raise is weak (preemptive) since you may cuebid to show strength, so check the weak box; check the box for "frequently bypass 4+ Ds - this means we would bid a 4 card M over a D suit; skip down to NT responses and write in the 1NT area 6-10- ; write in the 2NT area 11-12 and check invitational; in the 3NT area write 13-15. DONE.

2C BOX: Write 22+ in the 2C area; check 2D Resp as waiting; write in 2H = Bust, < 3 HCP and 2NT = Heart suit and 8+ HCP in the RESPONSES/REBIDS section; 2D, 2H, 2S are each filled in as 5 to 10 HCP and check the weak box for all 3. DONE.

OTHER CONV. CALLS: Check Weak Jump Shifts in Comp. & Not in Comp. DONE. **Proceed to the top left side.**

SPECIAL DOUBLES: Negative, check box and write in 3S (or your own partnership agreement). DONE.

NO TRUMP OVERCALLS: Direct: write 15-17 and check "Systems On" - this means you may bid the PIG, Stayman, or Transfers as if partner had opened 1NT, UNLESS the responder bids; Balancing (Pass-out) write 12+. DONE.

SIMPLE OVERCALLS: Write in 8-17 HCP; DONE. With 18+ HCP, you would either X then bid your own suit, X then bid NT, or X then raise in partner's suit. FYI: The advancer may cuebid the opener's suit to show support and 10+ HCP. *You will eventually need to decide whether a new suit is forcing and what a jump raise means.*

DEFENSE VS NOTRUMP: Write in NATURAL diagonally across the box. This means you would bid a long suit with 10+ HCP. DONE.

JUMP OVERCALL: Check weak box. DONE.

OPENING PREEMPTS: Check sound and write Vul under it. DONE.

OVER OPP'S T/O DOUBLE: Jump shift - check the weak box; DONE.

DIRECT CUEBID: Leave blank. DONE.

VS OPENING PREEMPTS DOUBLE IS: Check the takeout box. Write 16+ on the "other" line at bottom. DONE.

SLAM CONVENTIONS: Check Gerber and Blackwood. DONE.

LEADS: Circle the A in the AKx sequences, as we lead the A to show the K. The rest are standard leads. Length leads: check 4th best for both suits and NT. SIGNALS: Check the boxes **only** if you are using signals. DONE.

- **Do not use this sheet to keep score.** Save it to **reuse** each game so you don't have to mark a new one every time you play. You may have two or three partners and use a separate convention card with each partner.
- **Going over the convention card** is a quick way to generate agreements between you and a new partner.
- **When you fill out a score sheet,** which is found on the opposite side of the convention card, first write down your number and direction *somewhere* on the sheet so you don't forget them.

Building Bridges © 2022 Jeanne R. Wamack May not be reproduced in any form.

A sample of the older convention card:

On the other side of this card, write your pair number & direction, such as **3W**.

SPECIAL DOUBLES
After Overcall: Penalty ☐ _____
Negative ☑ thru __3S__
Responsive ☐ : thru ____ Maximal ☐
Support: Dbl.☐ thru ____ Redbl ☐
Card-showing ☐ Min. Offshape T/O ☐

SIMPLE OVERCALL
1 level __8+__ to __17__ HCP (usually)
often 4 cards ☐   very light style ☐
Responses
New Suit: Forcing ☐ NFConst ☐ NF ☐
Jump Raise: Forcing ☐ Inv.☐ Weak ☑

JUMP OVERCALL
Strong ☐   Intermediate ☐   Weak ☑

OPENING PREEMPTS
    Sound   Light   Very Light
3/4-bids   ☑   ☐   ☐
Conv./Resp. __VUL__

DIRECT CUEBID
    OVER: Minor   Major
Natural   ☐   ☐
Strong T/O   ☐   ☐
Michaels   ☐   ☐

SLAM CONVENTIONS
Gerber ☑ :   4NT: Blackwood ☑   RKC ☐   1430 ☐
_____
vs Interference: DOPI ☐   DEPO ☐   Level: _____   ROPI ☐

NOTRUMP OVERCALLS
Direct: __15__ to __17__ Systems on ☑
Conv. _____
Balancing: __12+__ to ____
Jump to 2NT: Minors ☐ 2 Lowest ☐
Conv. _____

DEFENSE VS NOTRUMP
vs: N
2♣   __A__
2♦   __T__
2♥   __U__
2♠   __R__
Dbl: __A__
Other __L__

OVER OPP'S T/O DOUBLE
New Suit Forcing: 1 level ☐ 2 level ☐
Jump Shift: Forcing ☐ Inv. ☐ Weak ☑
Redouble implies no fit ☐
2NT Over   Limit+   Limit   Weak
Majors   ☐   ☐   ☐
Minors   ☐   ☐   ☐
Other _____

VS Opening Preempts Double Is
Takeout ☑ thru ____   Penalty ☐
Conv. Takeout: _____
Lebensohl 2NT Response ☐
Other: __16+ HCP__

NAMES QUEEN JEANNE (1234567) & THE KING (7654321)

GENERAL APPROACH
STANDARD AMERICAN
Two Over One: Game Forcing ☐ Game Forcing Except When Suit Rebid ☐
VERY LIGHT: Openings ☐ 3rd Hand ☐ Overcalls ☐ Preempts ☐
FORCING OPENING: 1♣ ☐ 2♣ ☑ Natural 2 Bids ☐ Other ☐

NOTRUMP OPENING BIDS
1NT __15__ to __17__
3♣ _____
3♦ _____
3♥ _____
3♠ _____
5-card Major common ☐
System on over ____
2♣ Stayman ☑ Puppet ☐
2♦ Transfer to ♥ ☑
   Forcing Stayman ☐
2♥ Transfer to ♠ ☑
2♠
2NT __8-9 HCP__

4♦, 4♥ Transfer ☐
Smolen ☐
Lebensohl ☐ (____ denies)
Neg. Double ☐ _____
Other: _____

2NT __20__ to __21__
Puppet Stayman ☐
Transfer Responses:
Jacoby ☑   Texas ☐
3♠ _____

3NT ____ to ____

Conventional NT Openings

MAJOR OPENING
Expected Min. Length   4   5
1st/2nd   ☐   ☑
3rd/4th   ☐   ☑
RESPONSES
Double Raise: Force ☐ Inv.☑ Weak ☐
After Overcall: Force ☐ Inv.☐ Weak ☑
Conv. Raise: 2NT ☐ 3NT ☐ Splinter ☐
Other: _____
1NT: Forcing ☐ Semi-forcing ☐
2NT: Forcing ☐ Inv.☑ __11__ to __12__
3NT: __13+__ to ____
Drury ☐ : Reverse ☐ 2-Way ☐ Fit ☐
Other: _____

MINOR OPENING
                               NF
Expected Min. Length 4   3   0-2 Conv.
1♣   ☐   ☑   ☐
1♦   ☑   ☐   ☐
RESPONSES
Double Raise: Force ☐ Inv.☑ Weak ☐
After Overcall: Force ☐ Inv.☐ Weak ☑
Forcing Raise: J/S in other minor ☐
Single raise ☐ Other: _____
Frequently bypass 4+ ♦ ☑
1NT/1♣ __6__ to __10-__
2NT Forcing ☐ Inv.☑ __11__ to __12__
3NT: __13+__ to ____
Other: _____

DESCRIBE
2♣ __22+__ to ____ HCP
   Strong ☑ Other ☐
   2♦ Resp: Neg ☐ Waiting ☑

2♦ __5__ to __10__ HCP
Natural: Weak ☑ Intermediate ☐ Strong ☐ Conv.☐

2♥ __5__ to __10__ HCP
Natural: Weak ☑ Intermediate ☐ Strong ☐ Conv.☐

2♠ __5__ to __10__ HCP
Natural: Weak ☑ Intermediate ☐ Strong ☐ Conv.☐

OTHER CONV. CALLS: New Minor Forcing ☐ 2-Way NMF ☐
Weak Jump Shifts: In Comp. ☑ Not in Comp. ☑
4th Suit Forcing: 1 Rd. ☐ Game ☐ _____

RESPONSES/REBIDS
2H=BUST; <3 HCP
2NT=Hs & 8+ HCP

2NT Force ☐ New Suit NF ☐
2NT Force ☐ New Suit NF ☐
2NT Force ☐ New Suit NF ☐

LEADS (circle card led, if not in bold)
versus Suits	versus Notrump
x x x x x x	x x x x x x
x x x x x x x x	x x x x x x x x
(A)K x T 9 x	(A)K J x A Q J x
K Q x K J T x	A J T 9 A T 9 x
Q J x K T 9 x	K Q J x K Q T 9
J T 9 Q T 9 x	Q J T x Q T 9 x
K Q T 9	J T 9 x T 9 x x

LENGTH LEADS:
4th Best vs SUITS ☑ vs NT ☑
3rd/5th Best vs SUITS ☐ vs NT ☐
              Attitude vs NT ☐

Primary signal to partner's leads
Attitude ☐   Count ☐   Suit preference ☐

DEFENSIVE CARDING
                vs SUITS vs NT
Standard: ☐   ☐
  Except ☐ _____
_____
Upside-Down:
      count   ☐   ☐
      attitude   ☐   ☐

FIRST DISCARD
Lavinthal   ☐   ☐
Odd/Even   ☐   ☐
_____

OTHER CARDING
Smith Echo   ☐   ☐
Trump Suit Pref.   ☐   ☐
Foster Echo   ☐   ☐

SPECIAL CARDING   ☐   PLEASE ASK

All these agreements are what we've learned to play in *Building Bridges*. Don't worry if your card isn't completely filled out right now, you can add new skills and conventions later. *Can you believe how much you've learned?*
Remember that the lower left side (defensive carding, also known as signaling) isn't filled out - check what you and your partner have agreed to do, should you be signaling. If you are not yet signaling, leave the spaces blank.

Building Bridges © 2022 Jeanne R. Wamack May not be reproduced in any form.

A sample of the new convention card:

DOUBLES
- Negative ☑ Thru **3S** Penalty ☐
- Responsive ☐ Thru _____ Maximal ☐
- Support ☐ Thru _____ Rdbl ☐
- T/O Style **0-2 in opener's suit**
- Other _____

OVERCALLS
- 1-Lvl **8** to **17** Often 4 Cards ☐
- 2-Lvl **12** to **17**
- Jump Overcalls: Wk ☑ Int ☐ Str ☐
- Conv ☐
- Responses
- New Suit: F ☐ NFConst ☐ NF ☐ Tfr ☐
- Jump Raise: Wk ☐ Mixed ☐ Inv ☐
- Cuebids **10+** _____ Support ☑
- Other _____

DIRECT CUEBIDS
	Vs: Art	Quasi	Nat	Nat
	♣♦	♣♦	♣♦	♥♠
Michaels	☐	☐	☐	☐
Natural	☐	☐	☐	☐
Other	☐	☐	☐	☐

Describe _____

PREEMPTS
- 3-Level Style (Seat/Vul) _____
- Resp _____
- 4-Level Style _____
- Resp _____
- 4♣/4♦ Tfr ☐ Other _____

SLAMS
- 4♣ Gerber: Directly Over NT ☑ Over NT Seq ☑ Non-NT Seq ☐ _____
- 4NT: Blackwood ☑ RKC 0314 ☐ RKC 1430 ☐
- Control Bids _____
- Vs Interference _____
- Other _____

CARDING
Suits		NT
☐	Standard – Attitude	☐
☐	Standard – Count	☐
☑	Upside Down – Attitude	☑
☐	Upside Down – Count	☐

- Exceptions _____
- Other Carding: _____
- Smith Echo: Suits ☐ NT ☐ Reverse ☐
- Trump Signals _____

LEADS vs SUITS
CIRCLE CARD LED (if not bold):
Length Leads: 4th ☑ 3rd/5th ☐ 3rd/Low ☐
Attitude ☐ Small from xx ☐

x x x**Ⓧ**x x x x x x x**Ⓧ**x
H x x H x x**Ⓧ** H x**Ⓧ**x

After 1st Trick _____
Honor Leads:
ⒶKQ x (+) Varies ☐ _____
K**Ⓠ**Q x Q**🅙** x J**🅣** x T**🄐** 9 x
Interior Seq:
K J**🅣** x K T**🅙** x Q T**🄐** 9 x
Exceptions _____

NT OVERCALLS
- Direct 1NT **15** to **17** Systems On ☑
- Balance 1N **12+** to _____ Systems On ☐
- Conv ☐
- Jump to 2NT: 2 Lowest Unbid ☐
- Other _____

vs 1NT OPENING
	Strong		Weak
Dbl	**N**	Dbl	
2♣	**A**	2♣	
2♦	**T**	2♦	
2♥	**U**	2♥	
2♠		2♠	**R**
2NT		2NT	**A**
Other			**L**

vs TAKEOUT DBL
- New Suit F: 2 Lvl ☐ Tfr ☐
- Jump Shift: Wk ☐ Inv ☐ F ☐ Fit ☐
- Rdbl: 10+ ☐ Conv ☐
- 2NT Over: Nat Raise Range
  - ♣♦ ☐ ☐ ___ to ___
  - ♥♠ ☐ ☐ ___ to ___
- Other _____

vs PREEMPTS
- 2NT Overcall _____
- T/O Dbl Thru **3S** Penalty ☐
- 2NT Lebensohl Resp ☐
- Cuebid _____
- Jump Overcalls _____
- Other _____

SIGNALS
- Primary Signals to:
  - Declarer's Lead / Partner's Lead
  - Attitude ☐ / ☐
  - Count ☐ / ☐
  - Suit Preference ☐ / ☐
- Exceptions _____
- First Discard: Std ☐ Upside Down ☑
- Lavinthal ☐ Odd/Even ☐ Other ☐

LEADS vs NT
CIRCLE CARD LED (if not bold):
Length Leads: 4th ☑ 3rd/5th ☐ 3rd/Low ☐
Attitude ☐ 2nd from xxxx(+) ☐

x x x x x x**Ⓧ**x x x x x x**Ⓧ**x
H x x H x**Ⓧ** H x x**Ⓧ**

After 1st Trick _____
Honor Leads:
A K x x (+) Varies ☑ _____
K**Ⓠ**Q J x K Q**🅣** 9 Q**🅙** T x J**🅣** 9 x
Interior Seq:
A **Ⓠ**J x A J**🅣** x K T**🅙** x Q T**🄐** 9 x
Exceptions _____

OVERVIEW
Names **QUEEN JEANNE 1234567 & THE KING 7654321**
General Approach **STANDARD AMERICAN**
Min Expected HCP when Balanced: Opening **12** Responding **6**
Forcing Open: 1♣ ☐ 2♣ ☑ Other _____ 1NT Open: Str ☑ Wk ☐ Variable ☐
Bids That May Require Preparation _____

MINORS
1♣ Min Length: 5 ☐ 4 ☐ 3 ☐ NF 2 ☑ (4432 only ☐) NF 1 ☐ NF 0 ☐ Art F ☐
Resp _____ Transfer Resp ☐

1♦ **4+** _____ Bypass 5+ ☑ Raises
1NT **6** to **10-**   Single: NF ☑ Inv+ ☐ GF ☐
2NT **10+** to **12**   Jump: Wk ☐ Mixed ☐ Inv ☐
                                           After Overcall: Wk ☑ Mixed ☐ Inv ☐

1♦ Min Length: 5 ☐ 4 ☑ 3 ☐ Unbal ☐ NF 2 ☐ NF 1 ☐ NF 0 ☐ Art F ☐
Resp _____ Same as over 1♣ ☑

                                           Raises
1NT ___ to ___   Single: NF ☐ Inv+ ☐ GF ☐
2NT ___ to ___   Jump: Wk ☐ Mixed ☐ Inv ☐
                                           After Overcall: Wk ☐ Mixed ☐ Inv ☐

MAJORS
1♥/♠   Art Raises: 2NT ☐ 3NT ☐ Splinter ☐
1st/2nd Length: 4 ☐ 5 ☑   Other _____
3rd/4th Length: 4 ☐ 5 ☑   Drury: 2♣ ☑ 2♦ ☐ In Comp ☐
1NT: F ☐ Semi-F ☐ Bypass ♠ ☐
                                           Jump Raise: Wk ☐ Mixed ☐ Inv ☑
Other _____   After Overcall: Wk ☑ Mixed ☐ Inv ☐

NOTRUMP
1NT 15 to **17** (Seat/Vul) _____ **1NT** ___ to ___ (Same Resp: Y ☐ N ☐)
5-Card Major ☐ Sys On vs _____   3♣ _____
2♣: Stayman ☑ Puppet ☐ Other _____   3♦ _____
2♦: Nat ☐ Tfr ☑ Other _____   3♥ _____
2♥: Nat ☐ Tfr ☑ Other _____   3♠ _____
2♠: Nat ☐ Tfr ☑ Other _____
2NT: Nat ☑ Tfr ☐ Other _____   Other _____
Smolen ☐ Tfr: 4♣ ☐ 4♦ ☐ 4♥ ☐
Dbl: Neg ☐ Pen ☐ Other _____   Lebensohl ☐: _____

2NT 20 to **21** Puppet ☐ 3♠ ☐ _____
Conv ☐   Tfr: 3Lvl ☐ 4Lvl ☐   Neg Dbl ☐ Other _____

3NT ___ to ___   One Suit ☐

2♣ 22+ to ___   2♦ Neg ☐ Waiting ☑
                                           Steps ☐ _____ 2♥ Neg ☑
Very Str ☑ Str ☐ Nat ☐ Conv ☐   Other _____

2 LEVEL
2♦ 5 to **10** _____ New Suit NF ☐
Wk ☑ Int ☐ Str ☐ Conv ☐ Rebids over 2NT: _____ Other _____

2♥ 5 to **10** _____ New Suit NF ☐
Wk ☑ Int ☐ Str ☐ 2 Suits ☐ Rebids over 2NT: _____ Other _____

2♠ 5 to **10** _____ New Suit NF ☐
Wk ☑ Int ☐ Str ☐ 2 Suits ☐ Rebids over 2NT: _____ Other _____

OTHER
Jump Shift Resp **WEAK**
Vs (Very)Str Open _____ NMF ☐ 2Way NMF ☐ XYZ ☐ 4thSF: 1Rnd ☐ GF ☐

Questions to ask a new partner

Any time you sit down with a new partner to play bridge, you need to ask some questions to make sure each of you understands the other's bidding. If you know of a bid that is confusing or has caused you difficulties in the past, ask your new partner how *he* would have bid. Make your own list of questions/agreements, and add to it as you learn more bridge.

First, go through the convention card and check the point ranges, bids, rebids, leads and conventions that each of you play. Discuss how you play and what you promise with each bid, and let partner do the same. If you are in disagreement about point ranges, establish the boundaries with which you are both comfortable.

Suggestions for "Need to Know" items...

I play Standard American. With how many HCP do you open the bidding at the one level? I open with 12+ HCP or Rule of 20.

Conventions or special bids I play: Rule of 20+2, Preempts (weak twos), Stayman, Jacoby Transfers, strong 2C opener, TOX (takeout double), negative double, cuebid, Blackwood, and Gerber.

What is your opening 1NT count? Mine is 15-17. I open 2NT with 20-21 HCP.

Are all conventions (as in Stayman and Jacoby) **off** with interference? Then do you respond Stan. Amer.? Walk me through your bids.

I do not open 3NT, but I open all hands with **22+** points 2C. I will **rebid 2NT** to show 22-23 HCP, or **jump to 3NT** showing 24+ HCP if I have a balanced hand.

If I open a M, I always show 5+ in the M in any seat.

How many Ss do you promise over my 1H opener? How many Hs and HCP do you promise over my 1S opening bid?

A jump in your M shows <u>what</u> if no interference? (I play it as a Limit Raise with <u>4</u> of M) Minor? (I play Limit Raise with 5+ of m)

When you open a minor, how do you choose which m to open? I promise at least 4 Ds with a 1D opener, and at least 3 Cs if I open 1C, OR **more** Cs than Ds, with two rare exceptions. I do not bid a short club. Responding, I give preference to a 4+ M rather than bid a <u>long D suit.</u>

What are the point ranges for your 1NT, 2NT, and 3NT <u>responses</u>? Do you make these responses over both Ms and ms? Over a minor opening bid it means I have no 4+ c M. Over a M opening bid, I don't have support, and over a 1H bid, < 4Ss.

What are your requirements for V/NV preempts? I bid strong preempts when vul. (two of the top three or three of the top five honors and 8+ HCP), but I could be weaker when NV.

What are your requirements for overcalls level one and level two? I play Level 1 = 8+ HCP, Level 2 = 12+ HCP, esp when vul., *maybe* 11 HCP, NV, with a long suit (6+) and shortness. 1NT direct seat=15-17 HCP and pass-out or balancing seat= 12+ HCP.

What distribution do you promise with a Takeout Double (TOX)? I promise a full opening hand, 0-2 in opening suit, and even distribution with at least Jxx in every suit. I will TOX with 4/3 in the Ms over a m opener. If <u>you</u> TOX, I will jump with 10+ HCP and bid game with 12+ HCP.

If you are an overcaller with 18 HCP, how do you show me your strong hand?

How high do you play negative doubles? I will negative X thru 3S in case of a preempt by opponents.

How many HCP do you expect me to have if I double a two level preempt in the **first** seat? (16+) Balancing (last) seat? (12+)

Signaling: Discards? (standard, upside-down, or other) Count? (High/low to show a doubleton when **leading** your suit)

What is your defense if the opponents open a strong (15-17) 1NT? What if they bid a weak 1NT? I bid either "natural".

Do you double an artificial bid for a lead?   (Stayman, Jacoby Transfers, Blackwood, & Gerber)

What does a jump in your own suit (as a rebid) mean, as in point range? I will have 16-18 HCP, or 15+ with an unbal. hand.

What do you hold when the bidding goes 1 any suit/1 any suit/2NT and we are the only bidders? I promise 18-19 HCP.

What is your point range for opener's jump-shifts? I promise 19+ HCP.

I do/do not play reverses. If we decide to play reverses, what is the minimum point count?

How many points do you promise when you bid a new suit at the two level when I open, no interference? I promise 10+ HCP.

<u>When</u> do you add in support (distribution) points and <u>how many</u> for voids, singletons, doubletons and long, good suits in the opening seat, or as a responder?

Building Bridges © 2022 Jeanne R. Wamack May not be reproduced in any form.

BASIC BIDDING STUDY GUIDE

OPENING BID: 12-21 HCP →	*Minimum Response: "Stop" bid*	*Medium+ Response: Invitational bid*
1. A 5+ card Major, or equally nice,	6-9 (or 10- in NT) **HCP** (NF) Examples:	**10+ HCP**, no upper limit on points as yet.
2. 1NT (see † for 1NT responses)	1 any suit - simple raise (1H - 2H)	**New** suit bid at the 2 level Ex: (1S - **2C**),
3. Longer m: 4+Ds/3+Cs	1 any suit - 1NT (1C/D/H/S - 1NT)	See **Opener's REBIDS** below left.*

Limit Raise:	*NT Responses to opener:*	†*1NT responses: PIG, Stayman or Transfers (see guide card 2)*
10-12 HCP & Invites:	1 any suit - 1NT = 6-9 (10-)	**IF** the responder has *NO 4 or 5 c M suit*, he bids the **PIG**:
shows <u>4</u> of M/<u>5-6</u> of m	1 any suit - 2NT = (10+) 11-12	0-7 HCP: **Pass**; 8-9 HCP: **Invite** (2NT); 10+ HCP: **Game** (3NT)
Ex: 1H - 3H	1 any suit - 3NT = 13+ HCP	**Stayman:** 1NT - 2C = Responder has a least one 4 c M & 8+ HCP
		Jacoby Transfer: 1NT - 2D = Responder has 5 Hs, unknown HCP
Unknown bids: 1/1 bids - could be min, med, OR max.		1NT - 2H = Responder has 5 Ss, unknown HCP
Unlimited Bids: 1/1 (1C-1H) & 2/1 (1S-2D) bids.		*Defense over **interference** obstructing S'man or a Jacoby transfer:*
Opener MUST bid again, unless intervening bid		Bid a 5 c suit at the <u>lowest</u> level if weak, <u>jump</u> if strong (game force)

TWO MORE OPENING BIDS:

4. Rule of 20 + 2	**5. Preemptive Bids**	**Overcalls**
If # in 2 longest suits + # of HCP = 20	**2 level:** NV 5-10 HCP, with good trumps	**Level 1:** 8+ HCP & a 5+, 2 honor suit
...and your HCP are in your long suits	V 8-10 HCP, with...	**Level 2:** 12+ HCP & a 5+, 2 honor suit
...and you have 2 Quick Tricks:	2 of top 3 *or* 3 of the top 5 honors	**Takeout X** (TOX): Full opener and
AA, AK, A+KQ, KQ+KQ	**3 level:** 7-11 HCP, 7 trumps with honors	shortness (0-2) in the opener's suit.
Open the auction at the 1 level	**4 level:** 7-11 HCP; 8 trumps with honors	**1NT** direct seat = 15-17 HCP & stoppers
		1NT pass out seat = 12+ HCP & stoppers

Opener's REBIDS:	**Always...**	**There are 13 Trumps:** Count
1. Rebid suit with 6+ 2. Bid 2nd suit w/ 4+	Bid 4 card Majors "Up the hill" (Hs then Ss)	them & know which ones are
3. Bid NT if balanced 4. Raise partner's suit	Bid 5 card Majors "Down the mtn" (Ss then Hs)	missing. Usually draw ASAP.

Distribution Points added AFTER GOLDEN FIT: NEVER added in NT

SET:	NV	V	NVX	VX	**Opener & Responder with 3 Trumps**	-	**Responder with 4+ trumps**
-1	-50	-100	-100	-200	**1 point**	**Doubleton**	**1 point** *Add with careful consideration of*
-2	-100	-200	-300	-500	**2 points**	**Singleton**	**3 points** *actual hand strength; unbal hand,*
-3	-150	-300	-500	-800	**3 points**	**Void**	**5 points*** *strength in suits, mid-range cards.*
-4	-200	-400	-800	-1100			
-5	-250	-500	-1100	-1400			

Length Points (add ASAP)**:** Opener: **+1** for superb 5 c suit; **+2** for good 6 c suit; **+3** for 7

LEADS:	Partner's suit	**Opener**	**STRENGTH**	**Responder**
	Top of a sequence	12-15	Min hand	6-9 (10- NT response)
	4th card down in longest and strongest suit	16-18	Med hand	11 -12 (also 10+)
	Trump suit in partscore	19+	Max hand	13+

SCORING: See page 19

Minors=20 points each;   Majors=30 points each;   NT: 1st trick= 40 points, rest=30 points each   **GAME = 100 points**

Contracts:	**Combined HCP Requirements:**	**Title:**	**Bonus:**	**Vul/NonVul:**
Level one contract	18-20 HCP *Add 1-2 HCP for a NT contract*	Partscore	+50	NV or V
Level two contract	20-22 HCP *Add 1-2 HCP for a NT contract*	Partscore	+50	NV or V
Level three contract	22-24 HCP *Add 1-2 HCP for NT,* **3NT=Game**	Partscore M/m	+50	NV or V
Level four contract	25-28 HCP	**Game:** M or 3NT	+300 NV	+500 V
Level five contract	28-31 HCP *Borderline for slam if unbalanced*	**Game** in a minor	+300 NV	+500 V
Level six contract	31-34 HCP *33+ HCP if both hands are **balanced***	Small slam	+500 NV	+750 V
Level seven contract	35+ HCP *37+ HCP if both hands are **balanced***	Grand slam	+1000 NV	+1500 V

Why are more points required for NT?   The declarer cannot gain **extra** tricks from ruffing, and he's **balanced** - no long suits to run.
Why are 28-31 points borderline for slam?   If one partner is unbalanced (a long, strong suit and a void), his hand is **extra** valuable.
As you can see from the bonuses - DO NOT MISS YOUR GAMES, ESPECIALLY YOUR VULNERABLE GAMES!

Building Bridges © 2022 Jeanne R. Wamack May not be reproduced in any form.

STAYMAN: *Searching for a 4/4 fit*   Bid 4 card majors "**Up the hill.**"   *Optional if you are 4333.*

Requirements: **8+ HCP** & at least **one 4 card major.** Stayman (2C) asks, "Partner, do you have a 4 card major?"

OPENER	RESPONDER	MEANING
1NT	2C (2C = Stayman, not clubs)	"I have at least one 4 card major." *The opener will tell more about his hand...*

Answers:
2D — "I have NO 4 card major." *The Resp will bid 2NT (8-9 HCP) or 3NT (10+)*
2H — "I have 4 hearts & *may also have 4 spades.*"
2S — "I have 4 spades, but do not have 4 hearts because *I skipped them.*"

RESPONDER:
If you get a "**HIT**" on your suit, tell your HCP **in your suit**:
- 1NT - 2C - 2H - **3H** "I have **8-9** HCP. Do we have game?"
- 1NT - 2C - 2H - **4H** "I have **10+** HCP. We have game."
- 1NT - 2C - 2S - **3S** "I have **8-9** HCP. Do we have game?"
- 1NT - 2C - 2S - **4S** "I have **10+** HCP. We have game."

If you **DO NOT** get a hit on your suit, **tell your HCP in NT**:
- 1NT - 2C - 2H - **2NT** " I have **8-9** HCP (& 4 spades)."
- 1NT - 2C - 2H - **3NT** "I have **10+** HCP (& 4 spades)."
- *The opener can bid a SPADE contract if he also has 4 Ss.*
- 1NT - 2C - 2S - **2NT** "I have **8-9** HCP (& 4 hearts)."
- 1NT - 2C - 2S - **3NT** "I have **10+** HCP (& 4 hearts)."

† *Opener's Final Bid Chart:*
The opener will bid **game** over a 2NT/3M bid with **17 HCP**, consider game with a **good 16 HCP**, and will pass with **15 HCP**.

JACOBY TRANSFER: *Tells partner you have a 5 card suit*   **NO** minimum HCP requirement

OPENER	RESPONDER	MEANING	
1NT	2D (Opener says "**HEARTS**")	"I have 5 **hearts**; bid 2H at your next bid."	*Resp. bids suit **1 below** his suit &*
1NT	2H (Opener says "**SPADES**")	"I have 5 **spades**; bid 2S at your next bid."	*Resp. wants the big hand hidden.*

RESPONDER: After the transfer, the responder does "**THE PIG**"
- With 0-7 HCP — **P**ASS
- With 8-9 HCP — **I**NVITE (bids **2NT**)
- With 10+ HCP — **G**AME (bids **3NT**)

P: The responder **passes** if *weak*, as the transfer provides a better contract than a weak 1NT, even with a 5/2 fit.
I: The responder **invites** with **2NT** because the responder's 5 card suit could be the opener's **WORST** suit. Over 2NT, the opener will pass, bid 3M, 3NT, or 4M, depending on his HCP *(see † Opener's Final Bid Chart in Stayman section)* AND his holding in the transferred suit (support = 3-4 pieces).
G: The responder makes sure the team reaches game with **3NT**, & the opener will pass or correct to 4M with M support (3-4).

IF THE RESPONDER HAS NO 4 (& 8 HCP) or 5 CARD MAJOR, HE BIDS THE "PIG" DIRECTLY

With 0-7 HCP,	PASS	
With 8-9 HCP	INVITE...	Responder bids 2NT
With 10+ HCP	GAME...	Responder bids 3NT

WITH INTERFERENCE:

The responder reverts to STANDARD AMERICAN, except for Stayman, which may be shown with a double; 8 HCP required.
He bids his **5+** card suit, *M or m,* at the **lowest level** with **< 8** HCP. Opener passes.
The responder will **jump** with a **good** 5+ card M suit & **9-10+** HCP - a game forcing bid. The opener will pass, bid 3NT or 4M.
He can also bid NT: With 8-9 HCP, he'll bid 2NT & with 10+ HCP he'll bid 3NT... It is a partnership agreement if the NT bids show **stoppers in the interfering suit**.

APPENDIX B

Appendix B is for the **advancing player** seeking to improve his or her knowledge and understanding of the game. No peeking until you have played the game for a while, or have spent time studying the previous portion of this book. Appendix B is not for the frail or faint of heart.

Forcing bids - further information	106
Non-Forcing bids - further information	106
Penalty doubles	107
Miscellaneous	107
Tournament tips	107

Building Bridges © 2022 Jeanne R. Wamack May not be reproduced in any form.

Forcing Bids

You may be unsure about which bids are forcing bids, which doubles are for penalty, or what certain bids promise. The following lists should help you with your questions, but they are incomplete as every situation cannot be represented. For further explanation, consult a bridge book specific to your area of interest.

NF=Non-forcing, **F**=Forcing, **GF**=Game force, but typically in a M or NT, not in a m.

1. **An artificial bid** forces one round: Stayman, Jacoby Transfers, 2C opener, Blackwood, Gerber, & cuebids. Many responses force at least one round, but not all do.
2. A **reverse by the opener** forces one round: 1C-[P]-1S-[P]-2H. The opener has 16+ HCP, per PA. See pages 62-63.
3. **If neither partner has bid NT, a new suit by the responder is forcing.** If the opener rebids 1NT, responder must jump in a new, lower suit to force: 1D-[P]-1S-[P]-1NT-[P]-3C/3H=force; 2C/2H (or 2D) would be a sign-off/preference (NF). **Any change is PA.**
4. If opener rebids 2NT (after a 2/1 response) and **the responder continues the auction**, it's game forcing (GF): 1S-[P]-2D-[P]-2NT(a stop bid)-[P]-3C.
5. If the responder supports the opener's suit, **a new suit by the opener forces one round** and shows game interest: 1H-[P]-2H-[P]-3D= 17-18 HCP, or a strong, unbalanced 16 HCP.
6. As in 5, the same principle applies to the responder: 1C-[P]-1H-[P]-2H-[P]-3D=game interest and forces one round.
7. Any bid after the **opener jumps in his suit** forces game: 1C-[P]-1H-[P]-3C-[P]-3D/3H/3S=game force.
8. A **jump-shift by the opener** forces game: 1H-[P]-1S-[P]-3C. The opener has 19-21 HCP. The resp has at least 6 HCP=game.
    *The opener's jump-shift shows 19+ HCP. Without a jump-shift the opener's range is **12-18** HCP. Some rebids define opener's range: reverses, a new suit level three, jumps in opener's or responder's suit, 1/1 jump to 2NT, or continuing the auction: 1H-2H-3H.*
9. A **new suit bid at level one by a previously unpassed responder** forces one round: 1C-[P]-1H.
10. A **new suit bid at level two by a previously unpassed responder** forces one round: 1H-[P]-2C.
11. If the responder bids at the two level, a **new suit by the opener** forces one round: 1H-[P]-2C-[P]-2D.
12. If the responder bids at the two level, a **jump rebid by the opener** forces game (GF): 1S-[P]-2C-[P]-3S.
    *In 11 & 12 above, the responder's two level bid makes a **big difference** in the meaning of the opener's rebids.*
13. A **jump-shift by the responder** forces game, UNLESS there is a different PA (such as preemptive): 1C-[P]-1S-[P]-2C-[P]-3D.
14. A **reverse by the responder** forces game: 1C-[P]-1H-[P]-1NT-[P]-2S.
15. If the **responder raises the opener's second suit,** it is game forcing: 1H-[P]-1S-[P]-2D-[P]-3D.
16. A **new suit at the 3 level by either partner** forces a M or NT game: 1S-[P]-2D-[P]-3C. Opener's 3 level rebid shows 16+ HCP. If the opener has fewer HCP, he cannot bid 3C, he must bid something else. By responder: 1C-[P]-1S-[P]-2S-[P]-3D.
17. A **cuebid,** in response to the opener or overcaller, forces one round unless there is interference: 1H-[1S]-2S, or [1C]-1S-[P]-2C.
18. A **cuebid by the opener** shows 18+ HCP and forces game: 1D-[P]-1H-[1S]-2S.
19. **After an overcall, a new suit** bid by an unpassed responder forces one round: 1D-[1H]-1S=forcing.
20. A **takeout double** (TOX) *usually* forces one round, unless there is interference. NF if partner has length/strength in X'd suit.
21. After an interfering TOX, a new suit by the responder at the **one level** forces one round: 1D-[X]-1H.
22. After an inter TOX, a new suit at the **two level** is NF - strange, but true. The two level bid shows 6-9 HCP. To show a stronger hand, 10+, the responder must XX, then bid a suit to show 10+ HCP: 1D-[X]-XX. *The XX may stay in for penalty with no fit.*

As you can see, the general rule for forcing bids is to bid a new suit. However, you will eventually run out of new suits to bid, or a suit may be too short to bid, so the desire to continue the auction must be shown by jump bids, or continuing to bid over "stop"' bids such as NT.

Non-Forcing Bids

1. Any opening bid other than 2C is non-forcing: 1C, 1D, 1H, 1S, 1NT, 2NT, 3NT, or any preemptive bid: 2D, 2H, 2S, 3C, 3H, etc.
    Some partners may develop an agreement to bid over 1C to "rescue" opener from a 3 card C suit with < 6 HCP. Exaggerating HCP is dangerous, as partner will expect at least 6 HCP and may continue the auction, possibly bidding game. It is usually best to follow the rules and pass with fewer than 6 HCP, UNLESS the responder can <u>preempt</u> to clearly show a weak hand.
2. Responding in partner's suit at the lowest level is NF, even late in the auction: 1H-[P]-1S-[P]-2C-[P]-2H.
3. A new suit by the opener after a 1/1 bid is NF: 1H-[P]-1S-[P]-2C. *The response of 1S forced a rebid, but resp could be minimal.*
4. Rebidding the same suit at the lowest level by the opener or responder over a one level suit response is NF: 1H-[P]-1S-[P]-2H, or rebidding the same suit over a non-forcing bid does not force another round: 1H-[P]-1S-[P]-2C(NF)-[P]-2S= 6+ Ss & NF.
5. If the opener jumps in his suit or in partner's suit after a <u>one</u> level response, it is NF: 1H-[P]-1S-[P]-3H/3S.
6. If the responder jumps in his own suit it is NF, but is strongly invitational: 1H-[P]-1S-[P]-2C-[P]-3S.
7. Responding in NT is NF for opener OR responder: 1H-[P]-1S-[P]-1NT, 1C-[P]-1H-[P]-1S-[P]-1NT.
8. Rebidding the same suit after either partner bids lowest available NT is NF: 1S-[P]-1NT-[P]-2S, 1H-[P]-1S-[P]-1NT-[P]-2S.
9. If opener asks for a preference after a 1NT response, it is NF: 1H-[P]-1NT-[P]-2C-[P]-2H. Responder may have only two Hs.
10. Some NT rebids by either opener or responder strongly invite game, but are NF: 1H-[P]-1NT-[P]-2NT, 1H-[P]-1S-[P]-2NT, or 1D-[P]-1S-[P]-1NT-[P]-2NT.
11. After the opener rebids 1NT, a new lower suit by the responder is NF: 1C-[P]-1S-[P]-1NT-[P]-2H. Shows 5 Ss and 4-5 Hs.
12. A limit raise is NF: 1H-[P]-3H or 1D-[P]-3D.
13. Any new suit bid by a <u>passed</u> partner is NF, even if he extends the auction: P-[P]-1H-[P]-2C, P-[P]-1C-[P]-1S-[P]-1NT-[P]-2D.
    In the second example, the 2D bid is not a reverse because it is a lower ranked suit, and a passed hand cannot reverse.

14. A TOX forces one round UNLESS the advancer has length in the doubled suit. Pass converts the TOX to a penalty double.
15. After an enemy TOX, a new suit at the 2 level is NF, but a new suit at the one level *IS* forcing. See 21 & 22 in Forcing Bids.
16. Any game level bid is NF: 1C-[P]-3NT (strong), or 1S-4S (principle of "fast arrival" with a weaker hand: preemptive in nature).

Doubles for Penalty

1. Any double of a game-level bid, assuming a typical multiple bid auction, is for penalty.
2. Any double of a 1NT opening bid is for penalty, unless it is alerted as a convention. It may remain a penalty bid, according to the agreements of the convention.
3. A double of a 1NT overcall is *usually* for penalty.
4. If partner opens 1NT and the opponent overcalls, double is for penalty unless there is a different PA, such as X=takeout/Stayman.
5. If partner **preempts** and the opponent overcalls, double is for penalty. The preemptor is not expected to bid again.
6. If a player makes a TOX and his partner leaves the X "in" (does not bid a suit), the double converts to penalty.
7. If the opener bids a suit and the overcaller makes a TOX, a redouble (XX) is for penalty and shows 10+ HCP. See 22 in *Forcing Bids* on page 99.
8. If the auction is competitive or sacrificial, double is for penalty. These bids are often 3+ level bids.
9. There is a rule that can help you know when to penalty X - the Rule of 9 (or 10 if you prefer): Your **number of trumps** + your **number of trump honors** + the **level of the opponent's contract**. If the number is 9 or higher, make a penalty X.

Miscellaneous Reminders/Helpful Tips

1. If you and partner have a 1/1 auction and the **opponents** make you bid 2NT, as opener, you promise **16+** HCP and stoppers since partner promises only 6 HCP with his 1 level bid: 1C-[P]-1S-[2D]-2NT=16+ HCP.
2. If you have previously passed or there is interference, and you hold 5 of partner's M trumps and 7 HCP (with an unbalanced hand) or 8 -11 HCP, bid game - the principle of <u>fast arrival</u>. With medium+ HCP and no interference or previous pass, bid lower and slower to get the maximum information from partner you can, in anticipation of a game or slam contract.
3. If the responder must choose between a **5/2** or a **4/3** fit, he should usually opt for the **5/2** fit.
4. If the opponent preempts at the two level and your partner overcalls 2NT, it is the **equivalent** of partner opening 1NT: 15-17 & bal.
5. A 2NT bid by an unpassed responder is invitational: 1H - 1S - 2C - **2NT.**
6. If you have an extremely distributional hand with a long suit of your own or support for partner, usually bid game.
7. If you and partner are in a misfit and you have singletons or voids in his suit(s), NT will likely fail. Acquiesce to the **longest known suit,** even if it's a loathsome minor suit. It's hard to do, *but you will be a happier bridge player.*

Tournament Tips

Your first tournament experience is likely to feel a little overwhelming due to the number of players milling around. Always ask questions of directors or of more seasoned players from your club. These are general tips from my early experiences:

1. Memorize the start times of each session so you do not miss your scheduled games.
2. Have your partner's current masterpoint amount at hand, because you will need to know your points as you sign up for games.
3. Sign up early for games to reduce anxiety, and have a set meeting place in case you become separated from your partner(s).
4. Do not try to learn new conventions just before you go to a tournament.
5. Know the conventions/systems you play **well** - inside and out. Refresh more rarely played conventions w/ partner before you go.
6. Fix problems privately after the round is over. Do not get upset or berate your partner - be calm. Others are watching & learning about your strengths and weaknesses. Players love a good fight between opponents! *It means something went wrong.*
7. Do not socialize with players that come to your table such that you distract yourself from the business at hand - winning the session. Some players will come to your table with just that intent against you. (You'll know them because they never hush.)
8. Concentrate no matter how tired you feel. The event will end soon enough, and you will regret what your lack of focus cost you.
9. Take snacks and drinks with you in case you need a lift. A three hour+ session is a long event and takes a lot of brain power.
10. Try to stay in the hotel where the event occurs. It is less stressful and usually safer. Rest as much as you can; eat healthy meals.

Team Games

11. Try to keep all your scores in the PLUS column. Rarely sacrifice, but don't let them play in a two level minor contract either.
12. Don't risk your contract for an extra trick. Bid the SAFEST game or partscore and don't worry about the point difference in NT.
13. Double only if you are certain they will get set. If they don't get set, their score will often be the equivalent of a game score.
14. Bid game with at least a 40% chance of making it, because if game is there and you don't bid it, the big swing in points will be difficult to recover from.
15. Bid game in partner's suit with support and extreme or unusual distribution.
16. Bid slams with at least a 60% chance of making them.
17. If you have a difficult hand and feel as if you have made a huge blunder that will cost the team, **FORGET IT** and move on. The other team will find the hand difficult to bid as well, and may have made the same blunder you did, a *bigger* blunder than you did, OR your partners may have capitalized on their error and will have made a huge gain. You will NEVER KNOW until you compare scores. My worst scores have consistently come from **missing games** rather than from big errors on unusual hands.
18. If you get partners from the partnership desk, don't commit to the entire tournament yet. It may or may not be a heavenly match.
19. If you'd like, have 5-6 man teams when possible to relax between sessions. (Compact KOs are limited to 4 members.)

Building Bridges © 2022 Jeanne R. Wamack May not be reproduced in any form.

INDEX

1/1, 2/1   15, 26, 71

A

ACBL   1, 16, 20, 78-79, 81, 84, 87, 89
ACBL number   78-79
ALAS   48
ATAC   43
Abbreviation key   2
About the author   109
Ace   3-5, 7, 34-35, 37, 53, 59, 70, 93, 96-97
Ace ask   59, 70, 93
   using Blackwood   59, 60, 68, 70 , 81-82, 93-95, 99, 101, 103
   using Gerber   56, 59-60, 68, 70, 81-82, 93-94, 99, 101, 103
Adages   47, 82, compilation 95-96
Adjustments   53
Advancer   7, 27, 51, 62, 67, 74, 85, 99, 104
Alert   25, 57-58, 87, 93, 97, 104
Announce   16, 20, 27, 48, 78, 85, 89, 97, 99
Approve scores   3
Approximate HCP for levels 1-4   89, 95 Study guide 89
Artificial bid   20, 68, 85, 87, 89, 101, 103
Attitude   68
Auction   4-6, 8-11, 15-23, 25-32, 34-37, 39-40, 43, 48, 50-54, 59-62, 66-71, 73-78, 83-85, 87-88, 94, 96, 103-104
Automatic rebid   17, 19

B

Balanced hand   10, 13 16, 20, 24, 28, 40, 53-59, 66-69, 72-73, 76, 84-85, 88-89, 93, 97, 101
Balancing   28, 67, 88, 99, 101
Balancing seat   28, 88, 101
Bid   definition 3, 83
Bid boxes   3, 83
Bidding flow chart   82, 90-92
Bidding ladder   4-6, 8, 26, 75
Bidding ladder illustration   5
Big hands   71, 74-75, 77, 82, Chapter 13 p. 50, Study guide 94
Blackwood   73, 75, 79, 86, 90, 92, Chapter 15 p. 59, Study guide 93, 99
Block   36, 41, 43-44, 86-87, 93, 96
Boards   3, 7, 8, 11, 27, 35, 70, 78-79, 80-85
Bonus   11, 18-19, 61, 66, 71, 84, 95
Book   6, 8, 19, 84, 88
Break a new suit   46
Breakdown of Points Chart, The   98
Broken sequence   34, 46, 85, 87
Bust hand   57-58, 87

C

Call (see also Bid)   3
Cansino count   67, 96
Cappelletti, Allison Howard   40
Captain of the hand   56, 87, 95
Card sample (convention card)   100
Casino count   96
Clear a suit   42, 86

Closeout   52
Clubs   3, 83
Comfort zone   66
Competition   61
Contract definition 6, 83
Contract card   7, 66, 84
Convention (artificial bid) definition 7, 20, 26, 85
Convention card   7, 66, 70, 78-80, 82, 84, 99-101, sample card 100, written instructions 99-101
Count   5, 11, 13-14, 41-45, 54, 59, 69, 93-98, 101
Count your losers   42, 93
Counting   5, 15, 41-42, 48, 69
Cover an honor   68, 96
Cross-ruff/cross-trump   34, 42, 86
Cuebid   51, 52, 74, 76-77, 85, 93-94, 99, 101, Chapter 8 p. 32, Study guide 93

D

Danger zone   66
Dealer   6, 8, 9, 83
Declarer   6, 83
Defenders   6, 48, 68, 84
Defense   34-35, 64, 67, 78, Chapter 12 p. 46, Study guide 93
Definitions   81
Devalue   53-54, 94
Diamonds   3, 83
Direct seat   27-29, 51, 74, 88, 94, 101
Direction   3, 19, 78, 100
Director   3, 4, 8, 83
Discard(s)   41, 68, 78, 101
Discipline   18, 27, 71
Distribution   27, 85
Distributional hand   59, 66, 97, 104
Distribution points   53-55, 76, Study guide 94
Distributional value   27-28, 53, 55-56, 58, 71, 85
Double   7, 27-30, 32-33, 51, 59-69, 74, 78, 83, 85, 94,101-104
Doubleton   16, 20, 22, 34, 53, 68, 87, 97, 101
Down the mountain   13, 15-16, 84, 95
Draw   36, 42, 93-94, 98
Drop dead bids   18, 25, 55
Duck   41, 86, 96
Dummy   definition 6, 7, 13, 25-27, 34-49, 53, 67-70, 83-86, 93-96, 84
Dummy's duties 48
Duplicate board(s)   3, 83
Duplicate bridge   3, 4, 27, 61-62, 78, 83

E

Escape route   31
Establish   36, 41-42, 45-46, 53, 68, 86
Etiquette   5, 7, 78, 96, Chapter 1 p. 3, Chapter 18 p. 78
Evaluating your hand   5, 6, 14, 53-54, 94
Extra pizzazz   (See also distribution points) 11-12, 19, 22, 27, 53
Extreme distribution   53, 66, 98

F

Face down lead   6, 78
Fine tuning your hand   53-54
Finesse   20, 35, 41-47, 68-69, 82, 85-86, 96-97
   Chapter 10 p. 38, Study guide 93

Building Bridges © 2022 Jeanne R. Wamack May not be reproduced in any form.

First priority responses   13, 15, 88
Flat hand/flat distribution   67
Flow charts   90-92
Follow   38
Follow suit   5-6, 83
Forcing bids (F)   71, 94, 102-104
Four card suit bidding   10, 25, 27, 33 (mini review), 74, 81
Fourth from the longest and strongest   34
Frank Stewart: author, columnist, and bridge expert   29, 81
Free bid   28-29, 85
Free finesse   20, 35, 40, 85

G

Game   9, 11, 14, 15, 18, 19, 20, 22, 97, 98
Game force   50, 103-104 56, 59-60, 93, 94, 99, 101, 103
Gems of Wisdom   95
Gerber   Chapter 15 p. 59, Study guide 93
Golden Fit   9-13, 17, 21-22, 41, 43, 50, 53-54, 84-85, 88, 94
Guide card   3

H

HCP (high card points)   5
Hand   definition 4
Hearts   3, 83
High from the short side   41, 43, 45, 93, 96
High/hate   48, 49, 93
Hold up   41, 93, 96
Honor/Honor cards   3, 5, 83
HUGE hands   Chapter 14 p. 56, Study guide 93

I

Insufficient   8
Interference   7, 24-25, 31-33, 74, 89
Interference over 1NT opener   24-25, 89
Interior sequence   34, 36, 46, definition 85, 87, 95
Intervening   27-31, 71, 72, 74, 76, 85

J

Jack   3-7, 34, 36, 47, 68, 83
Jacoby Transfer   20-26, 28, 56-58, 89, 94, 99, 101, 103
    Jacoby Transfer chart   89
    Jacoby Transfer over 2NT   56-58,
    Jacoby Transfer when 5/4 in Ms   25
    Jacoby Transfer when 5/5 in Ms   22
    Jacoby Transfer when you have a 6 card M   22
    Jacoby Transfer when you have a minor suit   25
Jump bid   11, 18, 25, after TOX 27, 29, 32, 50-52, 57, 71-76, 84, 94, 98, 99
Jump-shift   52, 59, 97, 98, 99

K

Key   7
King   3-7, 39, 59, 83
King ask Blackwood   59, 93
King ask Gerber   59, 93
Known fit   23

L

LHO   7, 67-69

Ladder   4-8, 26, 75
Landing place   31, 85, 93
Lead(s)   6, 34-37, 48, 68-69, 84, 85, 95, 99, 101
    Chapter 9 p. 34,   Table 87
Lead table   87
Lead to strength   47, 93, 96
Lead to weakness   47, 93, 96
Lead worthy   27, 34, 98
Leader   6, 48, 84
Length   9, 13, 16-17, 20, 22-23, 28, 31, 35-36, 46, 50, 53, 57, 67, 71, 74, 76, 85-87, 89, 93-97, 99, 103-104
Length (Play of the Hand)   42-45
Length points   53, 94
Limit raise   11-12, 14-15,18, 32, 44, 69, 84, 88, 93-94, 99, 101, 103
Limited bid   13, 15, 44, 71, 87
Limited entries   40, 86
Long suit   4, 11, 17-19, 21-22, 25, 27-29, 34, 36, 38, 40-43 48, 51-59, 67-69, 73-74, 76, 85-88, 93-99, 101, 104
Longer minor   8-9, 13, 16, 20
Longest holding   41
Loser on loser play   42, 86
Low=like   48
Low=no   48

M

Major game   11, 21, 66, 84
Major opening bids   Chapter 2 p. 9, Study guide 88
Major responses   9-10
Major suits   6, 8, 9
Masterpoints   78-80, 87
Maximum hands   9, 98, see Chapter 13 p. 50
Medium hands   7, 9, 11-12, 14, 32, 52, 72-73, 76-77, 84, 98, Chapter 13 p. 50
Mini review (of four card suits)   31
Minimum hands   6, 9-14, 23, 31-33, 44, 50, 52, 55, 56, 62, 72, 75-76, 81, 88, 98, 101
Minor game   98
Minor opening bids   Chapter 3 p.13, Study guide 88
Minor responses   13-14
Minor suits   3, 8, 10, 14, 16, 87

N

Natural   20, 24, 25, 58, 70, 89, 93, 99, 101
Negative double   29, 85, Chapter 8 p. 31, Study guide 93
No Trump   5, 7-8, 14, 35, 41, 51-53, 73, 83, 99
No Trump game   14, 57, 88, 98, 103
No Trump responses   15, 25, 52, 93, 99, 101
Non-forcing bids (NF)   71, 94, 102-103
Non-vulnerable (NV)   7, 17, 18, 27, 61, 64, 95,

O

Odds   13, 39, 43, 66
One No trump opening bids   20, Chapter 5 p. 20, Chapter 6 p. 23, Study guide 89
One over one bids   15, 50, 52, 71, 72, 76, 84, 88, 94, 98, 103-104
Open/opener   4-36, 39, 41, 43-44, 46, 48, 50-60, 62, 66, 67-79, 81, 83-89, 93-99, 101, 103-104
Opener see open

Opener's rebids   23, 57, 72-75, 98, 103
Opening   4-5. 9-11, 13-34, 36, 39, 41, 43, 46, 48, 50, 51-53, 55-59, 62, 66, 68, 70-75, 78-79, 81, 84, 85, 87-89, 93-99, 101, 103-104
Opening a minor suit   Chart 16
Opening count   11, 17. 27, 29, 62, 66, 70, 95, 97-98
Opponent   3-8, 10, 13-14, 18, 20, 24-25, 27-29, 31-32, 34-36, 39-48, 50-51, 54-55, 60-61, 63-72, 74-76, 78-81, 84-87, 89, 93, 95, 101, 104
Opponent's bids shown in brackets   8
Overcaller   27, 29, 31, 34, 51, 55, 62, 74, 85, 93, 98, 101, 103-104
Overcalls   27, 28, 30, 33, 51, 66, 78, 82, 88, 93-94, 97, 99, 101, 104, Chapter 7 p. 27, Basic study guide 88, Advanced study guide 94

P

Pair number   3, 100
Partner   3-7, 9-37, 39, 41-44, 46-62, 66-79, 81-82, 84-89, 93-101, 103-104
Partnership agreement   7, 20, 28-29, 33, 49, 70, 74, 77, 95, 99
Partnership desk   79, 104
Partscore   11, 19, 27, 29, 34, 54, 61, 64, 66, 70, 74, 84, 87, 95, 97-98, 104
Pass   4-15, 18-25, 27-33, 35, 44, 50-52, 54-61, 64-67, 70-71, 73-79, 83-84, 88-89, 93-95, 98-99, 101, 103-104
Pass out seat   26, 75, 97
Pearson points   67
Penalty   5-6, 27, 29, 33, 61-62, 64-67, 70, 94, 95, 102-104
Penalty double   33, 66, 67, 94, 102, 104
Perfect sequence   34, 46, 85, 95
Phantom sacrifice   66, 87, 95
Pick up slip   3
PIG   20-25, 28, 44, 89, 95, 99
PIzzazz (See also distribution values)   11-12, 19, 22, 27, 53
Play for the drop   41, 45, 86, 93
Play of the hand   40-45, 68-69, 82, 96, Chapter 11 p.41, Study guide 93
Point scale, The   Chart   97
Points   5-20, 22, 26-28, 31-32, 36, 39-40, 44, 47-48, 50-56, 58-67, 69-71, 73-74, 76-83, 85-88, 94-98, 101, 104
Poor 10 points   14, 32, 88
Post mortem   35, 85
Preemptive bidding   17-19, 84, Chapter 4 p. 17, Study guide 88
Preference auction   76-77, 94
Previous passed hand   71, 88, 93, 104
Process of elimination   36
Promote   38-39, 46, 48, 68, 86-87

Q

Quantitative raise   59
Queen   3-5, 7, 83
Questions for a new partner   101
Quick tricks   17, 84, 88, 96

R

RHO   7, 18, 28, 30, 32-33, 38-39, 51, 67, 68-70

Rebids   11, 15, 23, 33, 51-52, 57, 71-77, 84, 88, 94, 98-99, 101, 103, Chapter 17 p. 71
    by opener   10-11,15, 51, 57 71-77, 84, 94, 98-99, 103
    by responder   11, 15, 74, 84, 103
Renege   5, 83
Responder   7, 9-15, 18, 20-25, 27-31, 50-53, 55-58, 60, 62, 66, 68, 71-77, 84-89, 94, 98-99, 101, 103, 104
Responses   9-11, 13-15, 20-26, 31, 44, 52, 56-57, 71, 75, 77-78, 88-89, 93, 95, 99, 101, 103
    to 1S   9-10, 88
    to 1H   9-10, 88
    to 1D   13-14, 88
    to 1C   13-14, 88
    to 1NT   20-26
Reverses   74-75, 77, 87, 94, 97, 101, 103
Review   33, 44, 52, 71-77, 80-81, 94, Chapter 17 p. 71
Revoke   5, 48, 83
Rich 10 points   14, 20, 32, 88
Round   3, 7, 13, 33-37, 41-44, 46, 48, 68, 70, 75, 79-80, 84, 93, 103-104
Ruff (see also trump)   5-6, 14, 17, 19, 21-22, 24, 26-27, 29, 33-37, 39, 40, 42-50, 53-54, 65-70, 83, 85, 86-87, 93-97
Ruff and sluff   46, 86, 96
Rule of 7   96
Rule of 10(9)   96
Rule of 11   49, 96
Rule of 15   67, 96
Rule of 17   18, 71, 96
Rule of 20 + 2 opening bid   17-19, 53, 77, 82, 88, 96, 98, 101, Chapter 4 p 17, Study guide 88

S

SA   7, 9, 25, 74, 99
Scoring   3,11, 19, 61-70, 82, 95 Chapter 16 p. 61, Study guide 95
Set
    contract 6-7, 17-19, 27, 29, 35, 38, 41-42, 61-71, 84, 95, 104
Set up or establish suit   34-38, 41-46, 54, 87, 95
Shape   9, 57-58, 60, 67, 74, 76, 85, 93, 98
Short side   41-43, 45, 66, 93, 96
Shortness (Play of the Hand)   17, 27, 42, 93, 96
Shortness points   22, 27, 53-54, 85, 94
Signaling   48, 68, 87, 96, 100, 101
    Standard   48, 68, 96
    Upside down   48, 68, 96
Singleton   7, 11-12, 20, 22, 26-27, 35-36, 42, 46-47, 49-50, 53-54, 60, 67, 71-72, 74, 84, 87, 89, 94-95, 101, 104
Sit behind   25
Skip bid (see also jump bid)   8, 86
Slough   46, 86
Sluff (slough)   46, 49, 86, 96
Somewhere to run   31
Spades   3, 5-8, 10, 12, 16, 18-19, 21, 54, 56-57, 68, 79, 83-84, 89, 93, 96
Split honors   39, 86
Split trumps   13, 43-45, 54, 67, 76, 96
Standard American (SA)   1-2, 7, 9, 17, 24-25, 81, 99-101
Standard American NT responses   24-25
Standard signaling   48, 68
Stayman   20, 23-26, 28, 44, 56-58, 68, 70, 81-82, 85, 87, 89, 93-94, 99, 101, 103-104

Building Bridges © 2022 Jeanne R. Wamack   May not be reproduced in any form.

Stayman and Transfers   Study guide 94
Stewart, Frank: author, columnist and bridge expert   29, 81
Stop bid   9, 26, 50, 71, 74, 76, 103
Stoppers   14, 18, 28-32, 41, 52, 55, 57, 67, 70, 72, 73, 85,
    87-88, 93-94, 96, 104
Strats, Stratifications   78-79, 87
Strain   57
Study guides   82-98
Suits   3-12, 14, 16-20, 22-23, 25, 27-29, 31-32, 34-35, 38,
    41-43, 45, 47-48, 52-54, 62, 67-71, 74-76, 78, 84-88,
    93-99, 101, 103
Switch   47, 49, 86
Systems on   28, 85, 93, 99

T

TOX (see takeout double)   7, 27-30, 33, 51, 67, 71, 74, 81,
    85, 88, 94, 97-98, 101, 103-104
Takeout double (TOX)   7, 27, 29-30, 32, 51, 67, 85, 101, 103
Temporizing bid   73-74, 87
Ten HCP, Responses with   10, 14-15, 25, 32, 52, 76, 84, 85, 94
Three Little PIGs, The   24
Tips   3, 5, 9-10, 13, 14, 15, 17, 24, 26, 32, 40, 43, 49, 51-53,
    55, 59, 69, 71, 74, 78, 82, 96, 102, 104
Tolerance   31, 85, 93
Top of a sequence   6, 34, 37, 87, 95
Top of nothing   35, 36, 46, 87, 95
Top suit (see also trump suit)   4-5, 83
Tournaments   Chapter 18 p. 78, Tips p.105
Transportation   18, 38, 41-45, 54, 74, 76, 86, 96
Trap   34, 36, 39-40, 46-48, 54, 72, 85
Traveller   3, 62-63, 83
Trick   6-8, 10-11, 14-15, 17-21, 26-27, 29, 34-48, 53-54, 56,
    61-64, 66-68, 70-71, 83-88, 93, 95-97, 104
Trump/trump suit   5-8, 11-15, 17-20, 24, 26-27, 33-36,
    39-47, 49-54, 59-62, 66-67, 69-71, 73, 76, 83-84,
    86-87, 89, 93-99, 104
Two club opening hand   93-94, 101, 103, Chapter 14 p. 56
Two No trump opening hand   Chapter 14 p. 56
Two No trump response   10, 11, 14-15, 21-24, 32, 50-52,
    55-58, 60, 71-76, 88, 93-94, 98-99, 101, 103-104
Two over one bids   15, 71-73, 84

U

Unbid suit   26-27, 29, 31-32, 34, 67, 70, 85, 87, 93, 95, 97
Unexpected lead   36
Unlimited bids   15, 32, 44, 50, 52, 71, 77, 88, 93
Unprotected honors   14, 19, 53-54, 85-86, 94
Unsupported   35-36, 85
Up the hill   13, 15-16, 23, 84, 88, 95
Upside down signaling   48, 49, 68, 78-79, 87, 93, 101, 104

V

Void   7, 11-12, 16, 18, 20, 22, 26-27, 29, 34, 39, 42-43, 46,
    50, 53-54, 59-60, 67, 71-72, 74, 83-86, 88-89, 94-95,
    97-98, 101, 104
Vulnerable (V)   6, 7, 17-19, 27, 29, 32, 61-62, 64-67, 69, 95

W

Watson, Louis: author of *Play of the Hand*   43
Win cheaply   47

Jeanne Wamack is a native of Birmingham, Alabama. She holds a Bachelor's degree in education from Auburn University and a Master's degree in education from the University of Alabama at Birmingham. She is a certified "Best Practices" teacher and is TAP certified by the American Contract Bridge League. She is also a certified "Easybridge" instructor, certified club director, and is a member of the American Bridge Teacher's Association. She is a Silver Life Master.

Jeanne began playing bridge at the age of eighteen, immediately developing a passion for the game. She played regularly until the birth of her children, then bridge become a sporadic hobby. After her children became teenagers, Jeanne returned to the game. To refresh her memory and to learn about the changes in bidding, she signed up for formal lessons. She found that taking lessons opened the doors to a more fascinating world of bridge.

After several years of club play, Jeanne was asked to instruct beginner classes at the Birmingham Duplicate Bridge Club. Though initially resistant to the idea, she stepped back into education and found a genuine love of coaching new players. Attempting to be a thorough facilitator, Jeanne sent out emails with tips and recaps of the week's discussion. Upon the realization she was spending hours writing chapters, the idea to compile the chapters into a book was born.

The book is known today as **Building Bridges.**

Jeanne entered *Building Bridges: An Introduction to the Card Game of Bridge* and the *Building Bridges Facilitator's Guide* in the American Bridge Teacher Association's "Book of the Year" contest. Coming in second to Larry Cohen was thrilling to the unknown author. She has written a second book, *Continuing Construction*, introducing next-step conventions and bidding techniques to the rising beginner player.

Jeanne has also developed the *Building Bridges* slide show to make presentations flow smoothly and to better meet the needs of those learning the game. The show is animated, displaying concepts with bright, attention-getting detail. It has become a student favorite.